AF544715

CELEBRATED IN THEIR TIME

CELEBRATED IN THEIR TIME

PHOTOGRAPHIC PORTRAITS 1910–1922
from the
GEORGE GRANTHAM BAIN COLLECTION

Edited by
AMY PASTAN

With an Introduction by
MICHAEL CARLEBACH

DOVER PUBLICATIONS, INC.
Mineola, New York

Copyright

Bibliographical Note

Celebrated in Their Time: Photographic Portraits 1910–1922 from the George Grantham Bain Collection is a new work, first published by Dover Publications, Inc., in 2009.

The photographic images in this book were downloaded from the files of the George Grantham Bain Collection at the Library of Congress' Web site. The edges were slightly cropped in some cases and some identifying numbers and words were removed. Marks, which were the result of damage to the original negatives, were restored on the downloaded electronic files and in some cases the contrast, brightness, and tone of the images were enhanced for reproduction in this volume.

Library of Congress Cataloging-in-Publication Data

Celebrated in their time : photographic portraits, 1910–1922 from the George Grantham Bain collection / edited by Amy Pastan ; with an introduction by Michael Carlebach.
p. cm.
Includes bibliographical references and index.
ISBN-13: 978-0-486-46754-2 (pbk.)
ISBN-10: 0-486-46754-6 (pbk.)
1. Celebrities—United States—Pictorial works. 2. Celebrities—Pictorial works. 3. Portrait photography—History—20th century—Sources. 4. Celebrities—History—20th century—Sources. 5. Bain, George Grantham, 1865–1944—Photograph collections. 6. Photograph collections—New York (State)—New York. 7. Photograph collections—Washington (D.C.) 8. Library of Congress. Prints and Photographs Division—Photograph collections. I. Pastan, Amy.

TR681.F3C447 2009
779.092—dc22

2009012693

Manufactured in the United States by Courier Corporation
46754601
www.doverpublications.com

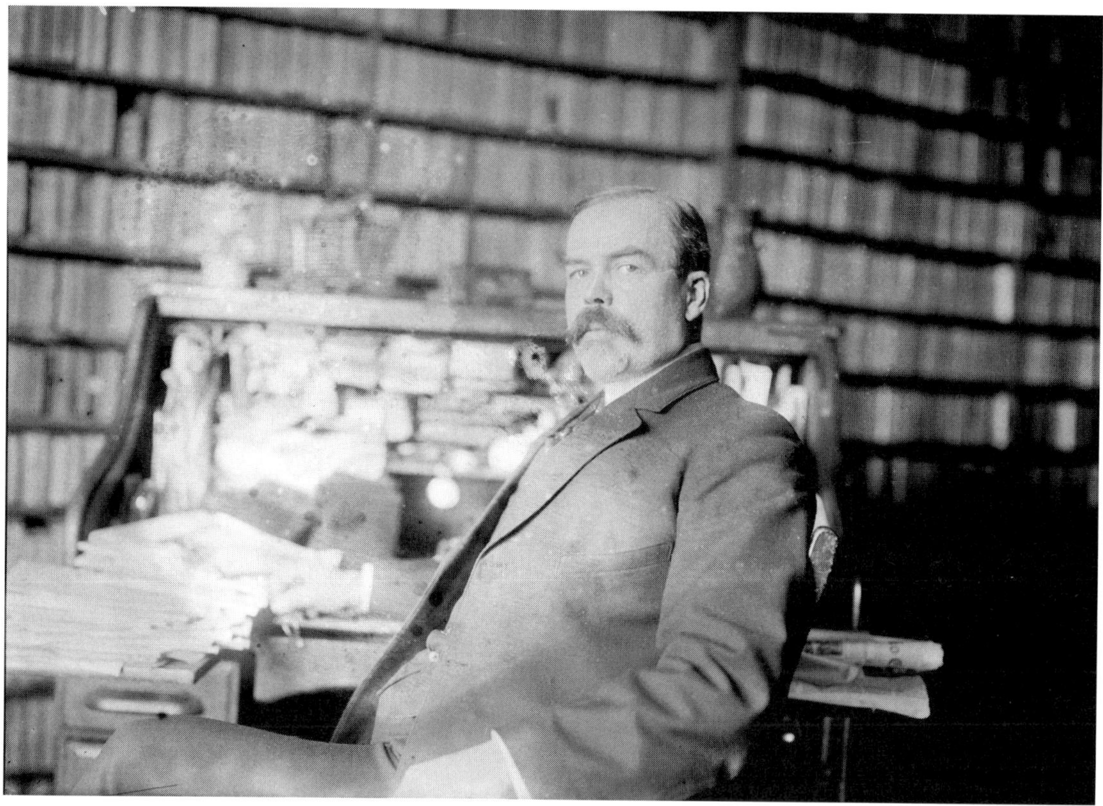

George Grantham Bain (1865–1944)

INTRODUCTION

George Grantham Bain, the man who collected and saw to the preservation of these pictures, was no photographer. His long career in journalism began in 1884 when he was hired as a reporter at the *Globe-Democrat* in St. Louis; a year later he joined Joseph Pulitzer's *St. Louis Post-Dispatch.* He proved to be a quick study, easily mastering the fine art of the interview and developing an instinct for the news. After only a few months, his editors sent him to Washington D.C. where he helped run the paper's principal out-of-state news bureau. At this point, and really for the rest of his life, Bain considered himself to be primarily a print journalist, a word man. But in the last years of the nineteenth century both the practice and character of journalism changed dramatically. A great many new readers were attracted to newspapers and magazines by cheap prices, varied and occasionally sensational coverage, and, especially, by pictures. Bain noted that editors were more likely to run his stories if they were illustrated, so, armed with rudimentary knowledge of photography picked up in college, he began taking a camera along on assignments. But actually taking the pictures was never more than a sideline for Bain; he had other, far more ambitious plans for news photographs.

The prodigious appetite of the press for visual material persuaded Bain to establish the country's first photographic syndicate, which was located at 15 Park Row in the heart of New York City's newspaper district. He hired and trained a staff of young men to comb the city for usable pictures, and began building what would become the nation's most important archive of early twentieth-century news pictures. At the same time, he purchased images from freelance photographers and augmented the News Service files with photographs sent in by client papers. Late in his life, Bain recalled that early in the century there "was a great need of news photographs when the use of halftone engraving developed; and there was no one in the whole United States to supply that need.... Hence my development as the pioneer of the news photograph business."

In the first decades of the new century, the Bain News Service and other syndicates supplied many of the images used by the periodical press. "The public demands pictures, and demands good ones," wrote the editors of *The Camera* in 1915. "The city editor, the managing editor, the magazine people, and the illustrated weeklies must have pictures, and it is the business of the camera man to see that they have them."[1] Photo staffs were small or nonexistent, and there was not yet competition from a reliable and effective wire service, so Bain and his colleagues in the picture syndication trade had things pretty much to themselves. At the heart of this business were photographs of people in the news. The famous and infamous were—naturally—fodder for the press, whether they liked it or not. So, too, were ordinary people caught up in noisome public events or captured unawares in some picturesque setting. It seemed that no one could long avoid the insatiable gaze of the press; the very concept of privacy was increasingly remote and passé.

Not surprisingly, there were strenuous objections to the new illustrated journalism endlessly promoted by Joseph Pulitzer, William Randolph Hearst, and Edward Willis Scripps, and not just from those seeking to avoid the prying eyes of the press. Silas Bent, who spent nearly a decade as a reporter at Pulitzer's *Post-Dispatch,* published scathing critiques of the journalistic practices he encountered in Missouri and elsewhere. The press was "merely incited to greater activity by *any* effort to escape," he wrote in 1926. Personal privacy could not be allowed to stand in the way of a dramatic scoop or exclusive. The fierce competition for readers and profits encouraged editors and publishers to "squeeze what they had more forcibly, and display it more enticingly."[2] Will Irvin, a well-regarded reporter at the turn of the last century, had nothing but contempt for the picture policies of contemporary newspapers. "As for photographs—what offenses were committed in their name," he wrote in *Collier's Magazine* in 1911. Photographs were essential in the news business, especially to illustrate what he called "pretty girl stories," and it was not uncommon for photographic agencies to supply papers with images of "foreign women in private life" to be used in stories like "Pretty Girl Who Whipped Burglar," or "Prominent Society Ladies of Evanston."[3]

Upton Sinclair, the famous muckraker and author of *The Jungle,* was even more caustic. In *The Brass Check,* which was privately published in 1920, Sinclair described with characteristic venom those who "print and publish our newspapers and magazines." They are the ones, he wrote, "who betray the virgin hopes of mankind into the loathsome brothel of Big Business."[4]

Heated diatribes against photographs and journalistic practice did little to dampen the public's enthusiasm for illustrations, though they did contribute to the idea that news photographers are, as a group, boorish, ill-mannered, and unscrupulous. The reputation of newspapers and their readers also suffered. Thus, the editors of *Time* once sneeringly described New York's lavishly illustrated *Daily News* as the "Manhattan gum-chewers' sheetlet."[5]

None of it made any difference. By 1900, photographs of people, events, and places in the news were a staple of the news, and George Bain's News Service was bound to succeed. Since portraits and candid views of newsmakers and celebrities were among the most sought-after images, Bain's photographers spent a good part of their time and energy

---

1 "The Ways and Wiles of the Camera Man," *The Camera,* vol. 19, no. 2 (February 1915): 94.

2 Silas Bent, "Journalism and Morality," *The Atlantic Monthly,* vol. 137, no. 6 (June 1926): 768.

3 Will Irvin, "Yellow Journalism," *Collier's Magazine* (February 1911). See also Edwin H. Ford, ed., *Selected Readings in the History of American Journalism* (Minneapolis: University of Minnesota Press, 1939): 412.

4 Cited by Cathy Covert, "A View of the Press in the Twenties," *Journalism History,* vol. 2, (Autumn 1975): 92.

5 "Camera Etiquette," *Time,* vol. III, no. 12 (March 24, 1924): 25.

making such pictures, and their work now comprises a formidable collection of portraits of people in the news during the first decades of the twentieth century. Bain organized and catalogued the pictures according to subject matter, and many pictures were identified by a brief caption scratched onto the surface of the glass-plate negative.

Sadly, the names and histories of the photographers who made these images are now gone. It was customary in the early days of photojournalism to deny photographers both credit and public praise for their work. It was a kind of enforced anonymity that eventually, and ironically, became a source of pride. "The newspaper photographer is not looking for publicity," wrote Charles Miller in *The Camera*. "All the cameraman needs," he added, "is a good, fast developer and the ability to deliver a wet print on the city editor's desk in record time..."[6] When a photograph supplied by Bain was published, the only credit was likely to be "George Grantham Bain," or "Bain News Service"; if anyone got credit, it was the company or the boss, not the photographer. There was nothing new about this practice; Mathew Brady did the same thing during the Civil War. By 1861, Brady's eyesight had deteriorated, and he seldom left his office and studio in Washington D.C. But he saw the possibility of creating a vast and profitable visual history of the conflict. He hired and provisioned the photographers, used his connections with the Washington elite to ensure access to the armies, and took credit for every image made by his employees. Even today, many still believe that Brady himself photographed the Civil War. So it was with George Bain. He saw the need for news pictures, hired, trained, and supplied the photographers, and took all the credit for the work they produced.

Although newspapers and magazines relied increasingly on photographs to augment the written word and attract readers, little attention was paid to the preservation of images. Newspapers routinely discarded used prints and negatives, which, in any case, were considered the property of the company, not the photographer. The idea that the pictures might constitute a significant and memorable visual history, or that they had inherent value beyond their immediate function as illustrations in an afternoon or morning paper, seemed not to have occurred to those in charge. Both Pulitzer and Hearst spoke warmly about "their pictures," but did nothing at all to preserve the work of their photographers.

One person who did see the potential of photographs as historical documents was Louis Wiley, the venerable business manager of the *New York Times*. In an address to the Camera Club of New York in 1928, the diminutive Wiley, (he was just over five-feet tall), noted, "No collection is being made of photographs of great current historical events." He felt that the "services of the camera to history...should be fittingly recognized,"[7] preserved, perhaps, by one of the great libraries at Harvard or Columbia. That never happened, of course, but some images from that time were saved.

George Bain knew both the historical and monetary value of his News Service collection, and he fiercely protected the pictures, even after wire service photography effectively dried up the market. Shortly after he died in 1944, David Jay Culver of Culver Pictures in New York purchased the Bain archive; four years later, he sold the bulk of the News Service collection to the Library of Congress. It resides there today, available—as it should be—to all Americans. It is, after all, our history.

MICHAEL CARLEBACH

[6] Chas. D. Miller, "The Staff Photog," *The Camera*, vol. 19, no. 5 (May 1915): 295.

[7] Louis Wiley, "Photographers as News-Reporters," *Photo-Era*, vol. LXI, no. 4 (October 1928): 184.

CELEBRATED IN THEIR TIME

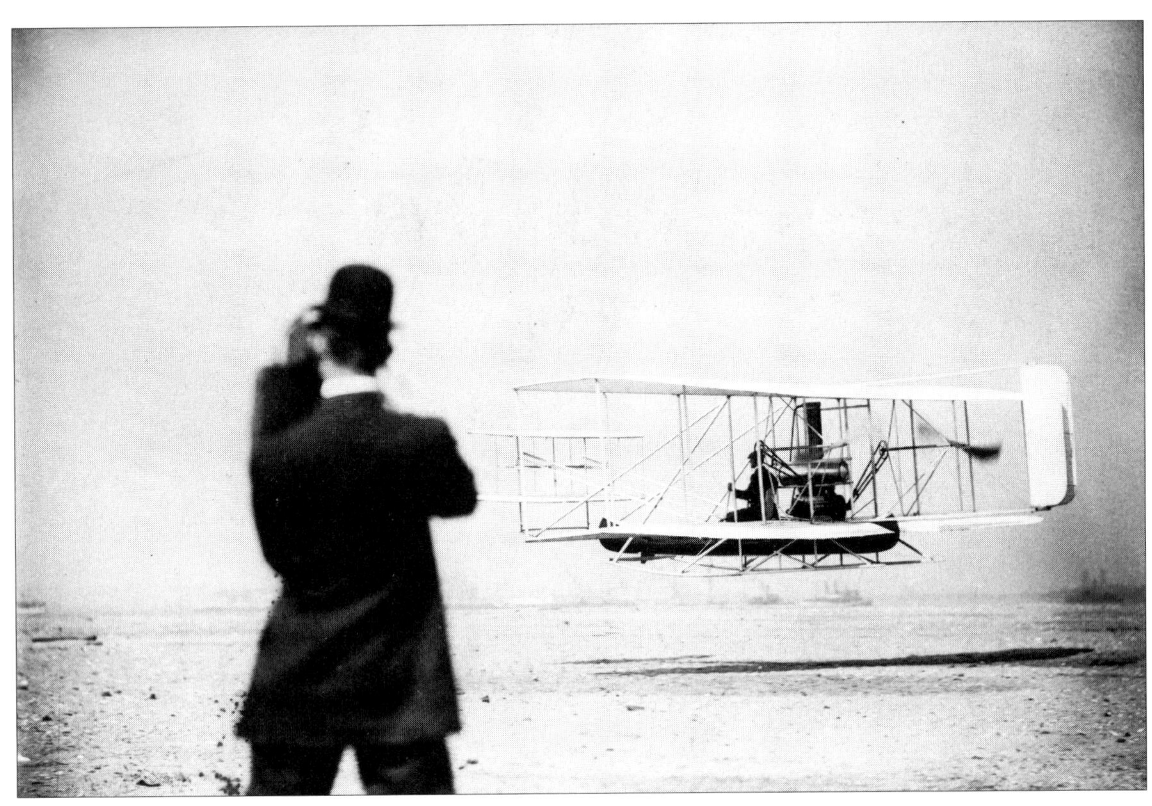

ORVILLE WRIGHT (1871–1948) AND WILBUR WRIGHT (1867–1912)

Orville and Wilbur Wright, brothers and inventors, built the world's first airplane to successfully sustain human flight. Their knowledge of machines was gleaned from years of owning their own bicycle business, and, even more importantly, from years of working with and flying gliders. They developed and patented a control system that enabled pilots to effectively steer a "flying machine." They made the first controlled, powered and sustained heavier-than-air flight at Kill Devil Hills, North Carolina, south of Kitty Hawk, on December 17, 1903. This photo shows the start of Wilbur's first flight over water on September 29, 1909 in New York.

CHARLES LINDBERGH (1902–1974)

Charles Lindbergh's non-stop flight across the Atlantic Ocean in a single-seat, single-engine airplane, made him a national hero. "Lucky Lindy," as the press called him, took off from Roosevelt Field on Long Island in the *Spirit of Saint Louis* on May 20, 1927 and landed at Le Bourget Airport in Paris thirty-three and one-half hours later. Lindbergh then promoted air travel and flew on goodwill tours for the U.S. government. The kidnapping and murder of his twenty-month-old son in 1932 forced his withdrawal from public life. Lindbergh initially opposed U.S. involvement in World War II, but later flew many combat missions in the Pacific. In later years he was involved in many environmental causes. He said: "The human future depends on our ability to combine the knowledge of science with the wisdom of wildness."

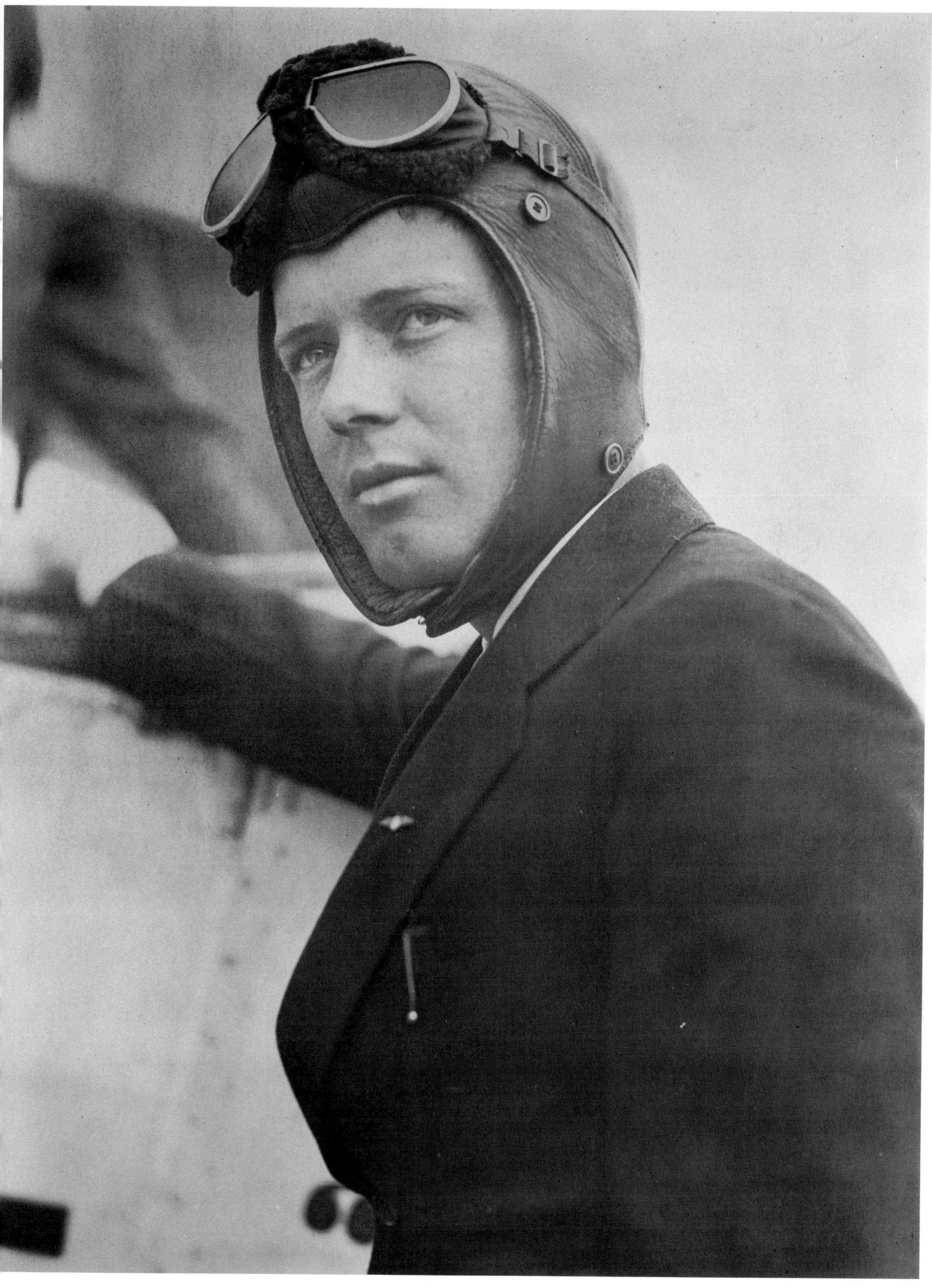

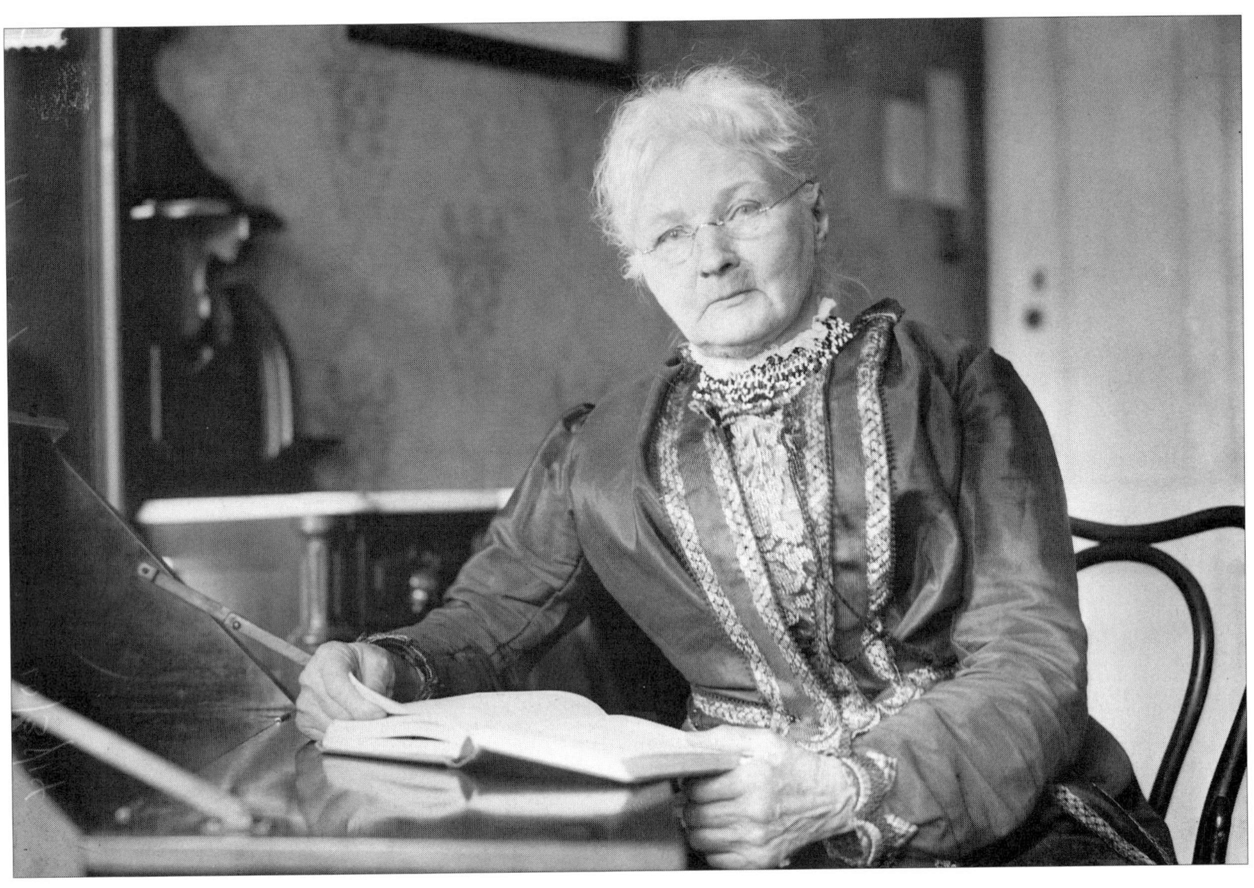

MARY HARRIS "MOTHER" JONES (1830–1930)

Mother Jones was a prominent American labor leader who worked passionately for the rights of workers. She was committed to fighting inhumane conditions in the railroad, steel, copper, coal, and textile industries and protested the use of child labor. Called "Mother" by the miners who adored her, she risked arrest and violence to strike for reforms. At a trial in 1902 for ignoring an injunction prohibiting striking miners from holding meetings, a West Virginia district attorney called her the "most dangerous woman in America." She was one of the founding members of the Industrial Workers of the World in 1905.

JANE ADDAMS (1860–1935)

Jane Addams was the leader of the United States settlement house movement. In 1889, she was a cofounder of Hull House in Chicago, which offered health, education, and social services to the urban poor. Addams was active in ending child labor, the struggle for women's rights, and in the women's peace movement during World War I. In 1931 she became the first American woman to be awarded the Nobel Peace Prize.

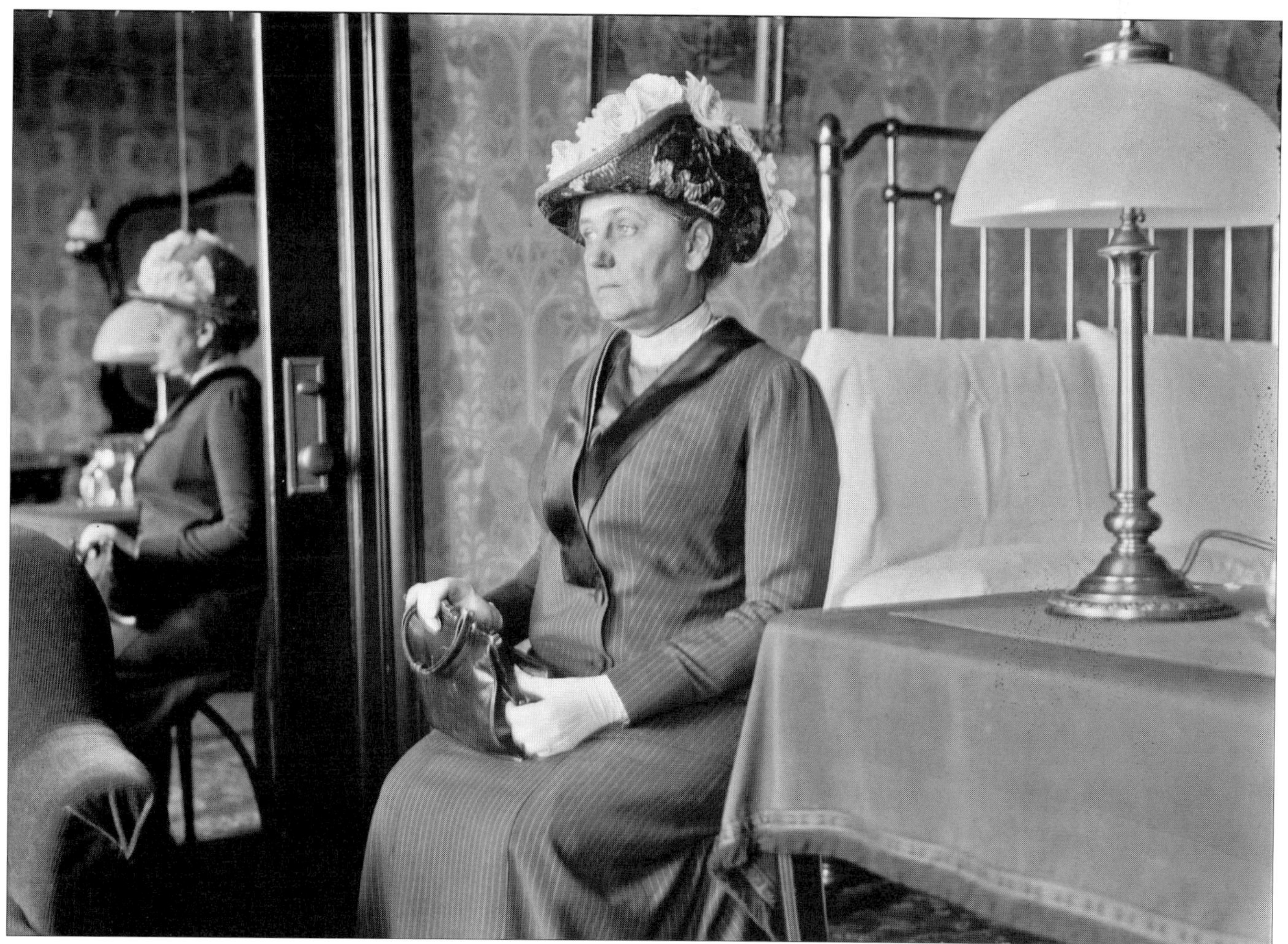

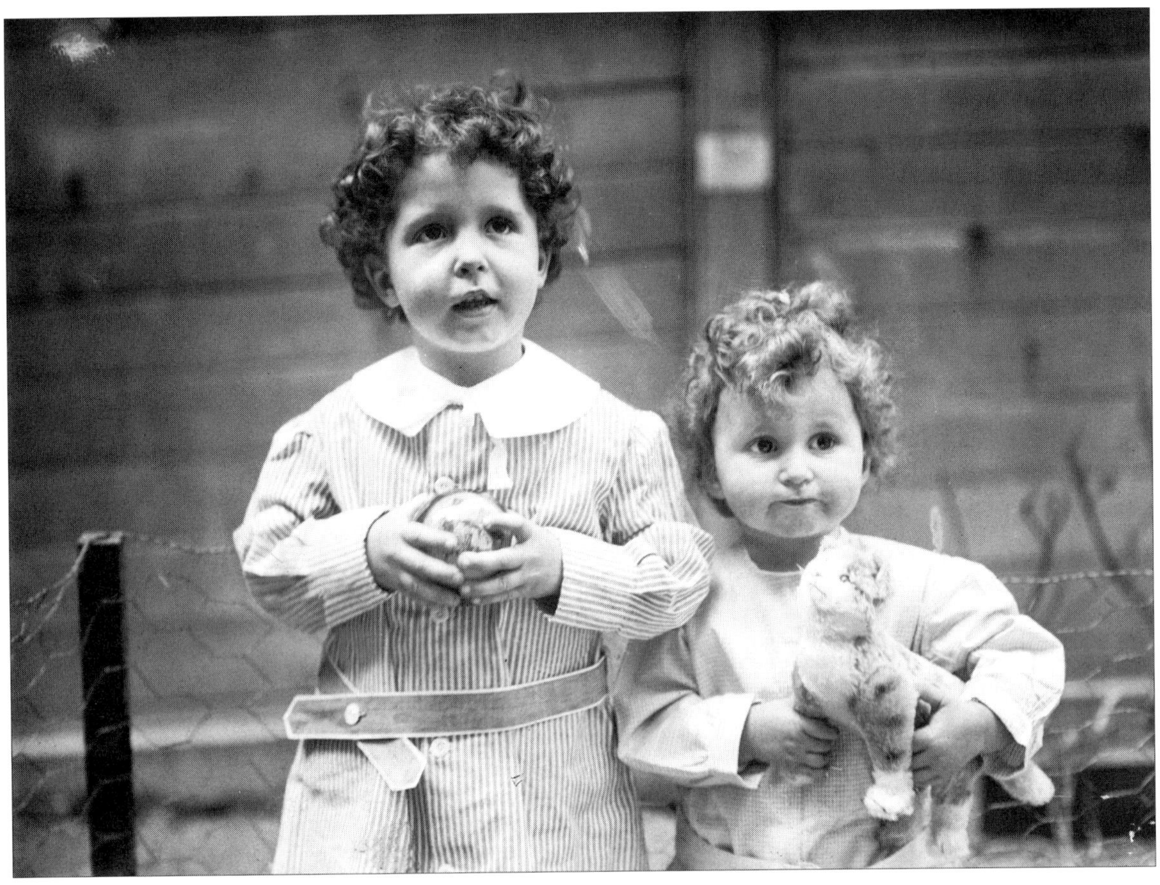

MICHEL NAVRATIL (1908–2001) AND EDMOND NAVRATIL (1910–1950)

Titanic survivors and orphans, these French brothers were identified as two-year-old Michel and four-year-old Edmond Navratil. (Originally, this photo was labeled Louis and Lola.) Their father, with whom they were traveling, died after placing the boys in the last lifeboat launched following the *Titanic*'s collision with an iceberg in the north Atlantic on April 14, 1912. Unable to speak English or identify themselves, the boys were briefly labeled the "*Titanic* orphans" but were soon reunited with their mother through illustrated newspaper articles. Michel became a professor of philosophy and died in Montpellier, France. Edmond became an architect and builder.

MARGARET "MOLLY" BROWN (1867–1932) AND CAPTAIN ARTHUR HENRY ROSTRON (1869–1940)

Early feminist Molly Brown was best known for her heroism in April 1912 during the sinking of the *Titanic.* Molly helped panicked passengers into lifeboats and tended to them aboard the rescue ship *Carpathia*. In this photo, taken on May 29, 1912, she presents a silver loving cup to the *Carpathia*'s Captain Rostron on behalf of the survivor's committee. Her life inspired the 1960 Meredith Wilson musical, *The Unsinkable Molly Brown.*

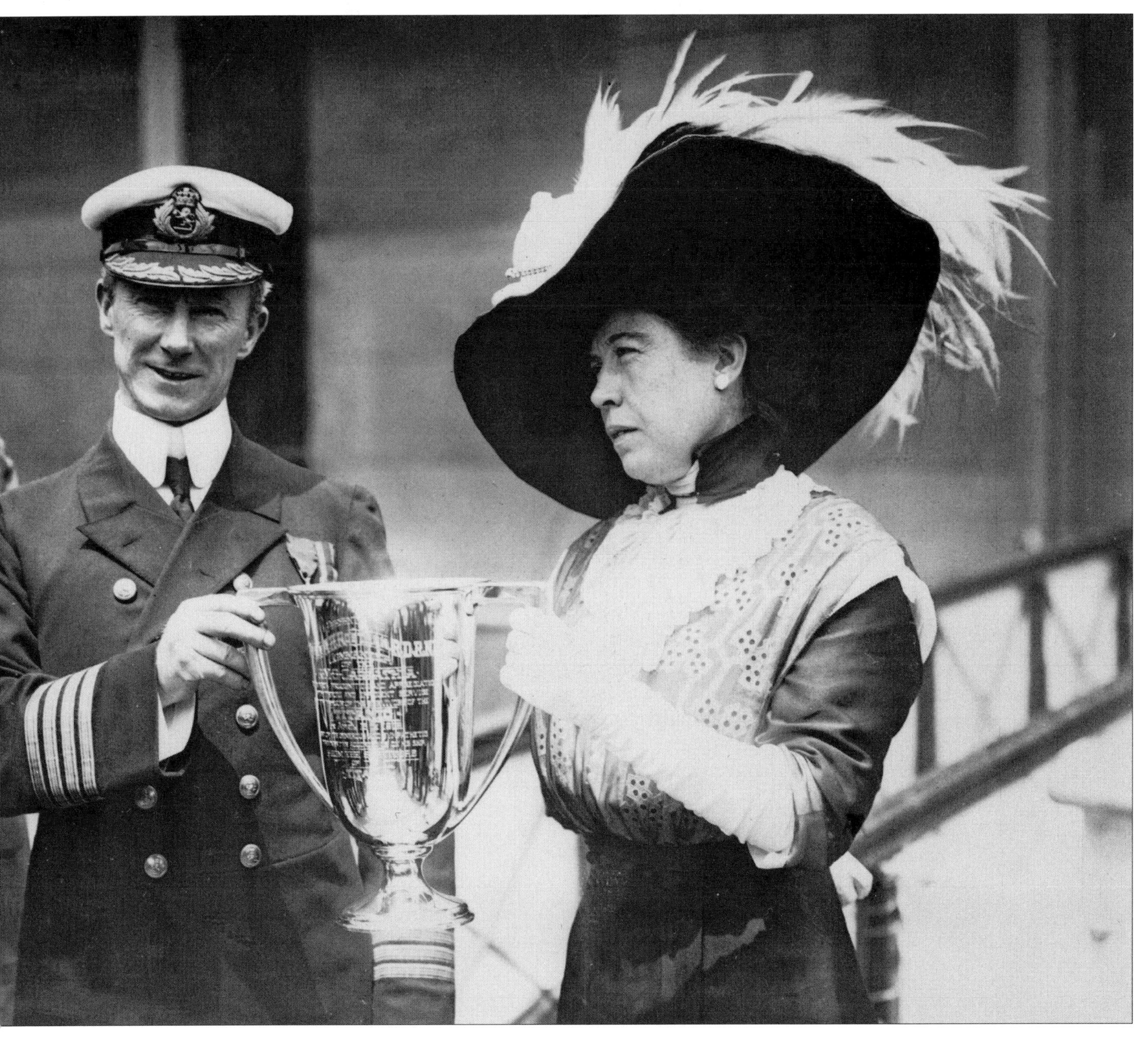

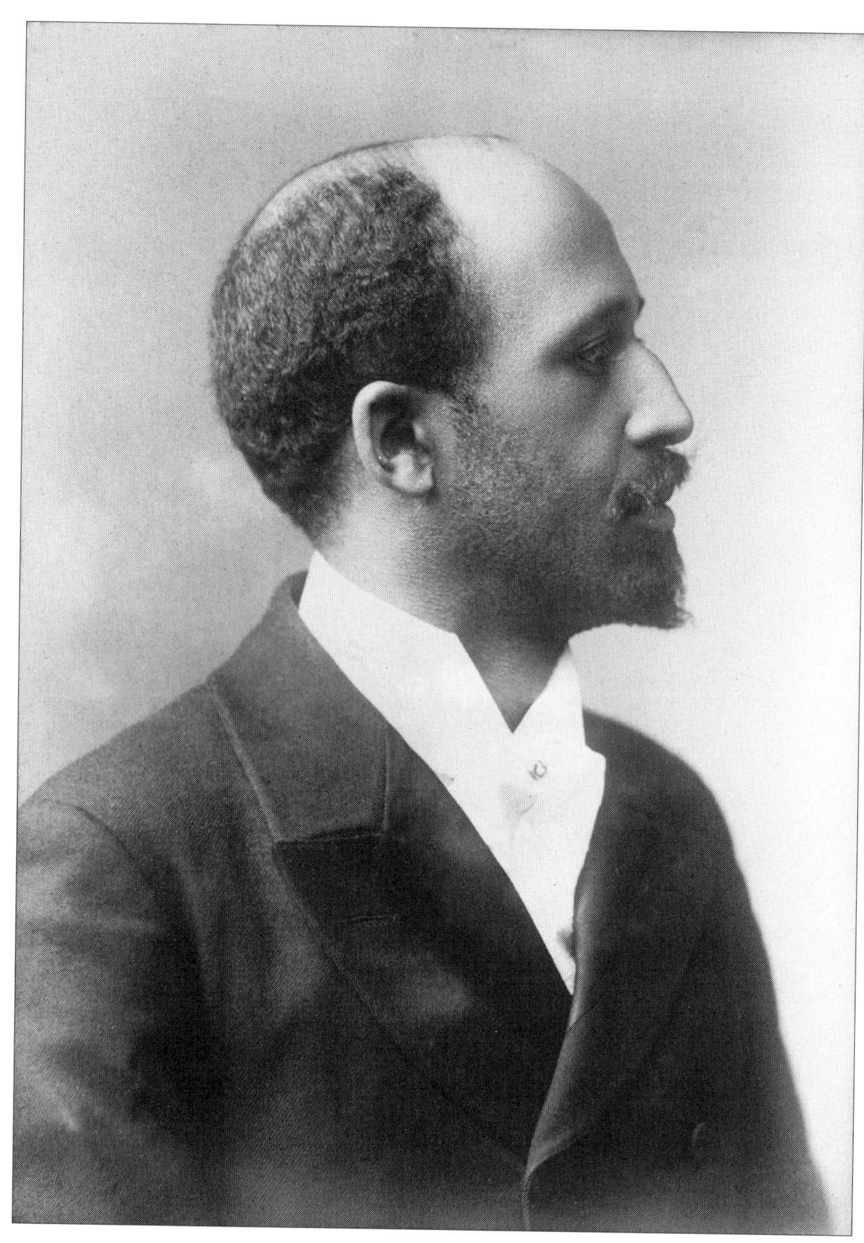

W. E. B. DU BOIS (1868–1963)

W. E. B. Du Bois was an African-American scholar and intellectual. He earned a doctorate from Harvard University and became a professor, writer, and authority on Black culture. He clashed with Black leaders such as Booker T. Washington, who urged integration into White society, writing *The Souls of Black Folk* (1903) to promote his views. Du Bois worked for the NAACP and edited their magazine *Crisis,* but broke with that organization in the 1930s. Growing increasingly disillusioned with the United States, he renounced his citizenship and in 1961 emigrated to Ghana where he died two years later.

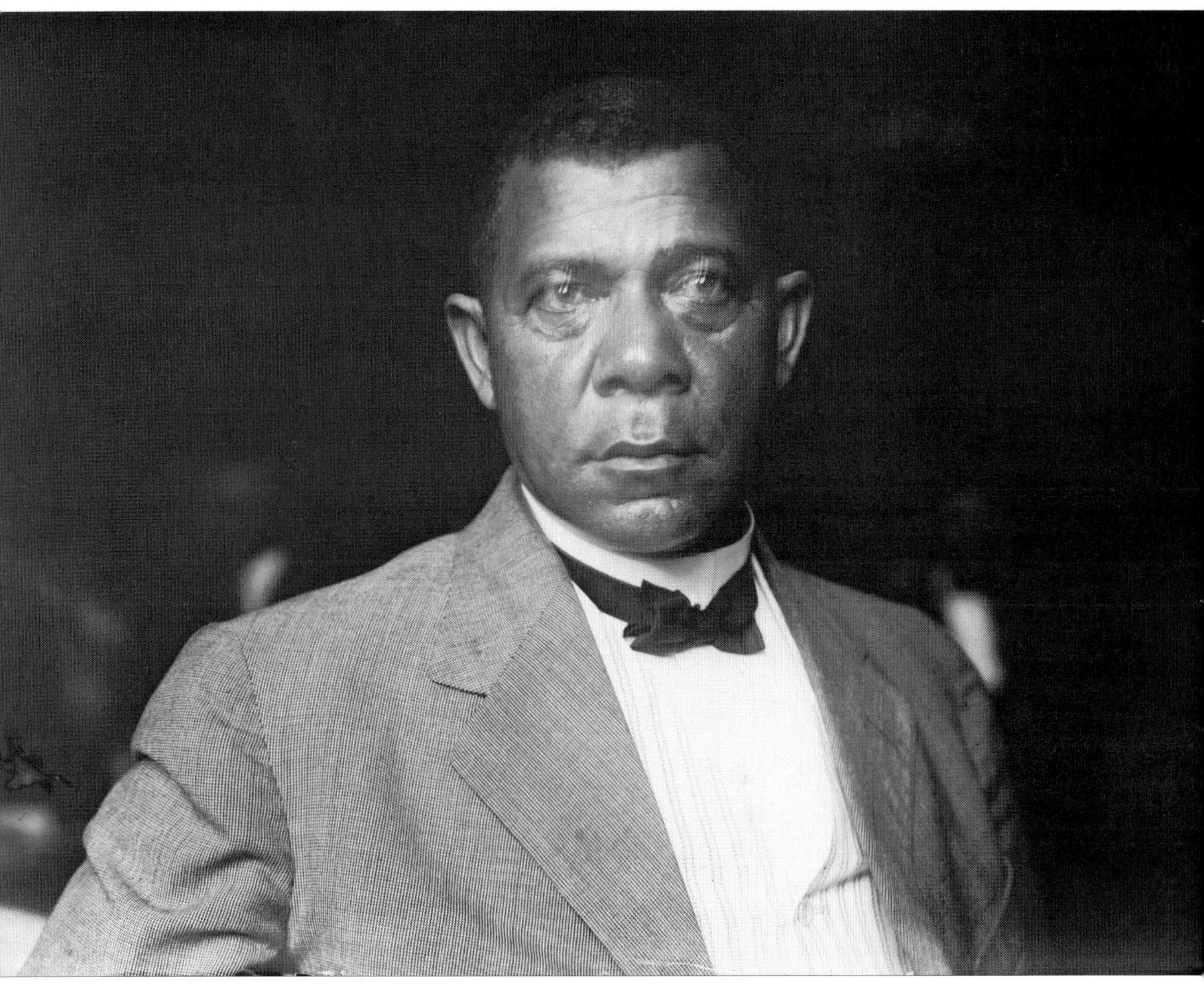

BOOKER T. WASHINGTON (1856–1915)

African American leader Booker T. Washington was born a slave in rural Virginia. After the Civil War he attended Hampton Institute and Wayland Seminary, and, on the recommendation of the president of Hampton, in 1881 was named the first head of Tuskegee Institute (now Tuskegee University), a new Alabama teacher's college. He remained Tuskegee's head until his death. Stressing the importance of education in improving the lives of blacks in America, Washington was the most prominent leader of the African American community during the last twenty-five years of his life. His 1901 autobiography *Up From Slavery* is an American classic.

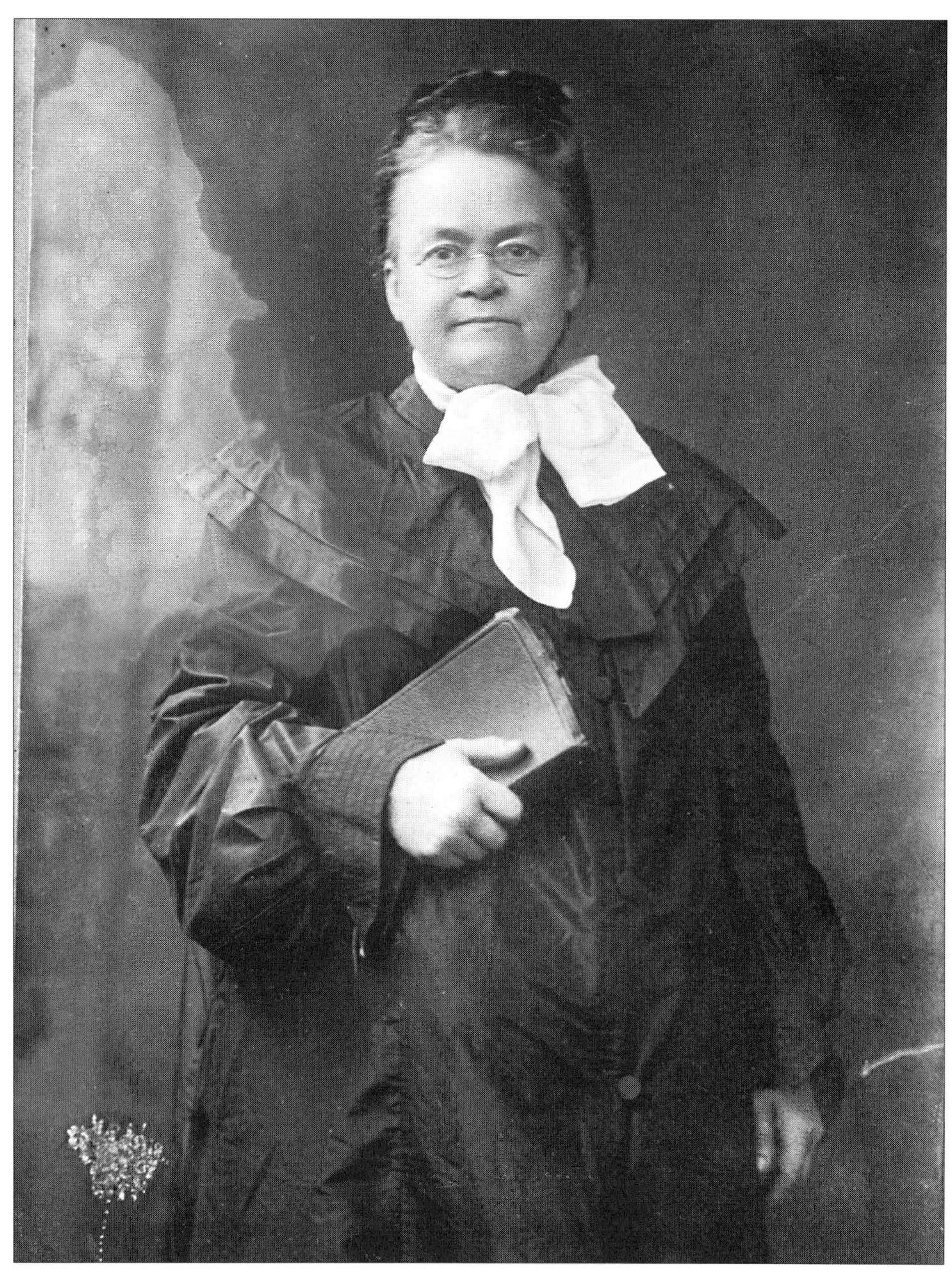

CARRY NATION (1846–1911)

Carry Nation was known as a bar room smasher and used radical means to lobby for a ban on alcohol in the years prior to Prohibition. She founded a branch of the Women's Christian Temperance Movement in Kansas. Guided by religious fervor, she vandalized saloons with a prayer book in one hand and a hatchet in the other. These "hatchetations," as she called them, resulted in Nation being arrested more than thirty times.

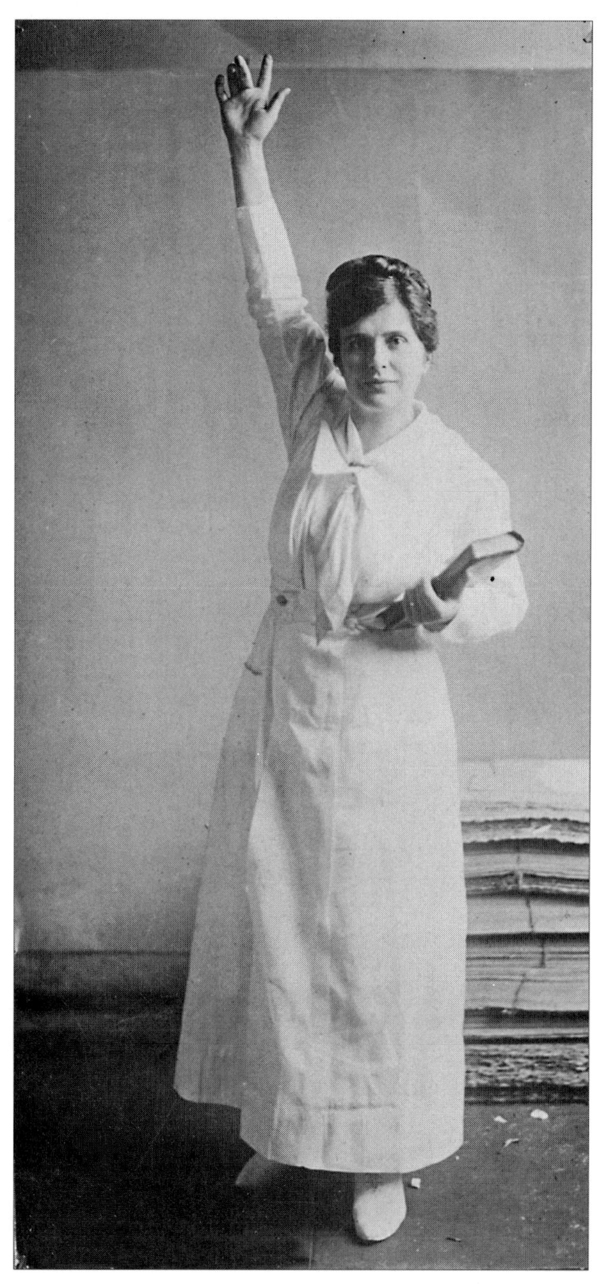

AIMEE SEMPLE McPHERSON (1890–1944)

A forerunner of modern televangelists, Aimee Semple McPherson was a religious sensation in the 1920s and 1930s. She spent years as an itinerant Pentecostal preacher before settling in Los Angeles where, in 1923, she founded the Foursquare Church which was filled to capacity three times a day, seven days a week. McPherson's sermons were media events and she was a skillful publicist and fundraiser. She was the first woman to be granted a broadcast license and to preach sermons on the radio.

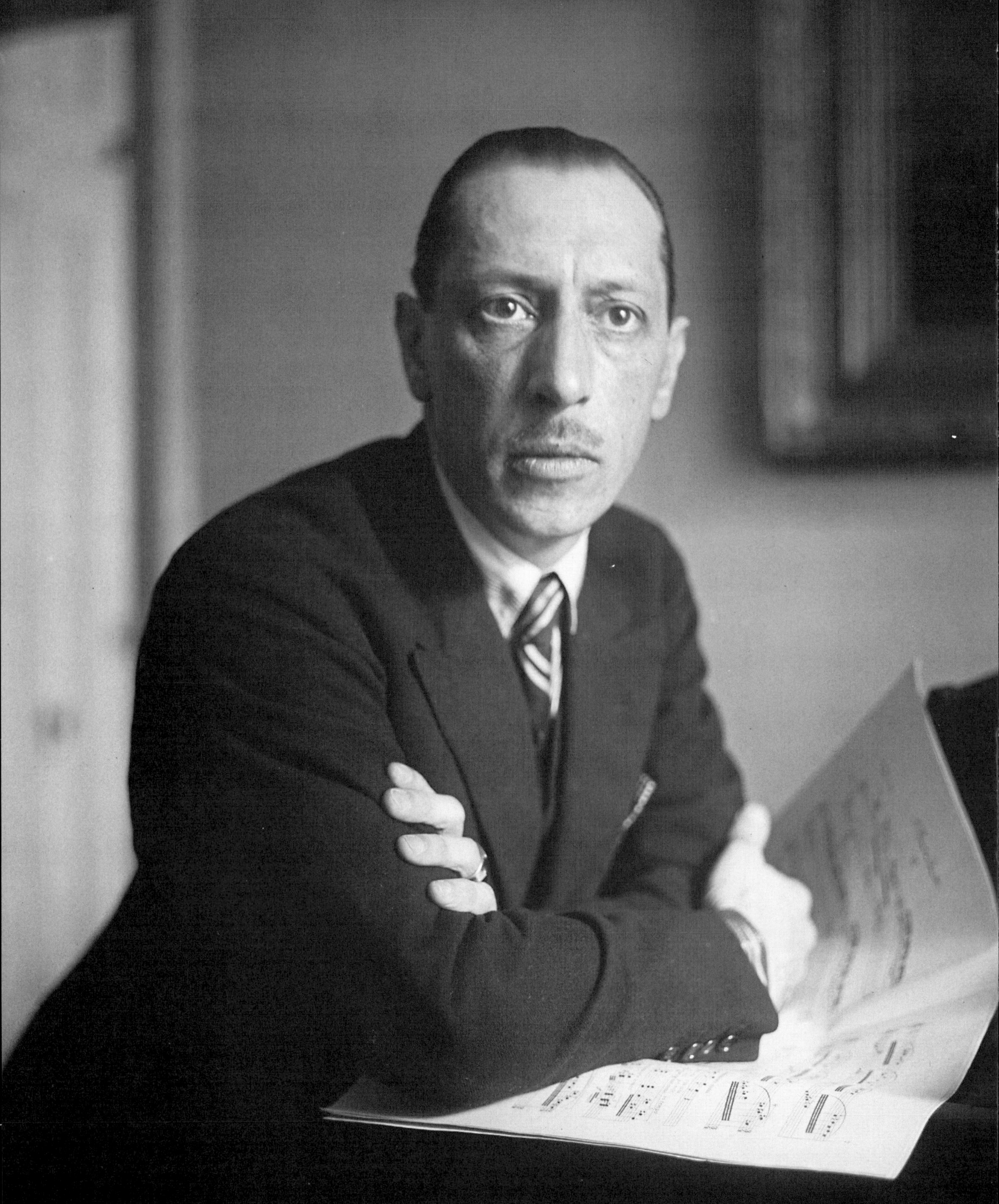

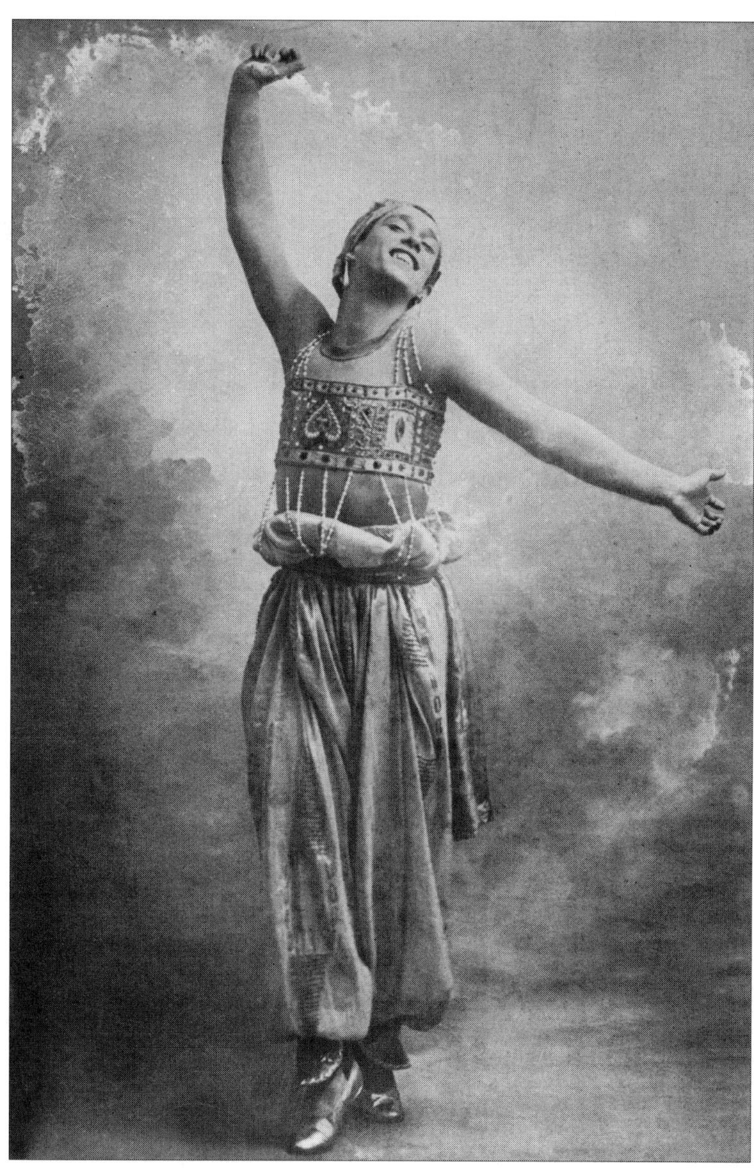

VASLAV NIJINSKY (1890–1950)

A Russian ballet dancer considered to be one of the most gifted male dancers of all time, Vaslav Nijinsky became a star in Diaghliev's Ballets Russes. His roles in Stravinsky's *Petrushka* (1911) and *The Rite of Spring* (1913), as well as Debussy's *Afternoon of a Faun* (1912) caused a stir when they premiered. His strong and suggestive choreography challenged tradition and heralded the age of modern dance.

IGOR STRAVINSKY (1882–1971)

Igor Stravinsky was a Russian-born composer, conductor, and pianist. The three ballets he composed for Sergei Diaghliev's Ballets Russes—*Firebird* (1910), *Petrushka* (1911), and *The Rite of Spring* (1913) won him worldwide fame. He was as innovator who tackled diverse musical forms—concertos, symphonies, and choral works. At the start of World War II in 1939, Stravinsky left Europe for America, establishing his home in the Los Angeles area where he lived until moving to New York two years before his death.

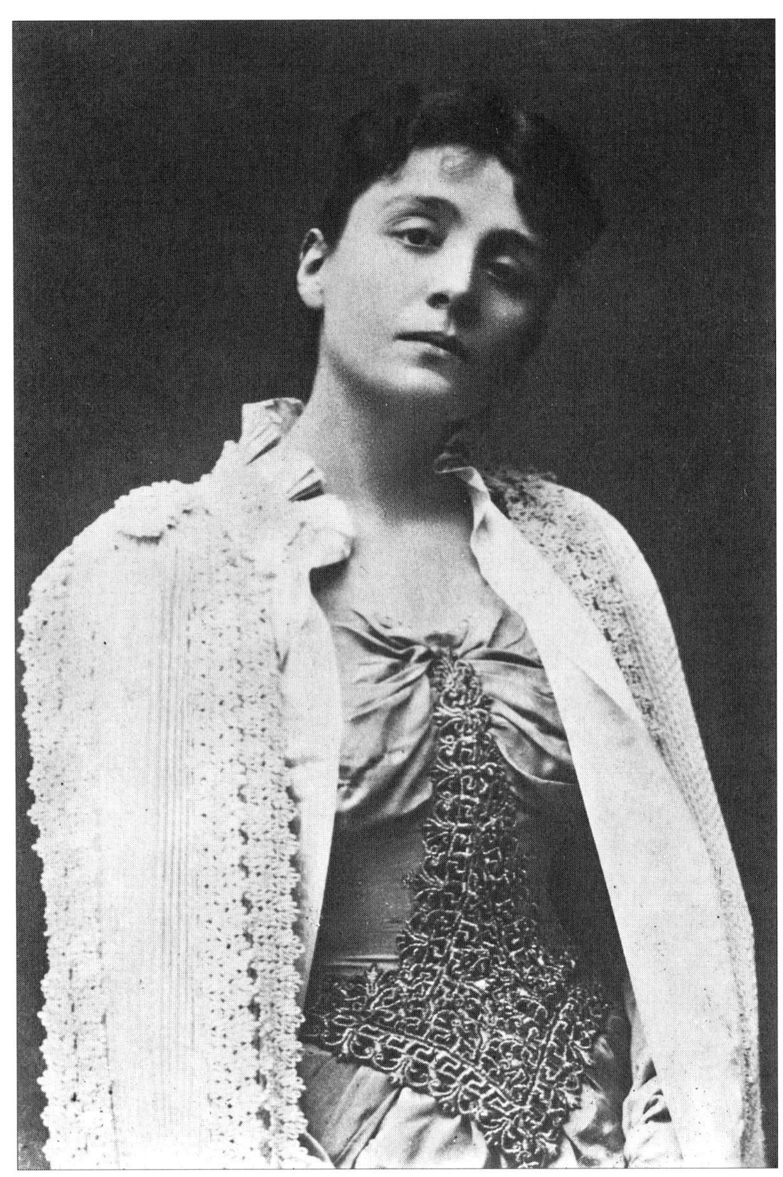

ELEANORA DUSE (1859–1924)

Eleanora Duse was an Italian actress who brought life to the plays of Henrik Ibsen, Gabriele d'Annunzio, and others. She toured Europe, South America, and the United States and won acclaim for her genius on stage. She was the first woman to appear on the cover of *Time* magazine (1923).

ENRICO CARUSO (1873–1921)

Enrico Caruso was one of the greatest operatic tenors in history. He sang at La Scala in his native Italy, the Royal Opera House at Covent Garden, London, and was leading tenor at the Metropolitan Opera in New York for seventeen years. He made his Met debut on November 23, 1903, as the Duke of Mantua in Verdi's *Rigoletto.* His fame endures in the hundreds of recordings that he made between 1902 and 1920.

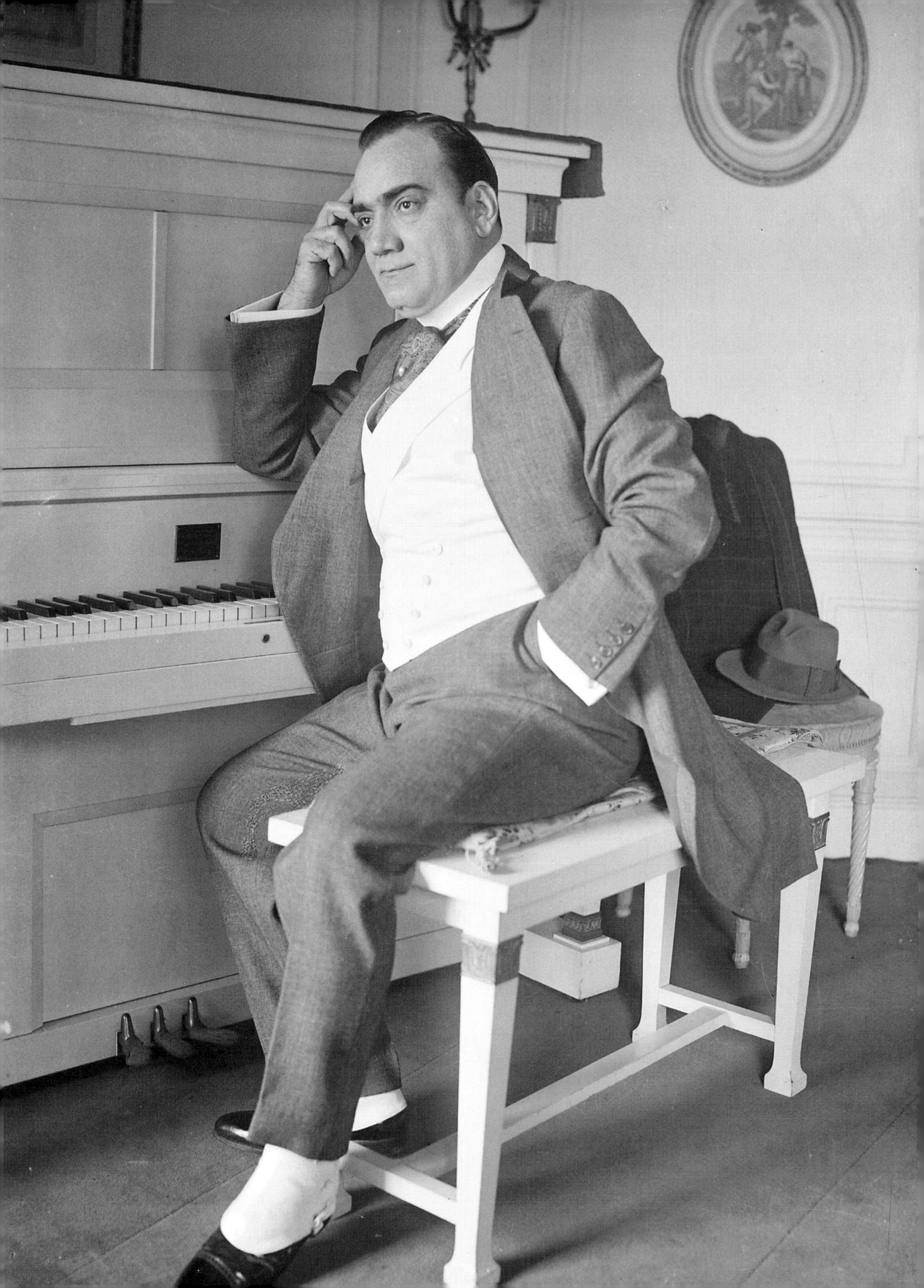

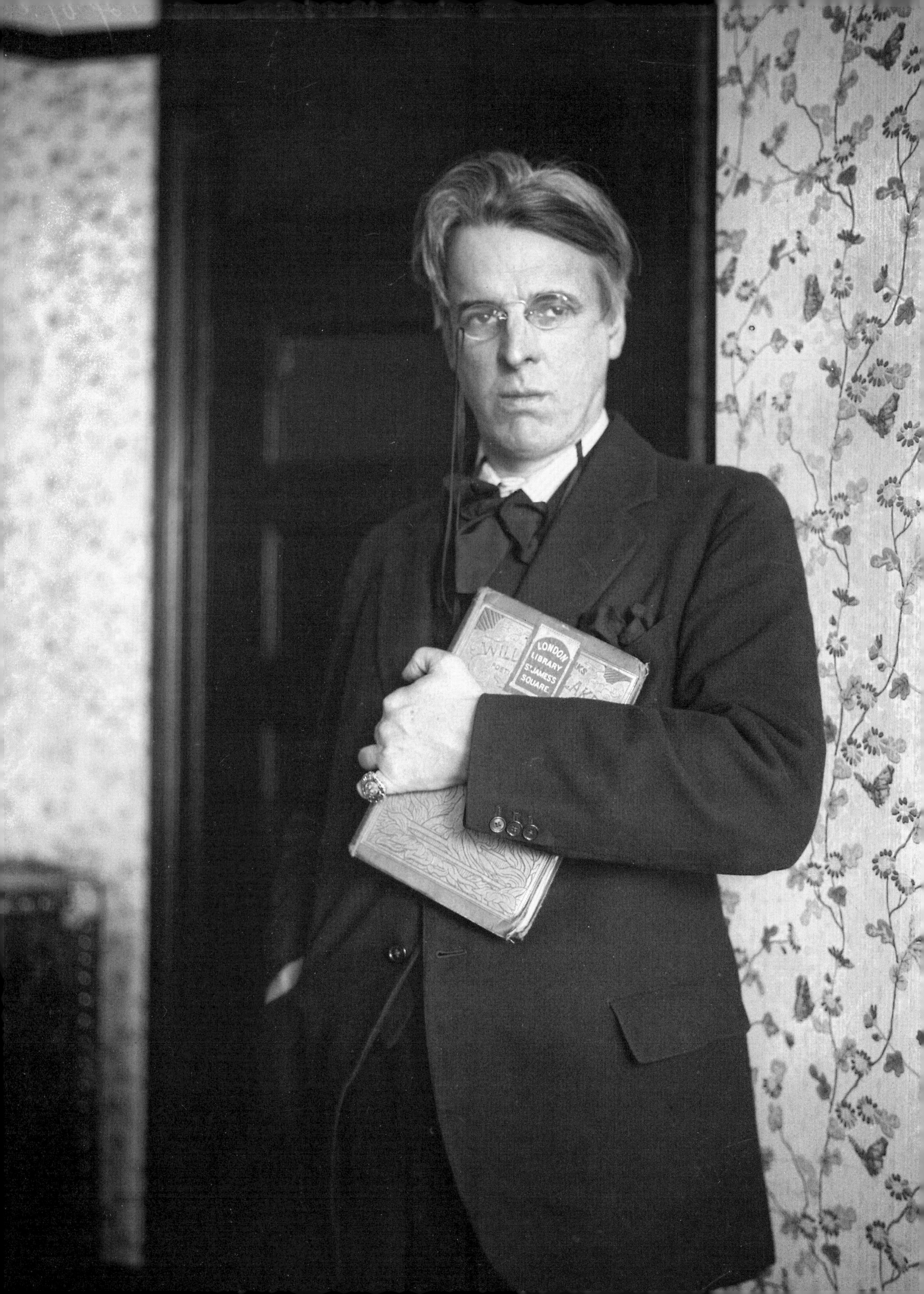
LONDON
LIBRARY
St JAMES'S
SQUARE

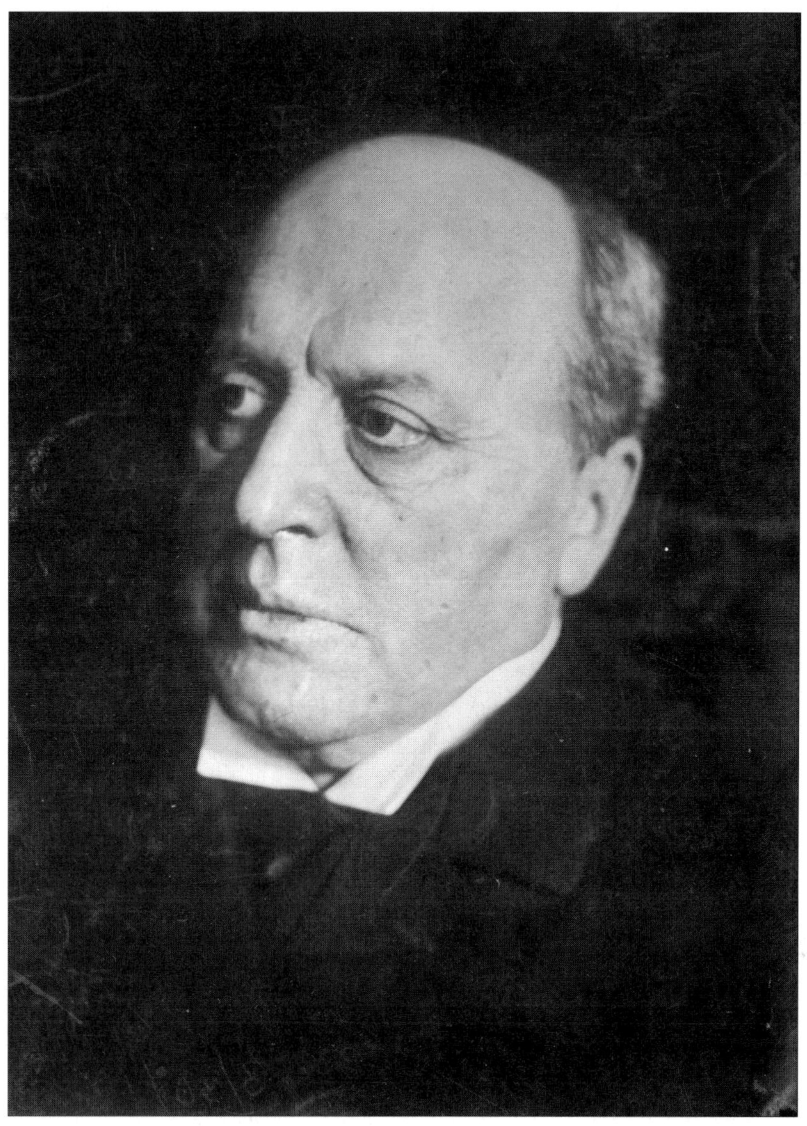

HENRY JAMES (1843–1916)

Henry James, a prolific author, was born in the United States but lived most of his life in England and became a British citizen. Born into a prominent American intellectual family, he was the brother of philosopher William James and diarist Alice James. Among his most famous novels are *Daisy Miller* (1879) and *Portrait of a Lady* (1881). His short story "The Turn of the Screw" is a classic.

WILLIAM BUTLER YEATS (1865–1939)

Born in Dublin, William Butler Yeats is considered one of the great poets of the twentieth century. His works draw on Irish myth and folklore, as well as Irish revolutionary politics. Yeats was awarded the Nobel Prize in Literature in 1923. He became a senator of the Irish Free States in 1922 and was active as a playwright and cultural leader. With Lady Gregory, Sean O'Casey, John Millington Synge, and others, Yeats played a major role in the early years of Dublin's Abbey Theatre, a major focus of Irish cultural life.

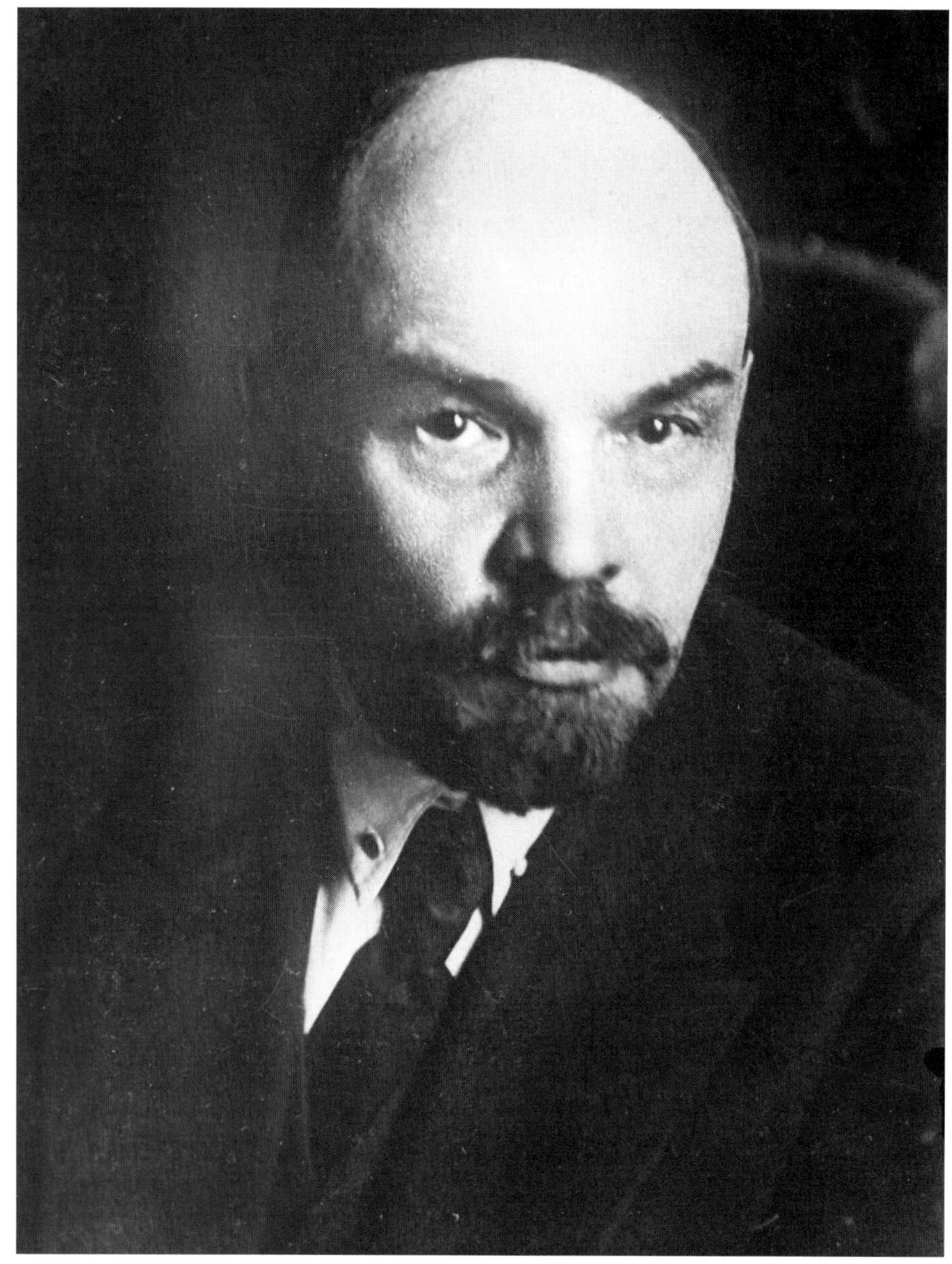

VLADIMIR ILYICH LENIN (1870–1924)

A mastermind of the Bolshevik Revolution in Russia in 1917, Vladimir Ilyich Lenin was also the first head of the Soviet state. He was originally exposed to radical thinking at Kazan State University and was eventually exiled to Siberia for involvement in subversive activities. He lived in Western Europe until 1917, when, sensing that change was possible in Russia, he returned to lead the October Revolution which established the Communist dictatorship. Lenin was considered a ruthless leader. He was seriously wounded in an assassination attempt in 1918 and died in 1924 following a series of strokes.

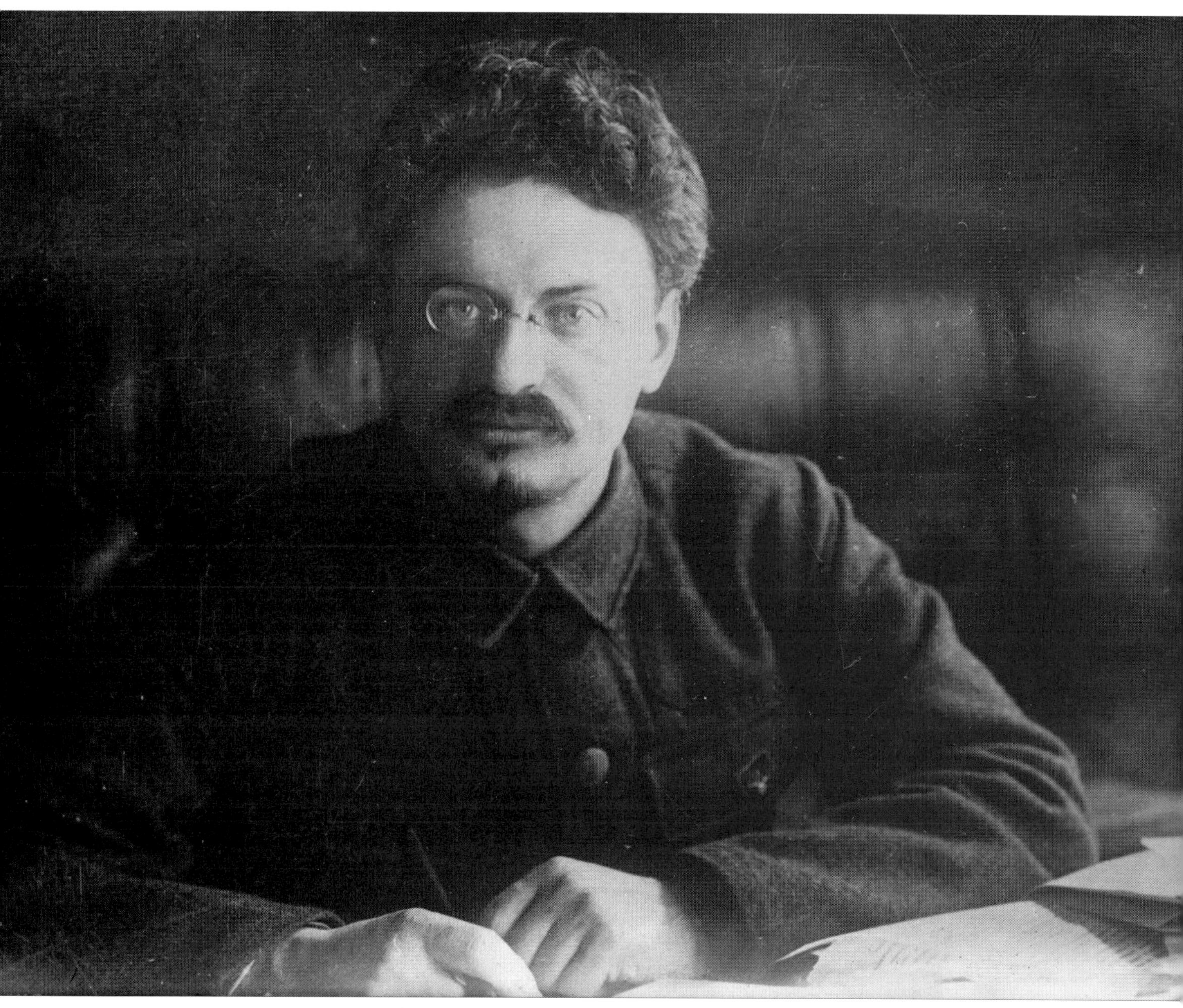

LEON TROTSKY (1879–1940)

Leon Trotsky was a key player in the Bolshevik regime in Russia and second in power to Lenin during the early years of communist rule. He became involved in underground activities as a teenager, was exiled to Siberia, and then lived abroad until 1917, just before the October Revolution. When Lenin died, Trotsky who was his supposed heir, was outmaneuvered by Stalin. While in exile in Mexico, Trotsky was assassinated in 1940 by an agent of the Soviet secret police.

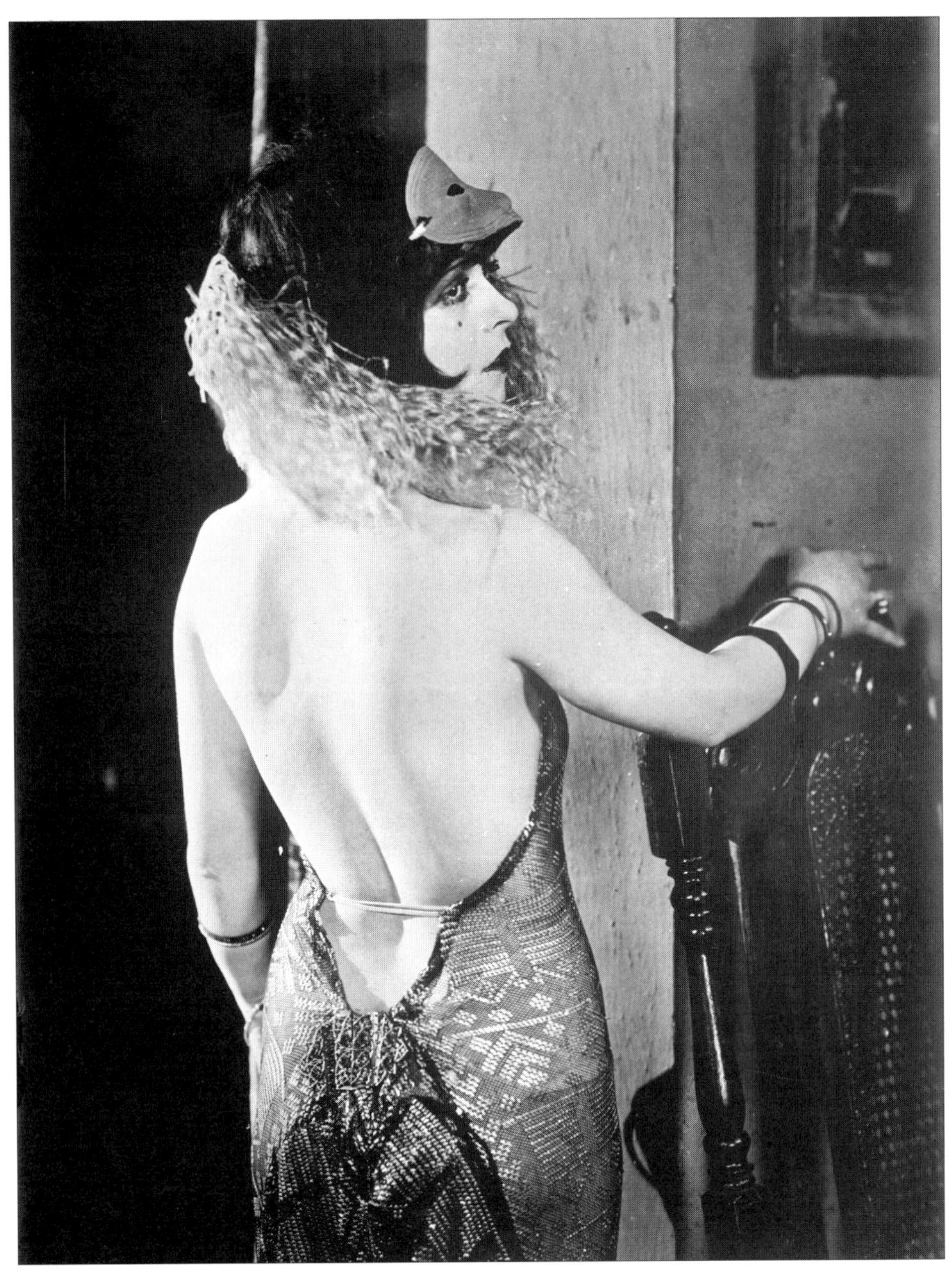

CLARA BOW (1905–1965)

Born in a Brooklyn tenement to an abusive family, Clara Bow starred in the film *It,* a 1927 romantic comedy based on an Elinor Glyn story, and became the famous "It" girl of the silent film era. *It* was her most popular film but it was also widely acknowledged that Bow had "it," meaning sex appeal. Later that year she starred in *Wings,* which won the first Academy Award for Best Picture. She continued to appear in films into the 1930s. The silent-screen actress was a model for many stars that came after her, from Marilyn Monroe to Madonna. Her last decades were troubled by mental illness. She once said: "Even now I can't trust life. It did too many awful things to me as a kid."

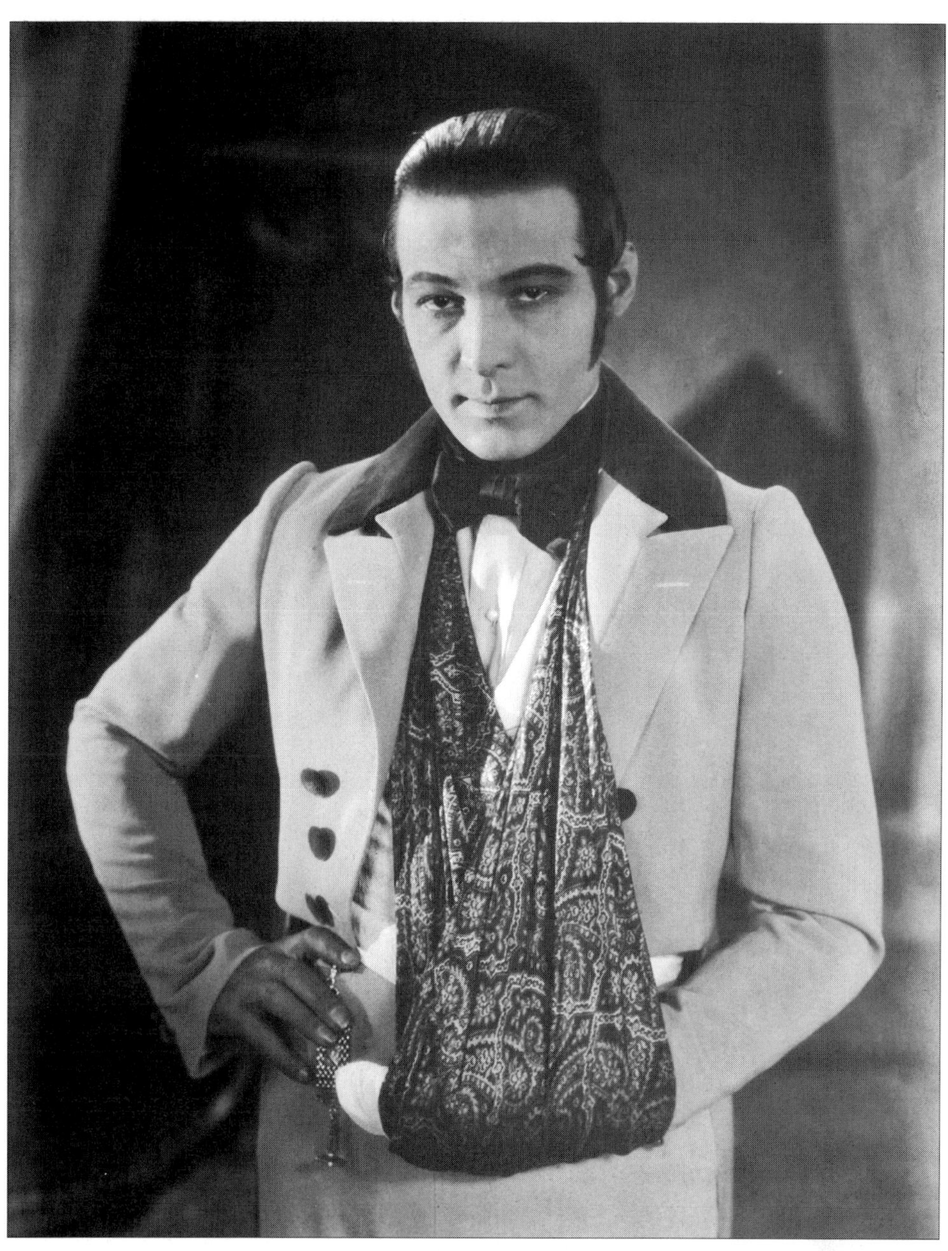

RUDOLPH VALENTINO (1895–1926)

Rudolph Valentino was one of the most popular film stars of the 1920s. He epitomized the Latin lover and drove women wild. Born in Italy, he arrived in New York in 1913 with no prospects. By 1917, he was getting small parts in films and hit the jackpot in 1921 with *Four Horsemen of the Apocalypse* and *The Sheik*. An estimated 100,000 people turned out for his funeral in New York after his sudden death at age thirty-one from complications following surgery for a perforated ulcer.

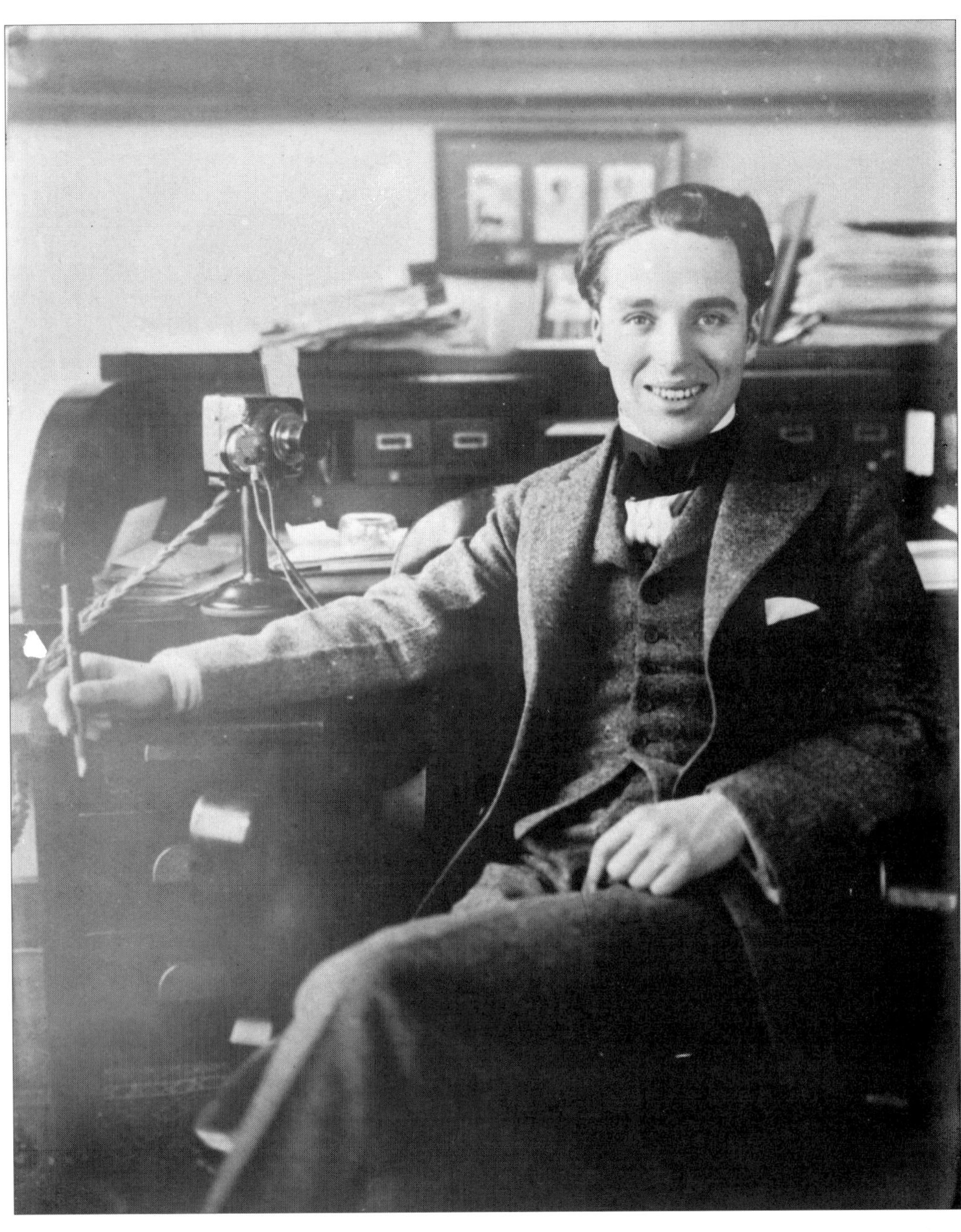

CHARLIE CHAPLIN (1889–1977)

Charlie Chaplin may be the best-known film star of the silent era. His popular character—the Tramp—clothed in a tattered suit and carrying a cane, is a well-meaning misfit who winds up in hilariously awkward situations. Chaplin was a master as both actor and director, controlling every detail on the set. In 1919 he cofounded United Artists with Mary Pickford, Douglas Fairbanks, and D. W. Griffith. His most famous films include *City Lights* (1931), *Modern Times* (1936), and *The Great Dictator* (1940).

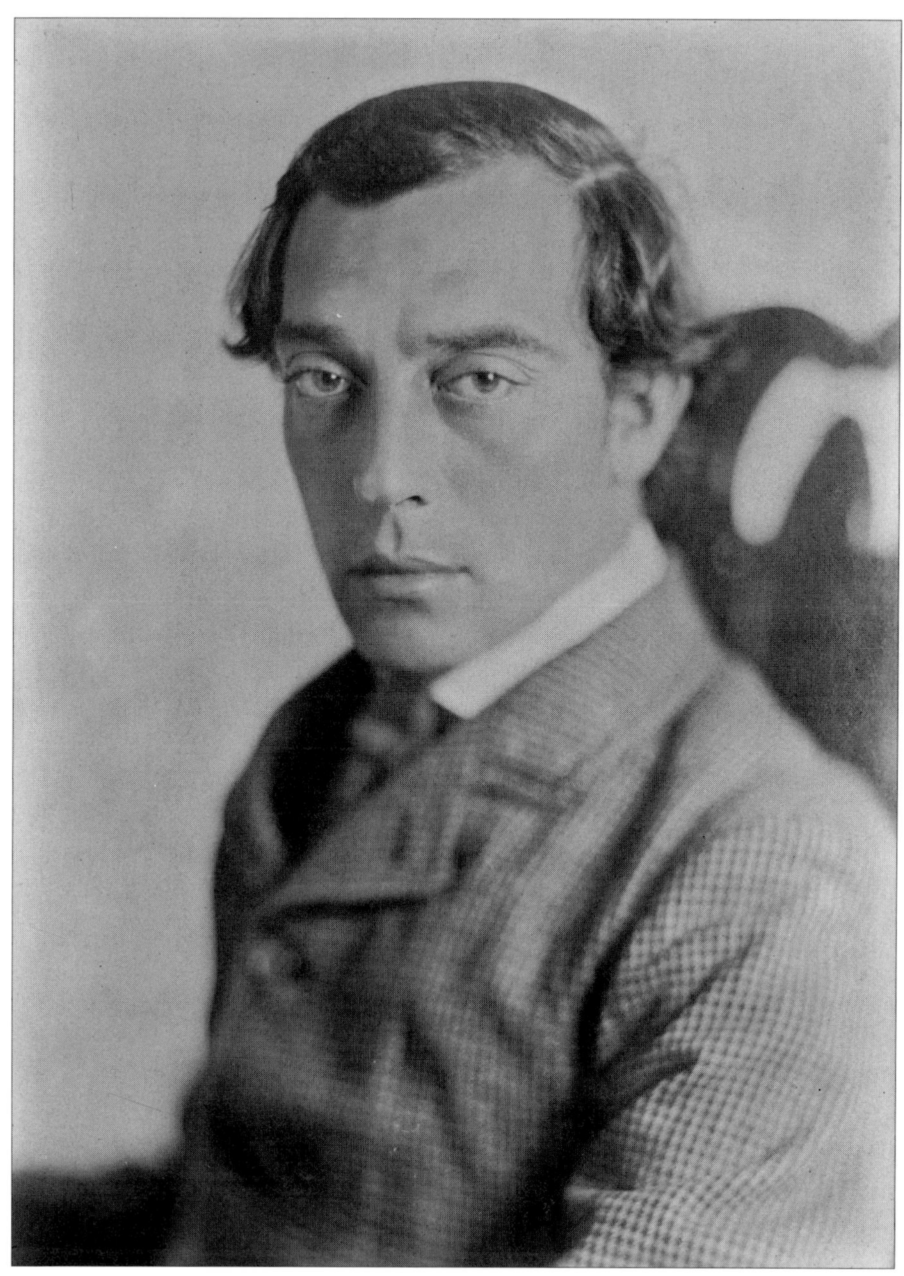

JOSEPH FRANCIS "BUSTER" KEATON (1895–1966)

Buster Keaton was an extraordinary silent film actor, who employed slapstick and sight gags to great effect. He is seen here in his masterpiece *The General* (1927), which is set during the American Civil War. Keaton plays Johnnie Gray, a Confederate train engineer whose locomotive—the "General"—is stolen by Union soldiers. Gray and his sweetheart cross enemy lines to reclaim the train and then return to warn the Confederates of the Union soldiers' advance. After a difficult transition period he had a successful second career in film and on television in the 1950s and 1960s.

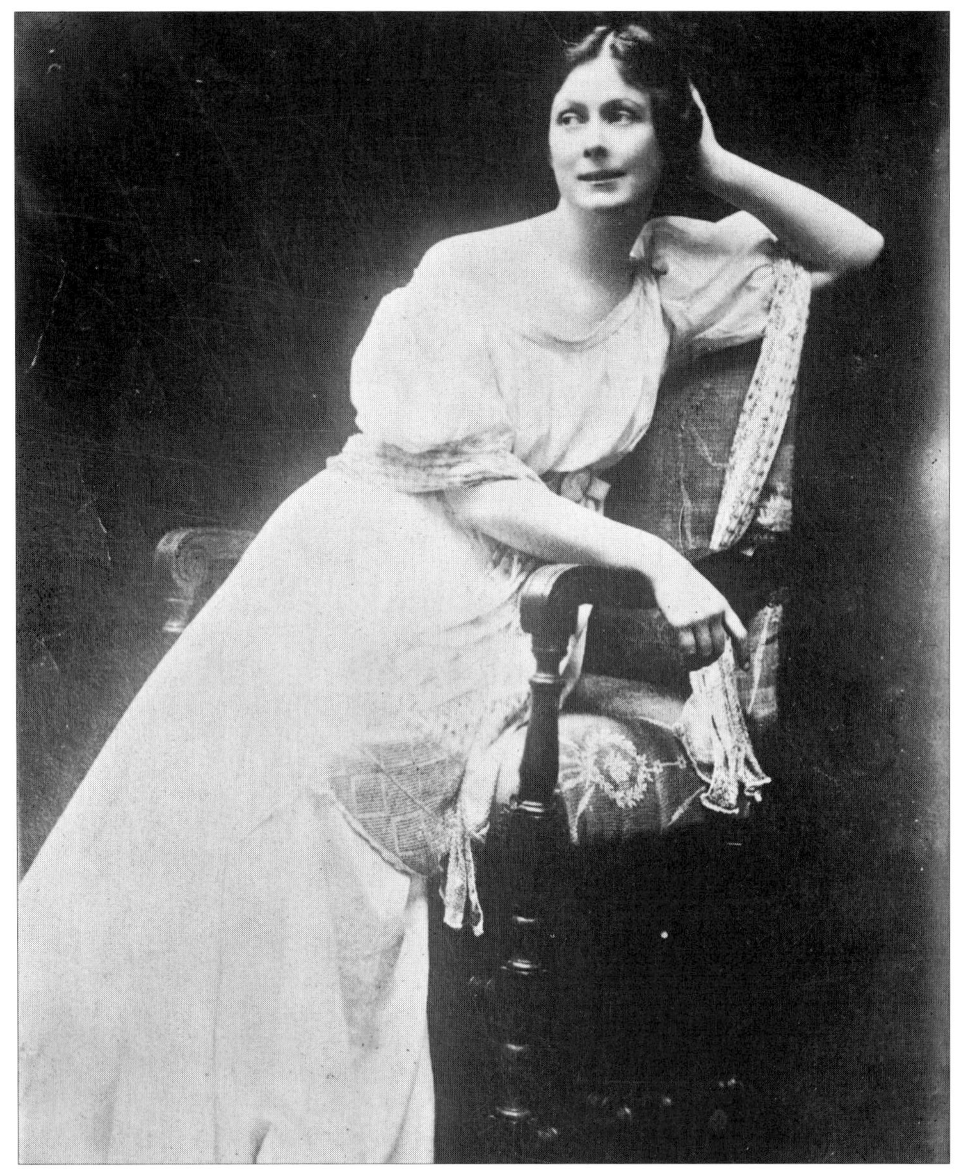

ISADORA DUNCAN (1878–1927)

Isadora Duncan was one of the creators of modern dance. Born in San Francisco and encouraged by her mother to explore the arts, she appeared in vaudeville shows as a teenager. Later, she took a natural, spiritual, and free approach to the medium, which was truly radical for her time. Audiences were both shocked and entranced by her athletic movements, which were performed in flowing robes and bare feet. She found her greatest popularity and celebrity in avant-garde circles in Europe. She died in a freak accident in Nice, France in 1927 when her long scarf became entangled in one of the wheels of an open automobile in which she was a passenger and strangled her.

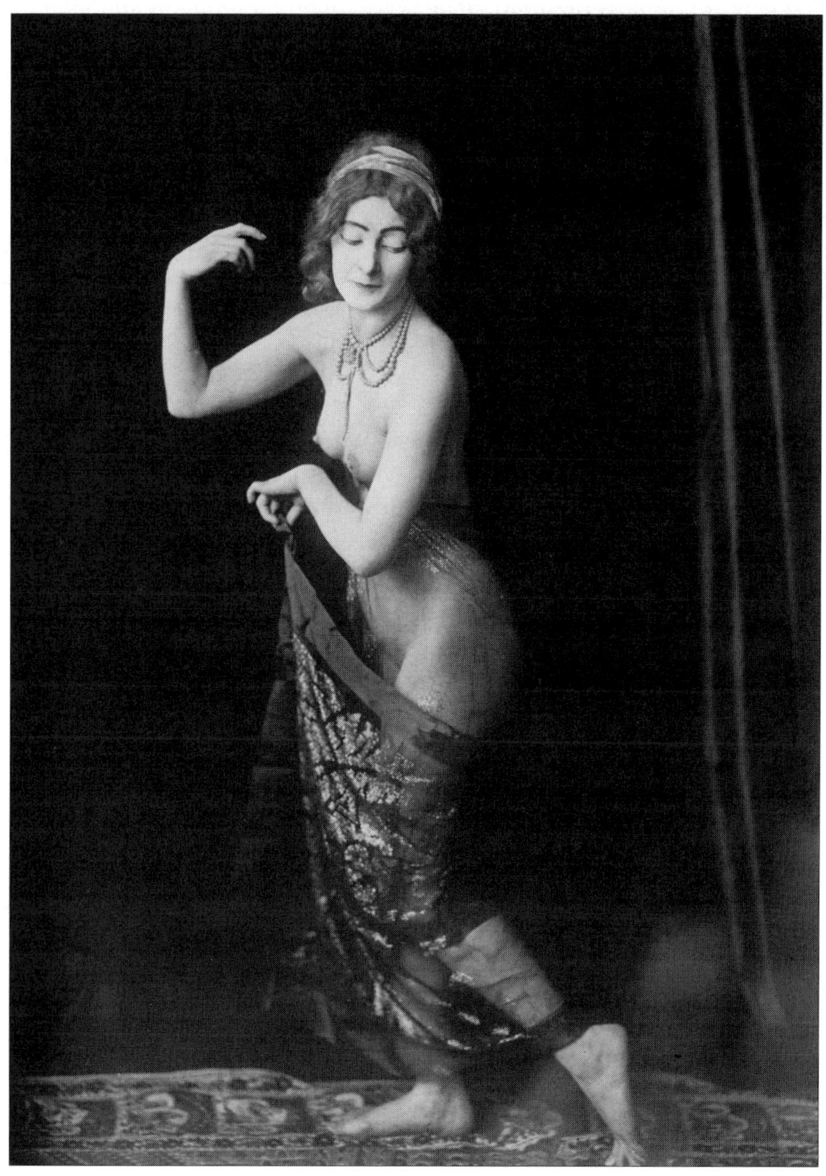

ADOREÉ VILLANY (N.D.)

Adoreé Villany was born in Rouen, France in the early 1900s. She was a self-taught dancer who often performed in the nude. Her pieces focused on mythical or classical themes and were coordinated with spoken monologues. Villany danced throughout Europe in rented spaces or private homes. In 1911, she was cited for obscenity by the Munich police, but continued, undaunted, to worship her body as art.

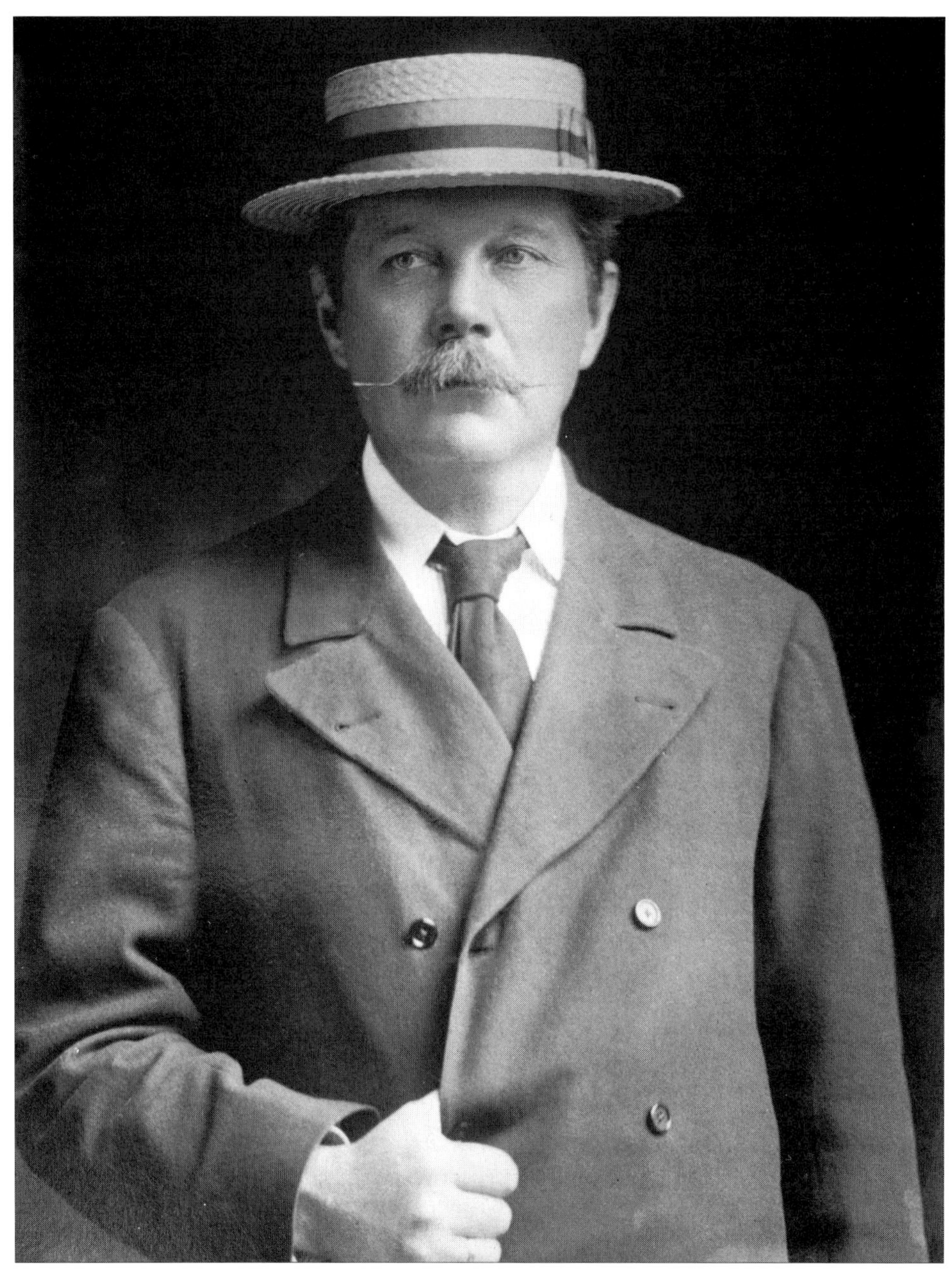

SIR ARTHUR CONAN DOYLE (1859–1930)

Sir Arthur Conan Doyle created the fictional detective Sherlock Holmes and revolutionized the crime fiction genre. While a practicing physician, Doyle launched the saga of Sherlock Holmes with *A Study in Scarlet* (1887). The character of Holmes was based on Doyle's former Edinburgh University professor Joseph Bell. The fifty-six Sherlock Holmes stories and four novels are easily the most popular works of detective fiction ever created—reprinted countless times and constantly imitated, parodied, and transformed into a never-ending sequence of plays, films, and television programs. Doyle also wrote historical novels and nonfiction. Later in life he turned to spiritualism and the occult.

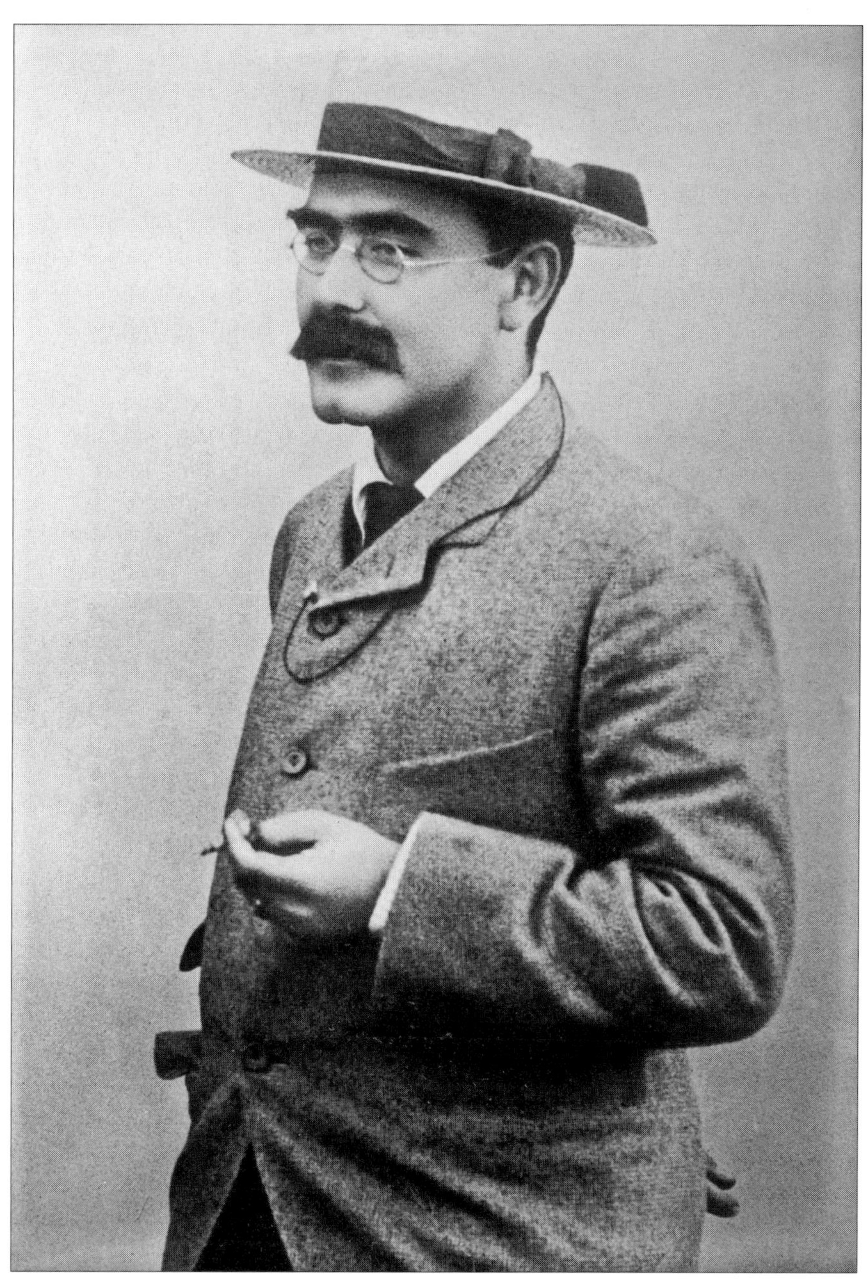

RUDYARD KIPLING (1865–1936)

Rudyard Kipling, English author and poet was born in Bombay (Mumbai), India during the British Raj. He is best known for his works *The Jungle Book* (1894) and *Just So Stories* (1902). His poems include "Mandalay" and "Gunga Din." Many of Kipling's stories are enduring classics including *The Jungle Book,* which was turned into a popular Disney film. He won the Nobel Prize in literature in 1907, making him the first English language writer to win—and the youngest winner at age forty-one. Later in the twentieth century, George Orwell and other critics stressed the imperialist, militarist, and racial prejudices expressed in much of Kipling's works. His legacy remains controversial.

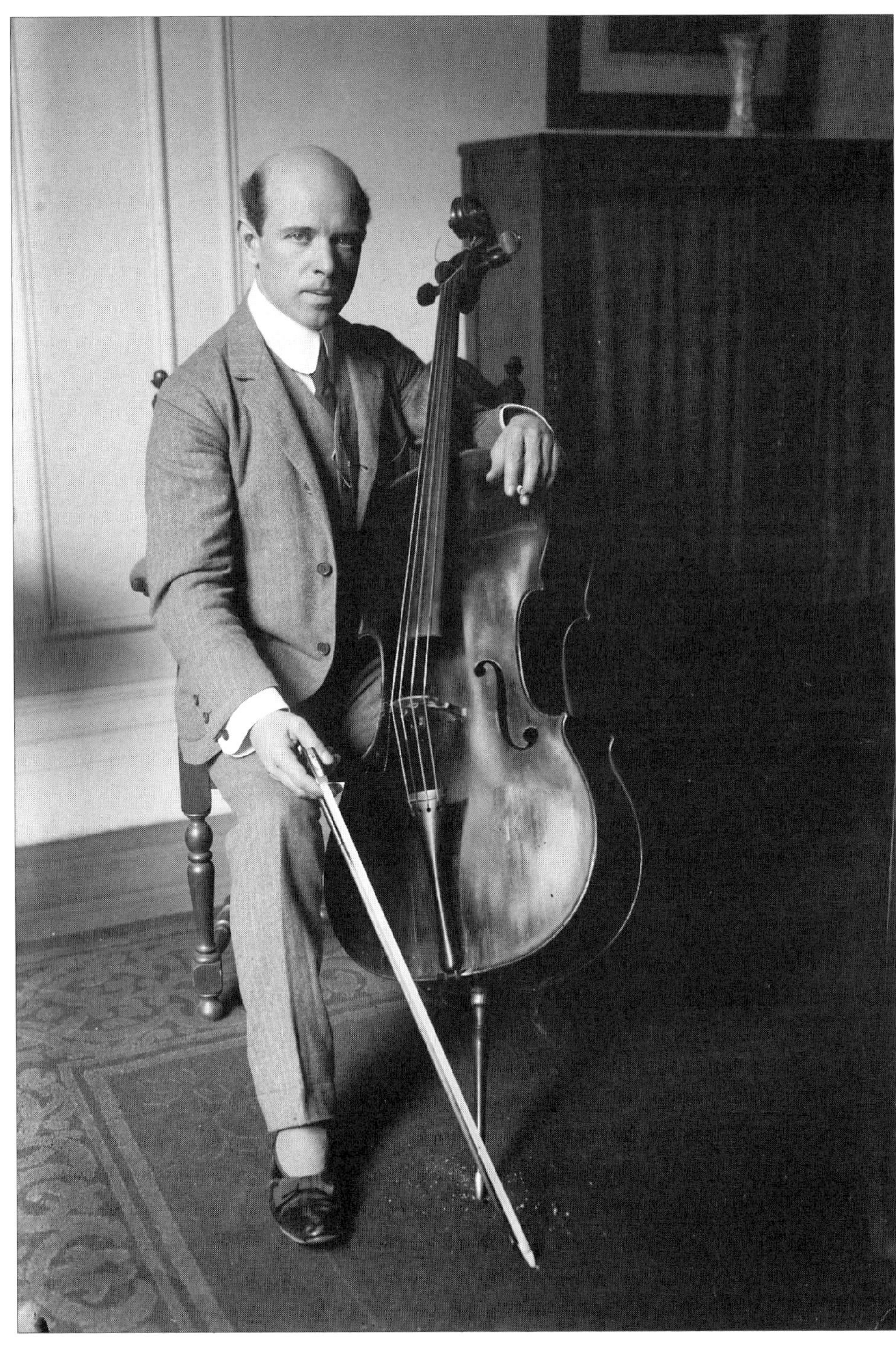

PABLO CASALS (1876–1973)

Born in Catalonia, Spain, Pablo Casals was a brilliant cellist who gave his first solo performance in Barcelona at the age of fourteen. Following the defeat of the Spanish republican government in 1939, Casals vowed not to return to Spain until democracy was restored there. He didn't live to see that day. He made an exception to his rule of not performing in countries that recognized the Franco regime by playing at the White House on invitation from President John F. Kennedy. In 1963 he was awarded the Presidential Medal of Freedom.

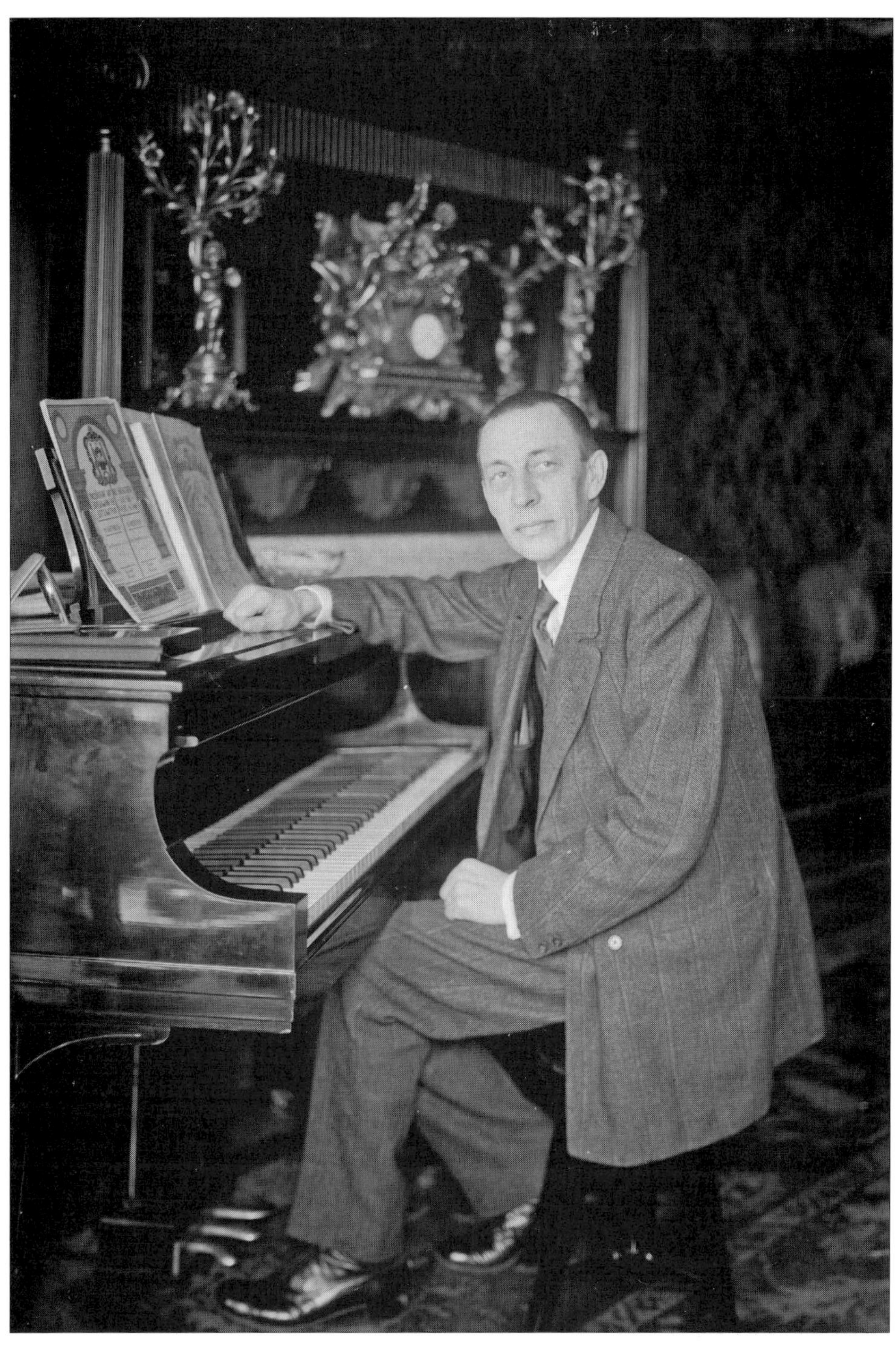

SERGEI RACHMANINOFF (1873–1943)

Russian composer, conductor, and virtuoso pianist Sergei Rachmaninoff was greatly influenced by the music of Tchaikovsky and Rimsky-Korsokov. He left those influences behind when Revolution broke out in Russia. He arrived in the United States in 1918, already a well-known performer, receiving a recording contract from the Victor Talking Machine Company. His best-known compositions are *Symphony No. 3* (1936), *Rhapsody on a Theme of Paganini* (1934), and *Symphonic Dances* (1940).

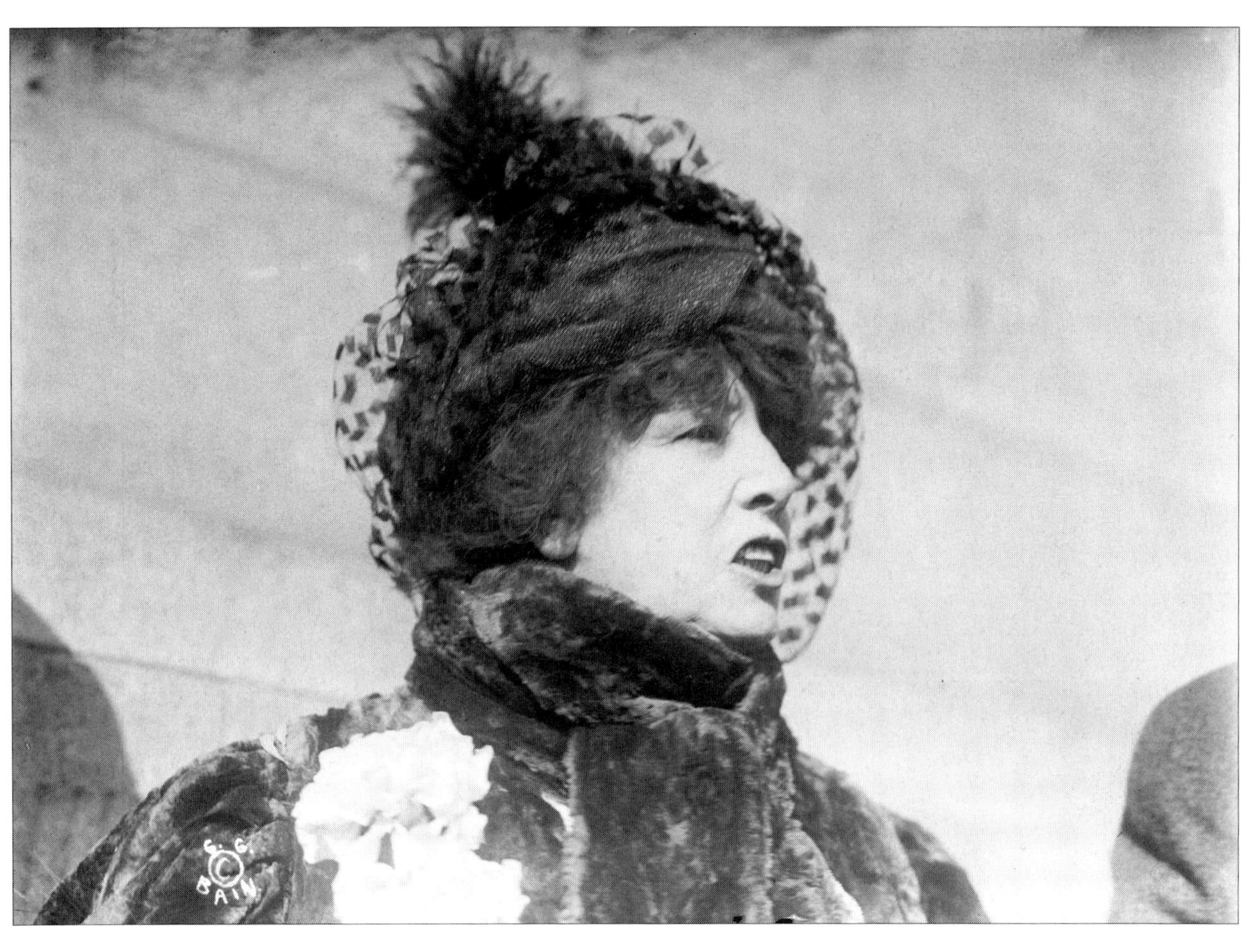

SARAH BERNHARDT (1844–1923)

Sarah Bernhardt was a French actress who rose to fame on the stages of Europe in the 1870s and was soon in demand in the United States, earning the nickname "The Divine Sarah." Bernhardt appeared in several early silent films and continued her stage career even after she had a leg amputated in 1915 due to gangrene from an acting injury.

GEORGE BERNARD SHAW (1856–1950)

George Bernard Shaw was originally a theater and music critic who later became one of England's most successful playwrights. He had an extraordinary gift for combining comedy, satire, and drama. Among his most famous plays are *Major Barbara* (1905), *Androcles and the Lion* (1912), and *Pygmalion* (1913). The latter, an amusing take on class distinctions in British society, was the basis for the musical *My Fair Lady* in 1964. Shaw won the Nobel Prize in Literature in 1925.

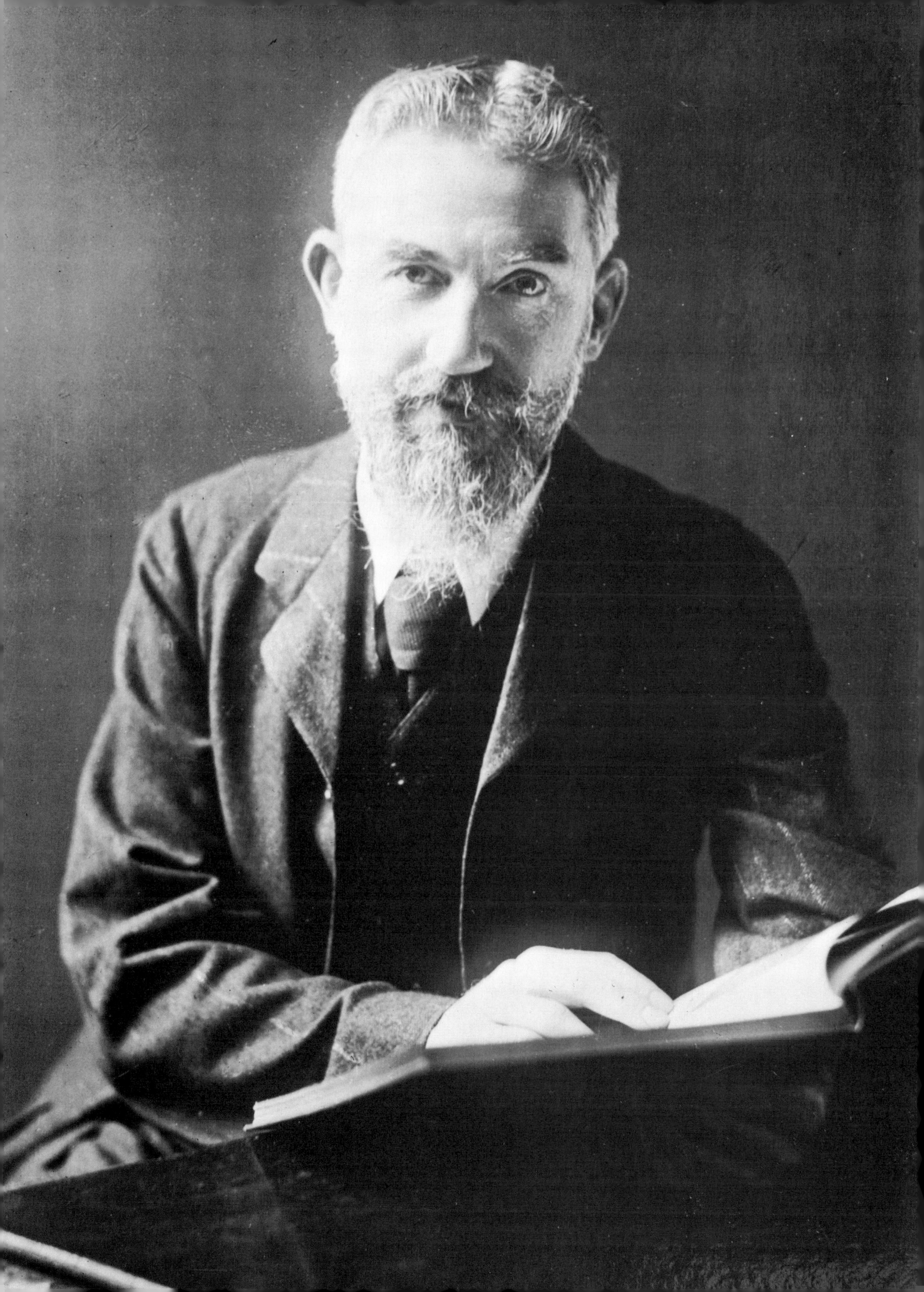

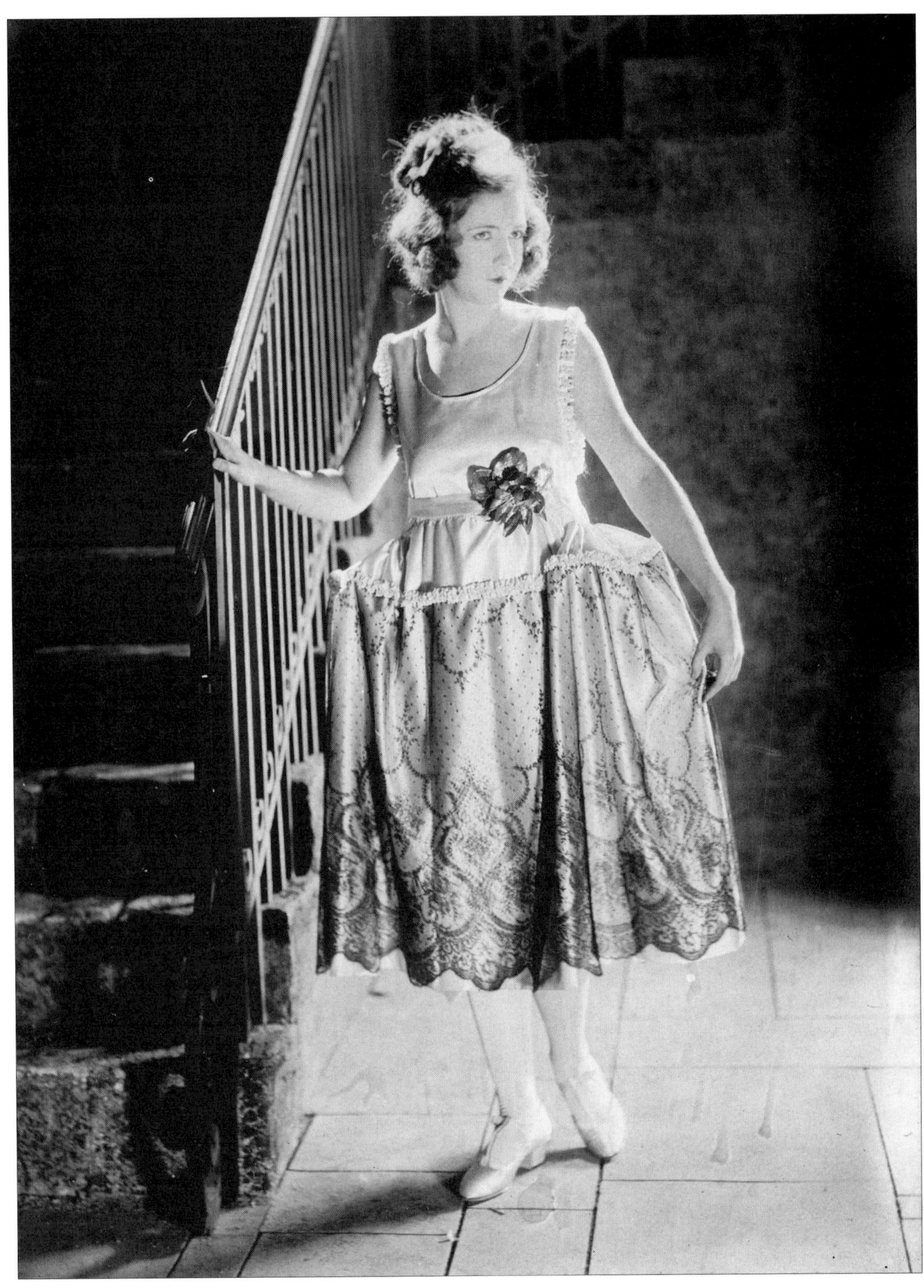

DOROTHY GISH (1898–1968)

Dorothy Gish lived in the shadow of her famous older sister Lillian. But like Lillian, Dorothy was a pioneer of the silent movie era, acting in several of director D. W. Griffith's classic productions. The sisters made their debut in the silent film *An Unseen Enemy* (1912) and starred together in *Orphans of the Storm* (1921).

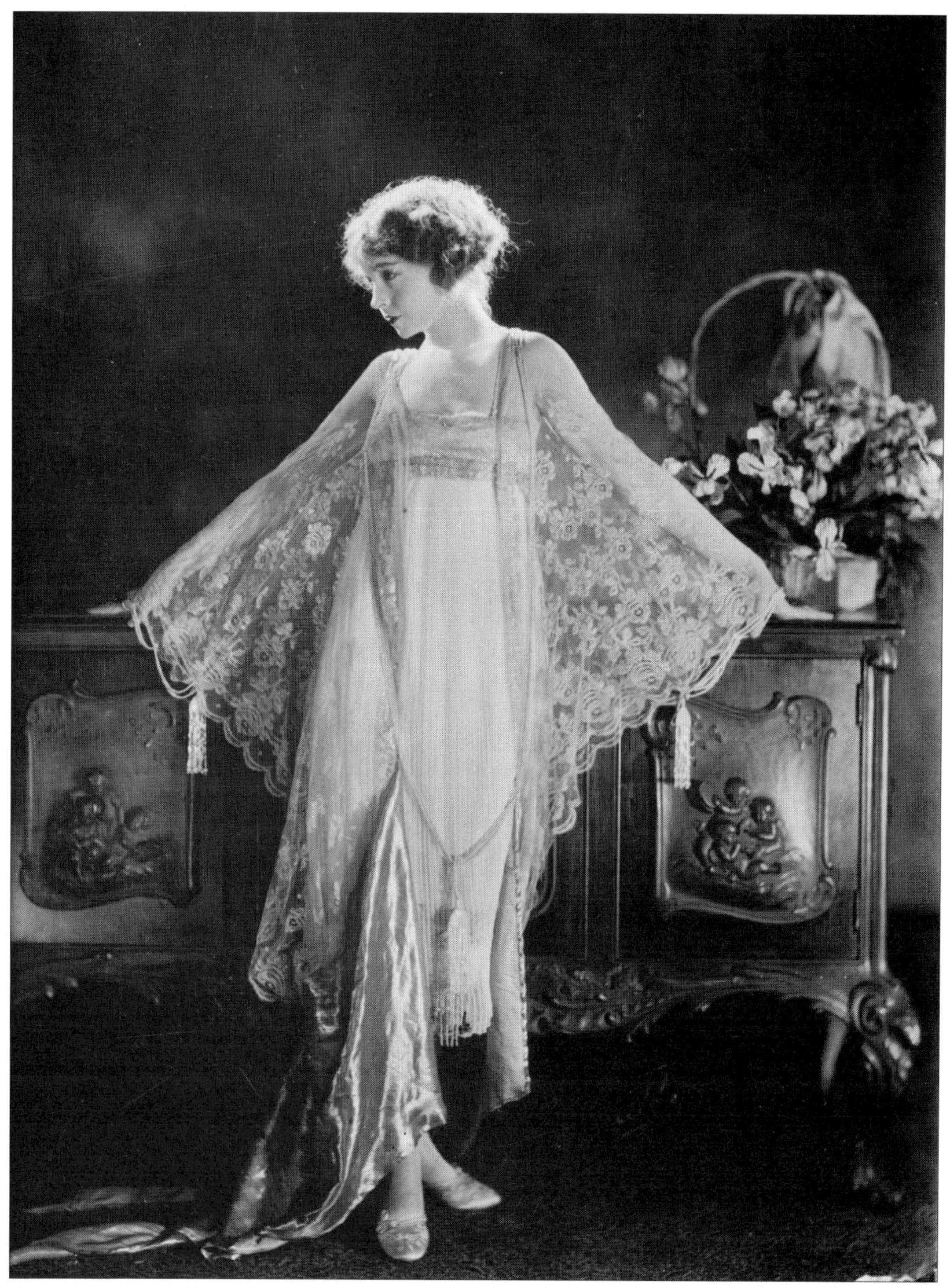

LILLIAN GISH (1893–1993)

A consummate actress with delicate beauty and obsessive devotion to her art, Lillian Gish dazzled silent screen audiences from the day she debuted in D. W. Griffith's *An Unseen Enemy* (1912). She later had a leading role in Griffith's *The Birth of a Nation* (1915). Her powerful portrayals from that period are unforgettable. After the silent film era, Gish, whose acting career spanned seventy-five years, worked in radio and television and won many awards for her achievements, including an honorary Academy Award in 1971.

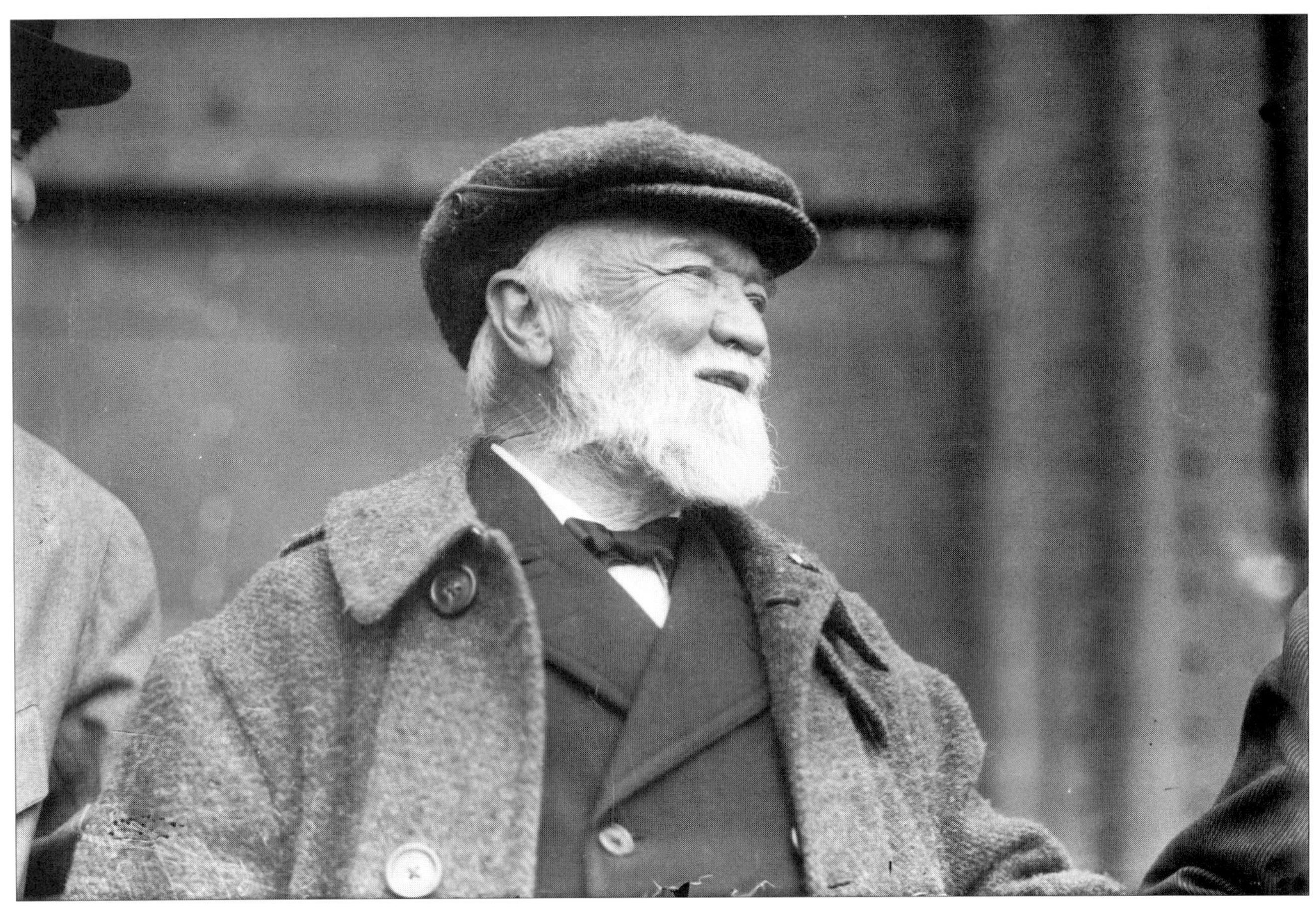

ANDREW CARNEGIE (1835–1919)

Andrew Carnegie was a Scottish-born American industrialist, businessman, and a major philanthropist. He built Pittsburgh's Carnegie Steel Company, which later merged with Elbert H. Gary's Federal Steel Company and several smaller companies to create U.S. Steel. With the fortune he made from business, he turned to philanthropy and interests in education, founding the Carnegie Corporation of New York, Carnegie Endowment for International Peace, and Carnegie Mellon University in Pittsburgh. At the time of his death in 1919 he had given away over $350 million to found schools, libraries, and support many other charitable initiatives.

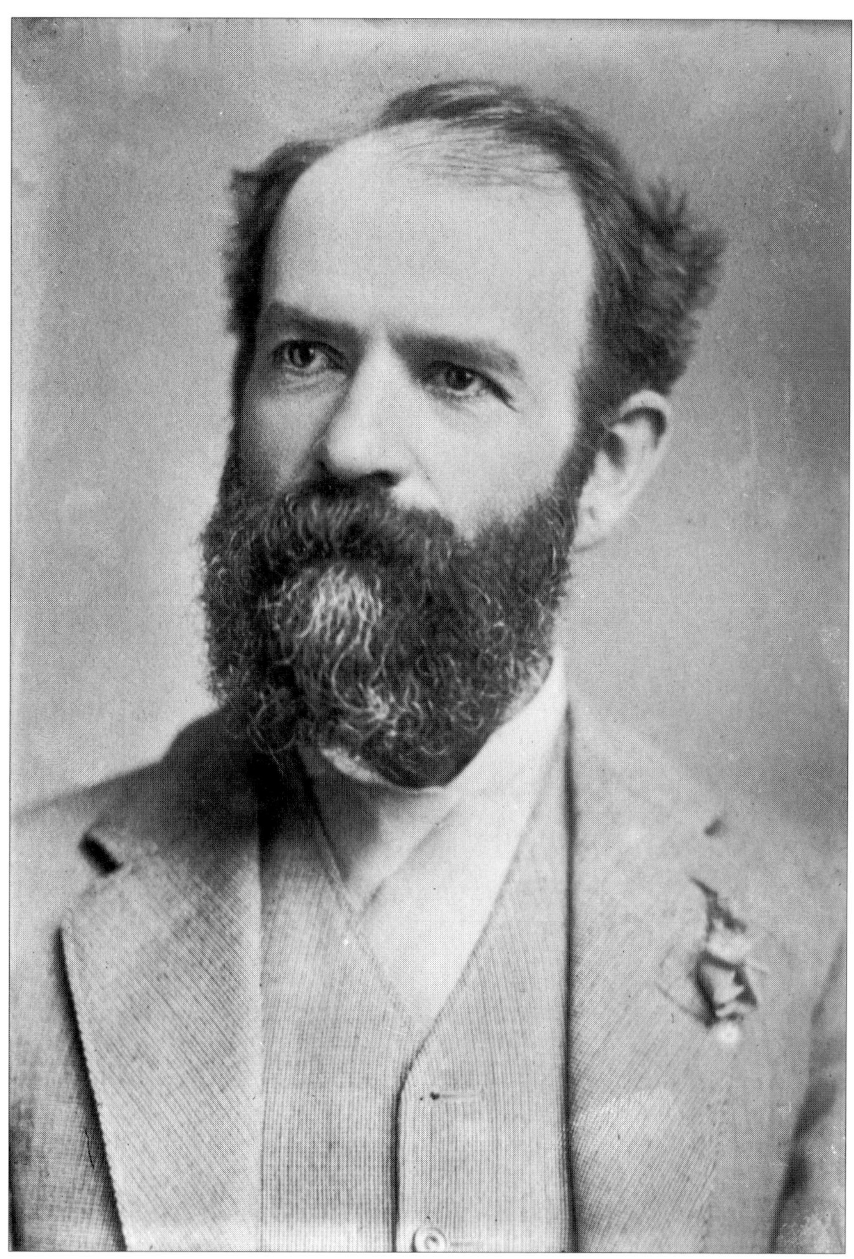

JASON "JAY" GOULD (1836–1892)

Jay Gould was an American financier who became a leading American railroad developer and speculator. Gould had a reputation as a robber baron. He pioneered the practice of declaring bankruptcy as a strategic maneuver and used stock manipulation and insider trading to build capital and to execute or prevent hostile takeovers. By 1882 he controlled about 15 percent of the nation's railroad mileage. When he died in 1892 of tuberculosis, his estate was estimated at $72 million for tax purposes. Often vilified and the subject of baseless malicious rumors during his lifetime, recent historians have taken a more balanced view of his business tactics and accomplishments.

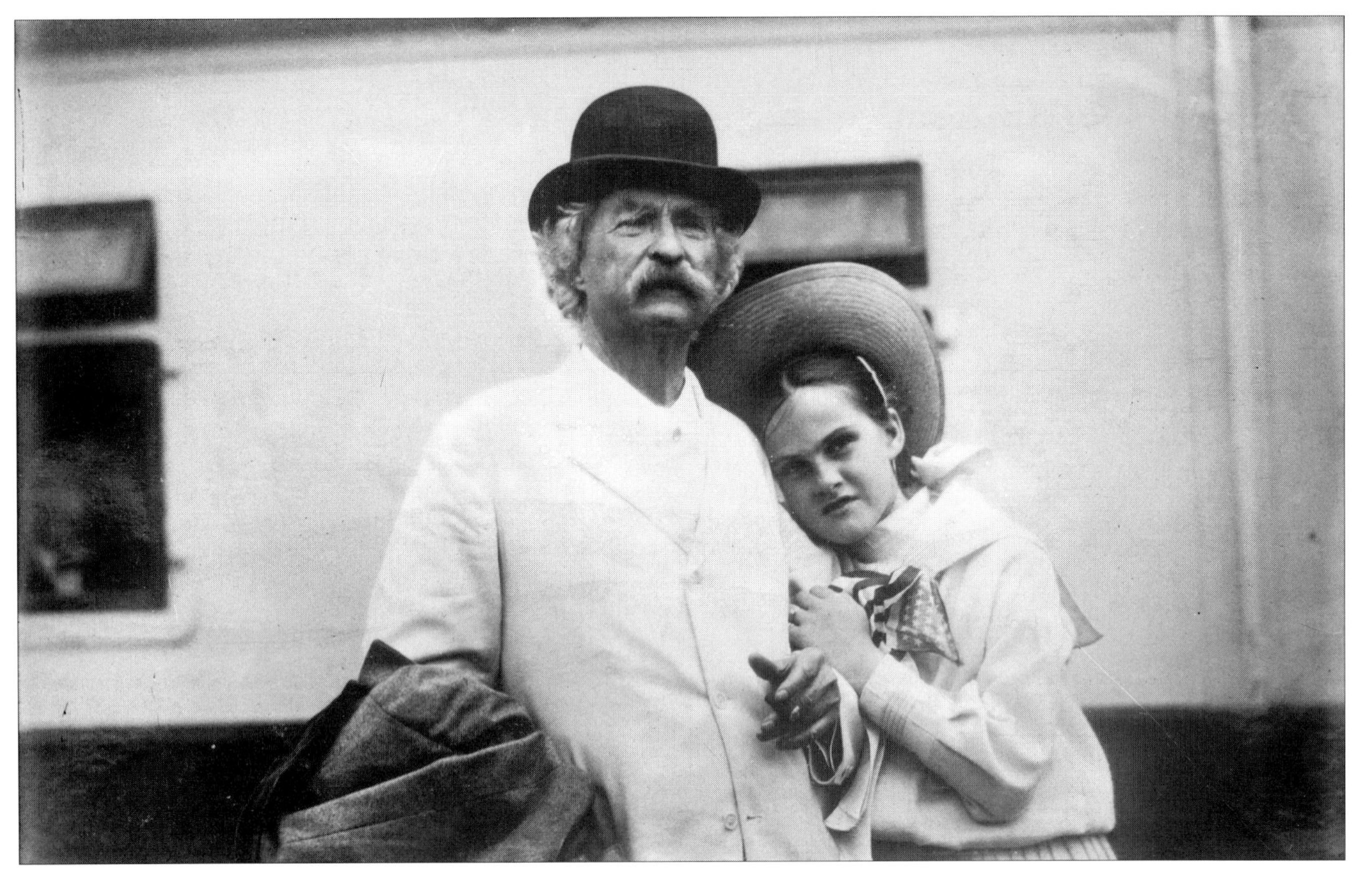

MARK TWAIN (1835–1910) AND DOROTHY QUICK (1896–1962)

Dorothy Quick was eleven years old when she met Mark Twain on a ship returning from Europe to the United States. The young girl instantly recognized the famous author and followed him around the ship until he finally noticed her. It was the beginning of a friendship that lasted until Twain's death. Miss Quick became a writer herself, publishing poems and mystery stories. Her last published book was *Enchantment: A Little Girl's Friendship with Mark Twain* (1961).

UPTON SINCLAIR (1878–1968)

Pulitzer Prize–winning author Upton Sinclair wrote over ninety books. Known as a political activist, he achieved fame with his 1906 muckraking novel *The Jungle,* which dealt with conditions in the U.S. meat packing industry and caused a public outcry. Sinclair's exposé contributed to the passage of the Pure Food and Drug Act and the Meat Inspection Act in 1906. Sinclair ran unsuccessfully for the House of Representatives and Senate as a socialist in 1920 and 1922. In 1934 he staged a more effective effort, after gaining the Democratic nomination for governor. Running on a platform called End Poverty in California, Sinclair received over 800,000 votes, but his opponents were able to portray him as a communist, and he lost the election.

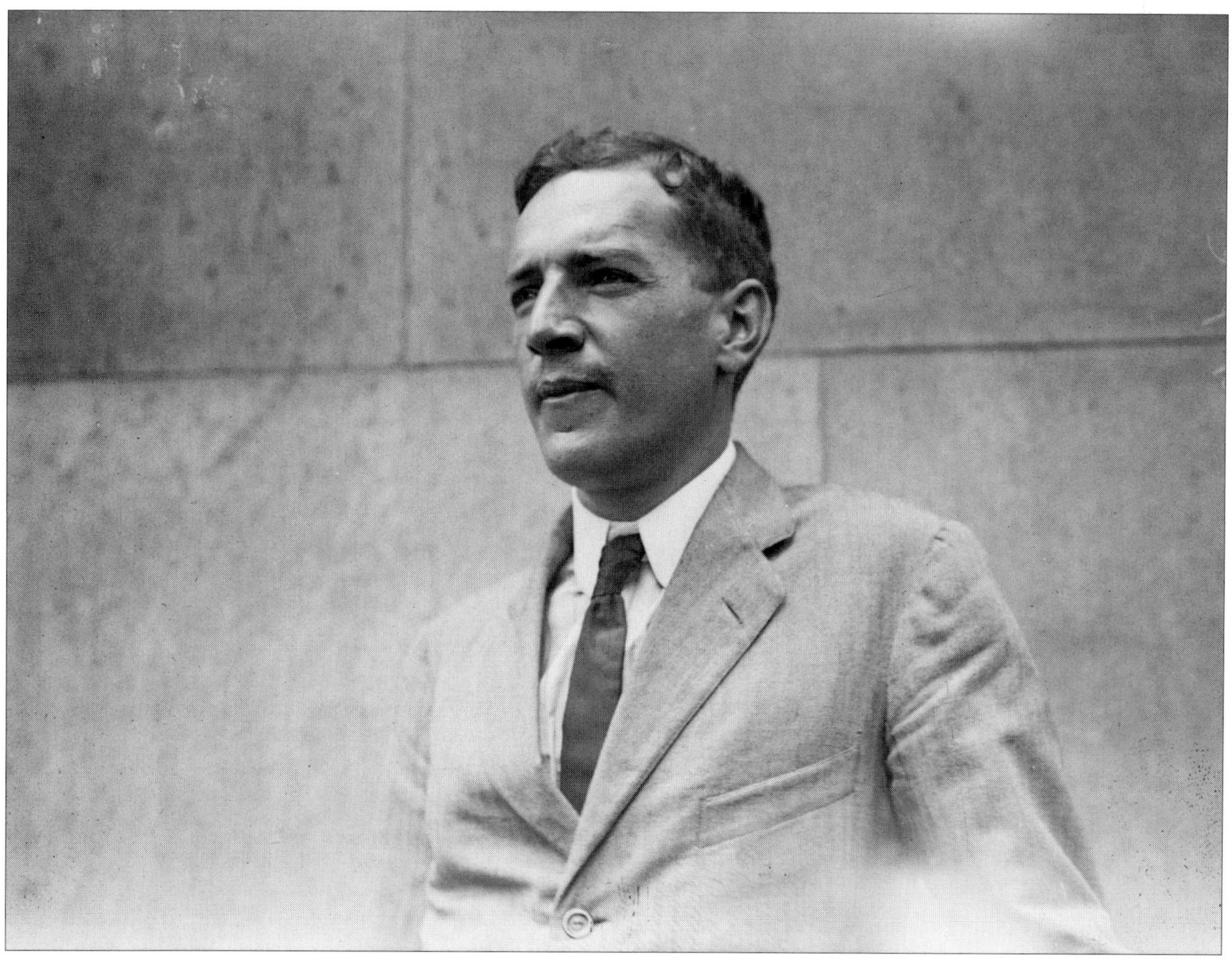

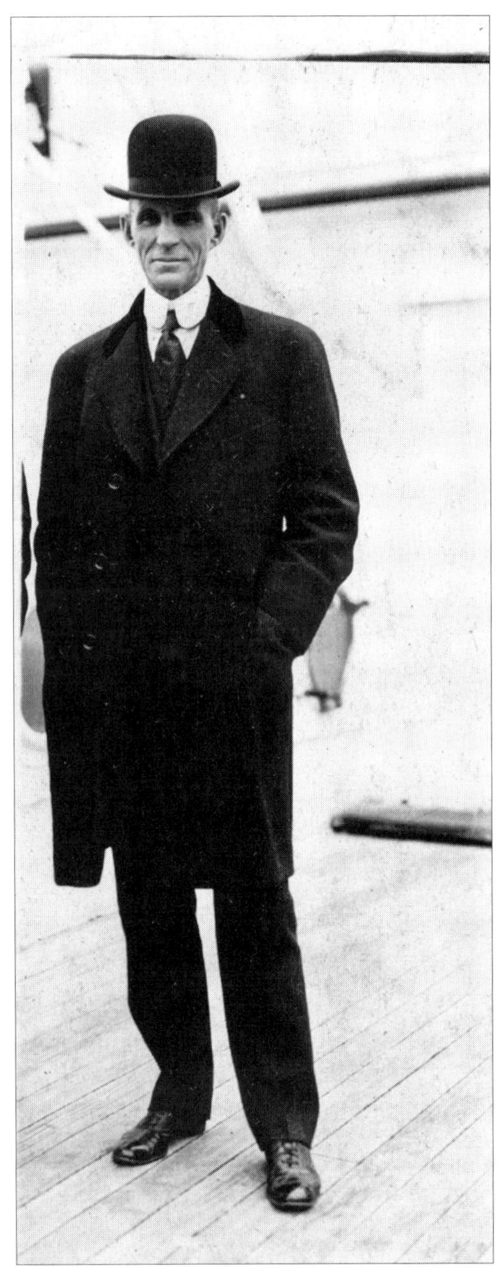

HENRY FORD (1863–1947)

Henry Ford, founder of the Ford Motor Company, used assembly lines in the mass production of his automobiles and revolutionized American industry. His Model T, introduced in 1908, was affordable and easy to drive. By World War I, over half the cars in America were Model Ts. Ford's success made him one of the richest men in the world. When production of Model T ended in 1927, over fifteen million had been produced, a record which stood for forty-five years. Ford and his engineers used their expertise in assembly-line production to aid the massive U.S. war effort in World War II, reducing the time to produce one *B-24* bomber from one day to one hour.

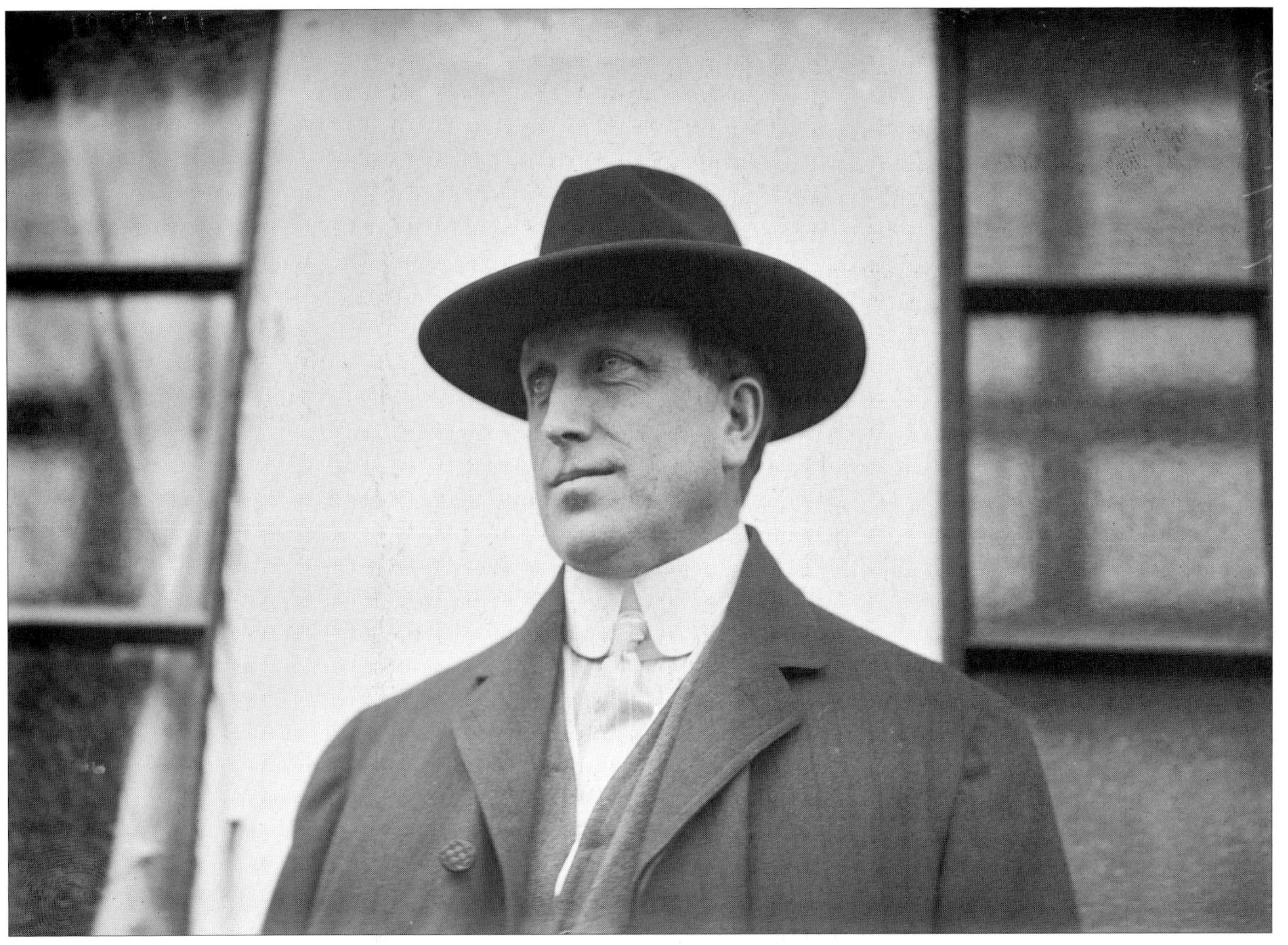

WILLIAM RANDOLPH HEARST (1863–1951)

William Randolph Hearst, an American newspaper magnate and publisher, took over the *San Francisco Examiner* from his father in 1887 while he was still a student at Harvard, making it a great success. He later acquired the *New York Journal*, engaging in a circulation war with Joseph Pulitzer's *New York World* which led to the rise of "yellow journalism," and fed the frenzy that pushed the United States into the Spanish-American War in 1898. Hearst eventually created the largest newspaper and magazine empire in the world. He is especially remembered today because his life story was a source for the lead character in Orson Welles' classic film *Citizen Kane* (1941), and for building and lavishly furnishing the unique Hearst Castle on his 240,000 acre ranch in San Simeon, California.

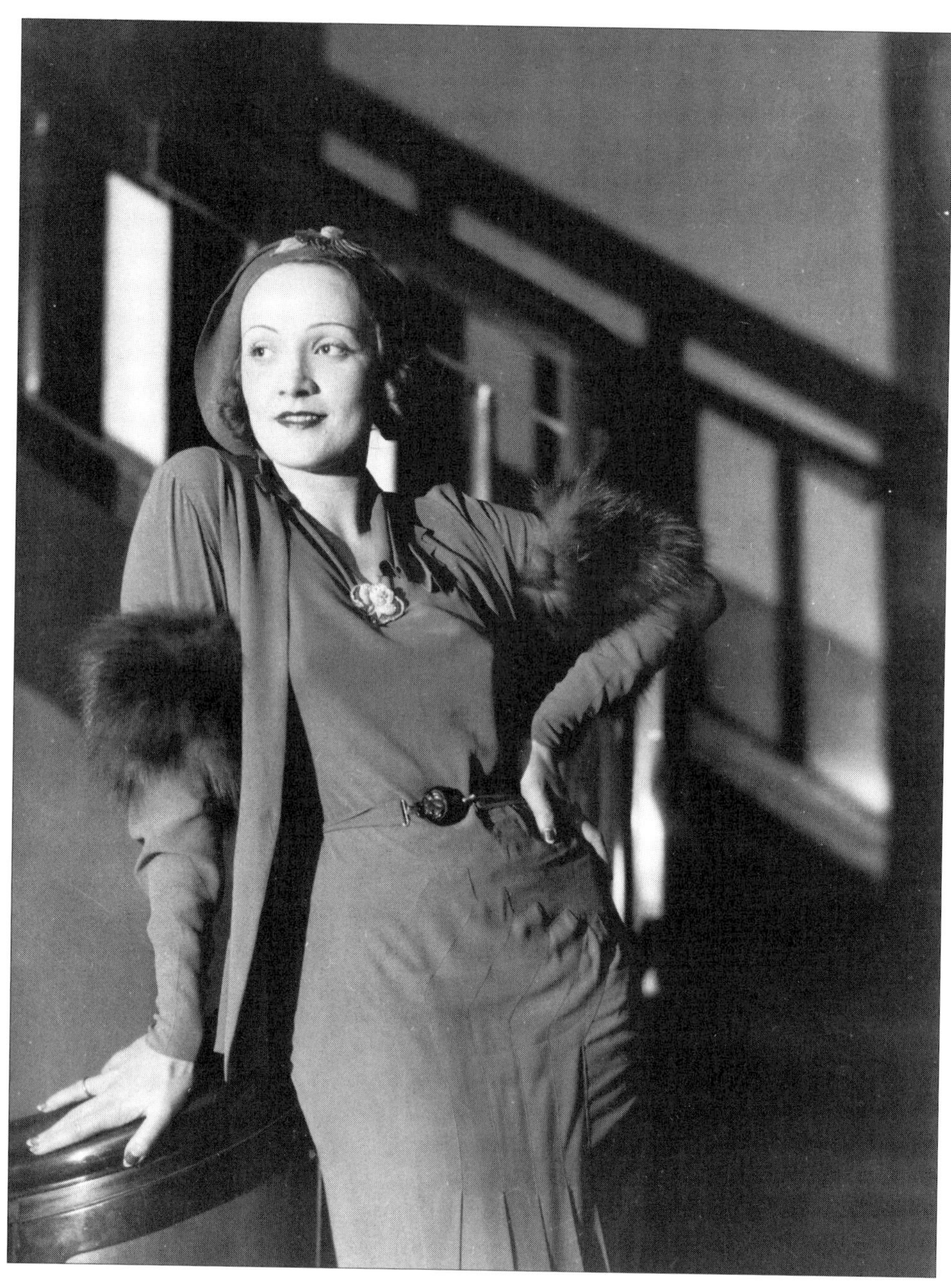

MARLENE DIETRICH (1901–1992)

German-born Marlene Dietrich began her work as a cabaret singer, chorus girl, and film actress in Berlin in the 1920s, winning fame for her performance in Josef von Sternberg's *The Blue Angel* (1930). That role propelled her to Hollywood, where she starred in *Shanghai Express* (1932), and *Desire* (1936). During World War II, the anti-Nazi Dietrich was a frontline entertainer for the American troops. From the 1950s to the 1970s she performed internationally in cabarets and on stage. By the end of her career she had become a fashion and entertainment icon of the twentieth century. Long after she retired, Dietrich made a cameo film appearance in *Just a Gigolo* (1979).

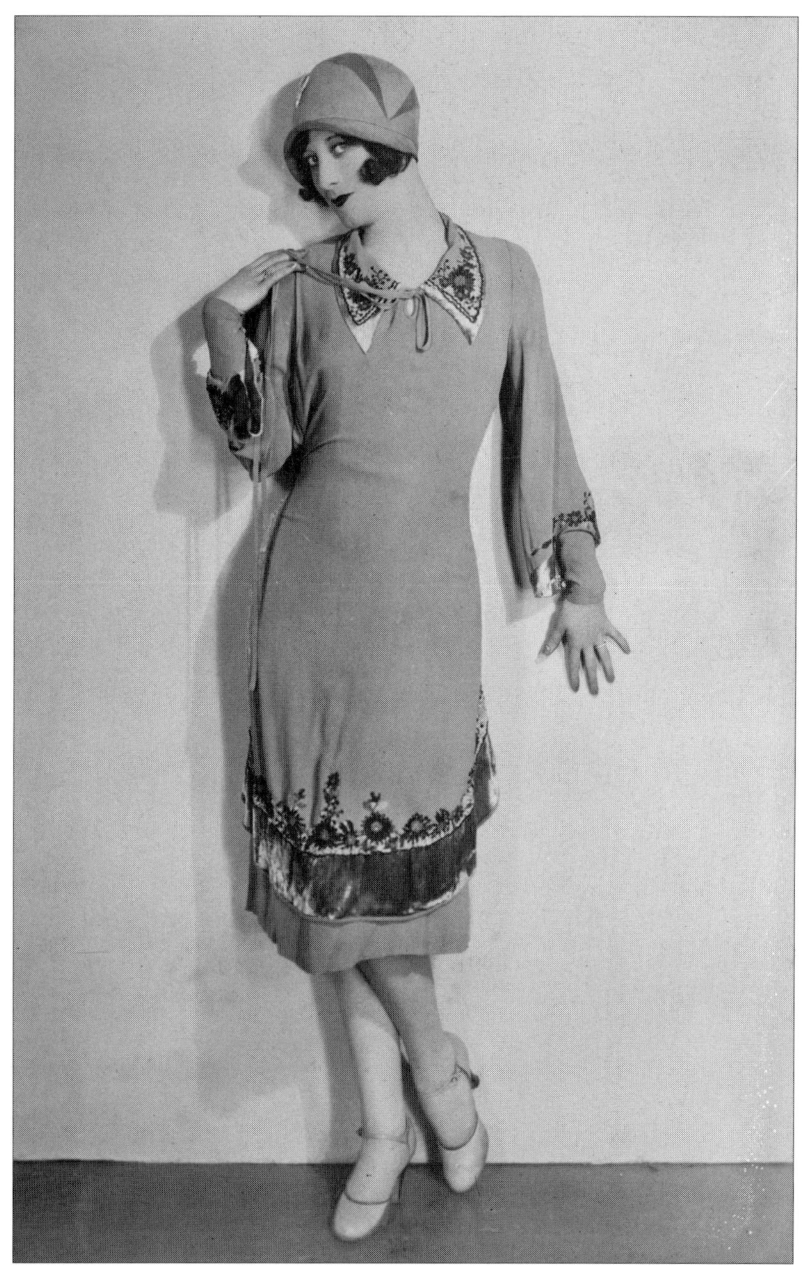

JOAN CRAWFORD (c. 1905–1977)

Starting out in show business as a glamorous flapper, Joan Crawford soared to fame at the Metro-Goldwyn-Mayer Studios in Hollywood in the 1920s. She often played tough, hardworking women who rose to success. She made eighty films in her forty-five-year career and won the Academy Award for Best Actress for *Mildred Pierce* in 1945.

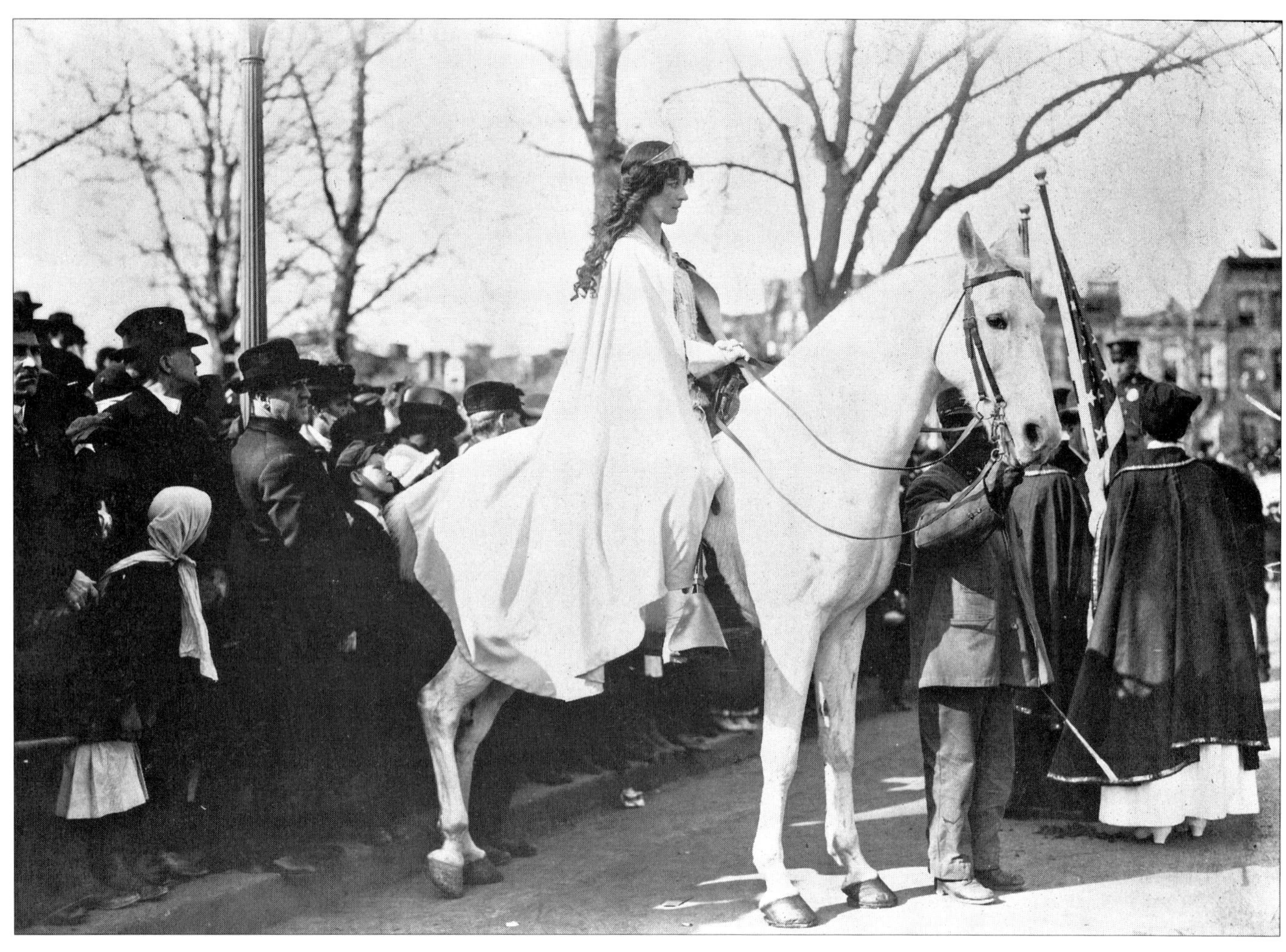

INEZ MILHOLLAND (1886–1916)

Activist Inez Milholland was a leader of the women's suffrage movement and a frequent speaker for the National Women's Party. In this photograph she heads a suffrage parade on March 3, 1913, in Washington, D.C., the day before Woodrow Wilson's inauguration. Milholland was also a labor lawyer and children's advocate. She was a member of the Greenwich Village–based group that published the socialist magazine *The Masses,* and protested U.S. involvement in World War I as a passenger on the *Peace Ship,* financed by industrialist Henry Ford in 1915 to mobilize representatives of the warring nations to end the hostilities. Perhaps as a result of her relentless campaigning for women's rights and other causes, Milholland died of pernicious anemia at the age of thirty.

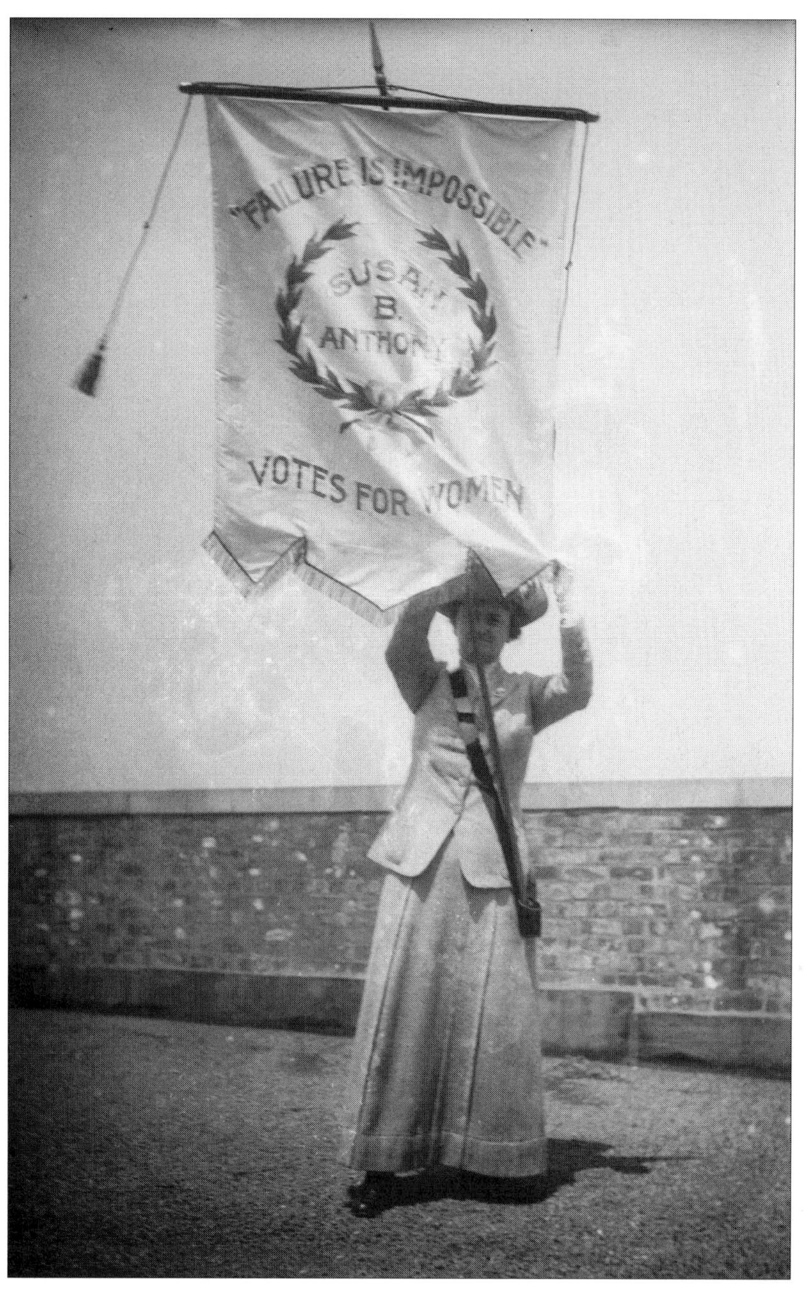

SUSAN BROWNELL ANTHONY (1820–1906)

Susan Brownell Anthony played a pivotal role in the effort for womens's suffrage in the United States. As a young woman she was active in the anti-slavery and temperance movements. In 1869 Anthony and Elizabeth Cady Stanton founded the National Women's Suffrage Association, an organization dedicated to gaining the right to vote for women. Anthony became president of the NWSA in 1892. Though she gave thousands of speeches for the cause, she didn't live to see women win the right to vote in America in 1920. Anthony was honored as the first woman to appear on U.S. coinage with her appearance on the dollar, which was minted for only four years.

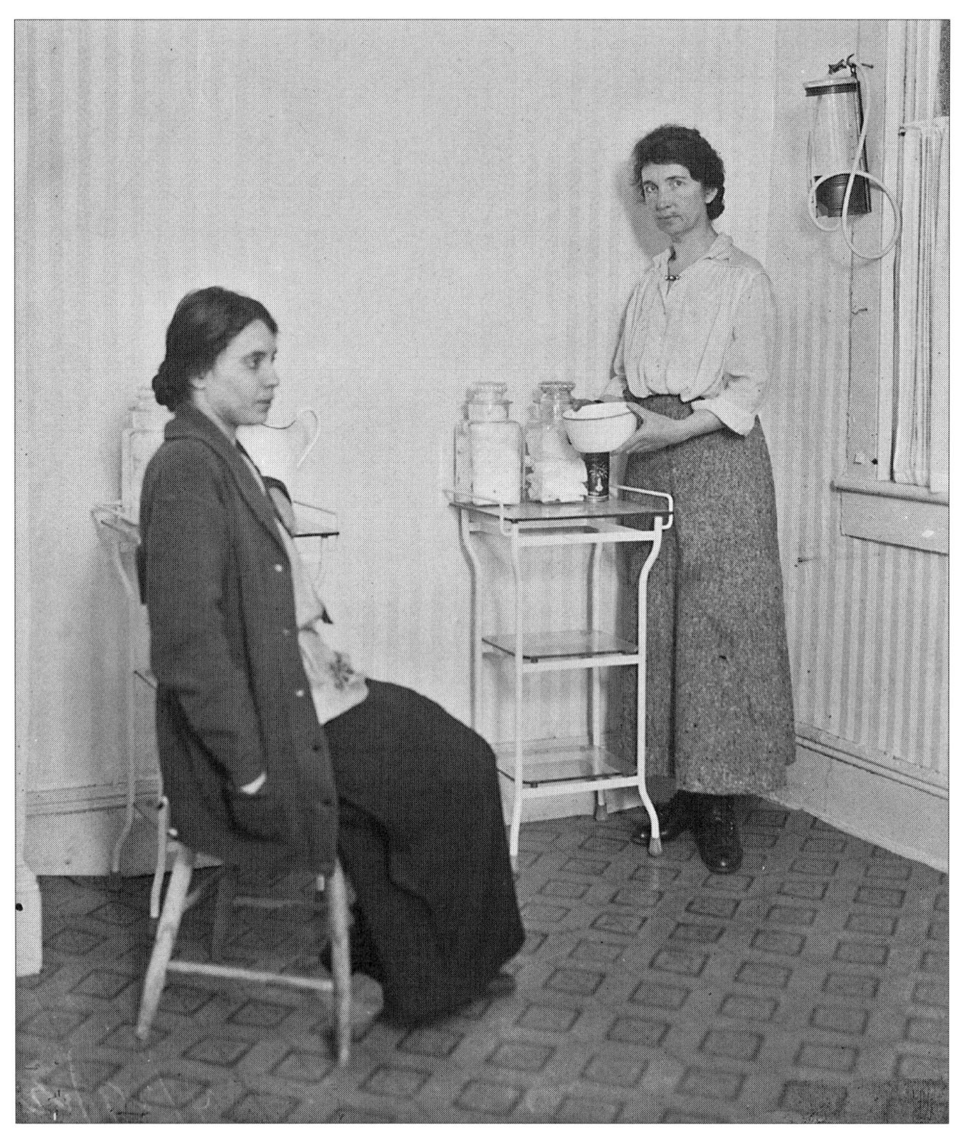

MARGARET SANGER (1879–1966)

Margaret Sanger was a nurse and a pioneering women's health advocate who witnessed the toll unwanted pregnancies took on women's lives. In violation of the Comstock Act of 1873, she distributed birth control information, writing articles such as *What Every Girl Should Know* (1916). From 1916 to 1917, Sanger established the first birth control clinic in America in the Brownsville section of Brooklyn, New York, suffering many arrests for her daring work. Ultimately, she helped change the law so that doctors could offer birth control to their patients.

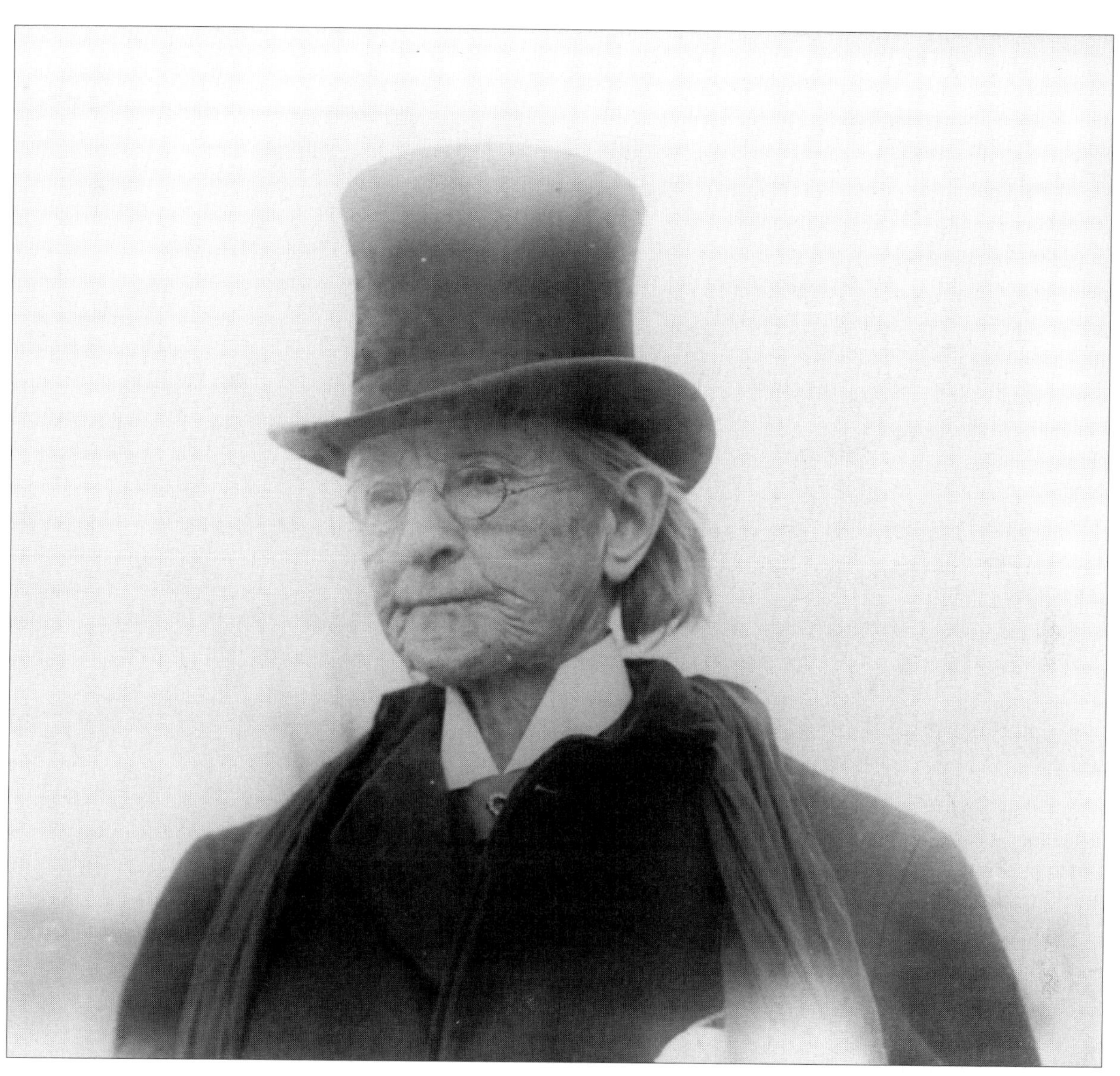

DR. MARY EDWARDS WALKER (1832–1919)

Dr. Mary Edwards Walker was the first woman ever awarded the Congressional Medal of Honor. An 1855 graduate of the Syracuse Medical College, she volunteered to join the Union Army as a civilian surgeon at the start of the Civil War, but at first was limited to working as a nurse. In 1863, however, Walker was commissioned by the Army of the Cumberland and became the first female surgeon in the United States Army. Captured by Confederates and later released in a prisoner exchange, she again served as surgeon during the Battle of Atlanta, and was recommended for the Medal of Honor by General William Tecumseh Sherman and others. In her later years Walker was an outspoken campaigner for women's rights, temperance, and other causes. In 1917 Congress revised the standards for awarding the Medal of Honor and revoked Walker's medal along with hundreds of others. President Jimmy Carter restored her medal posthumously in 1977.

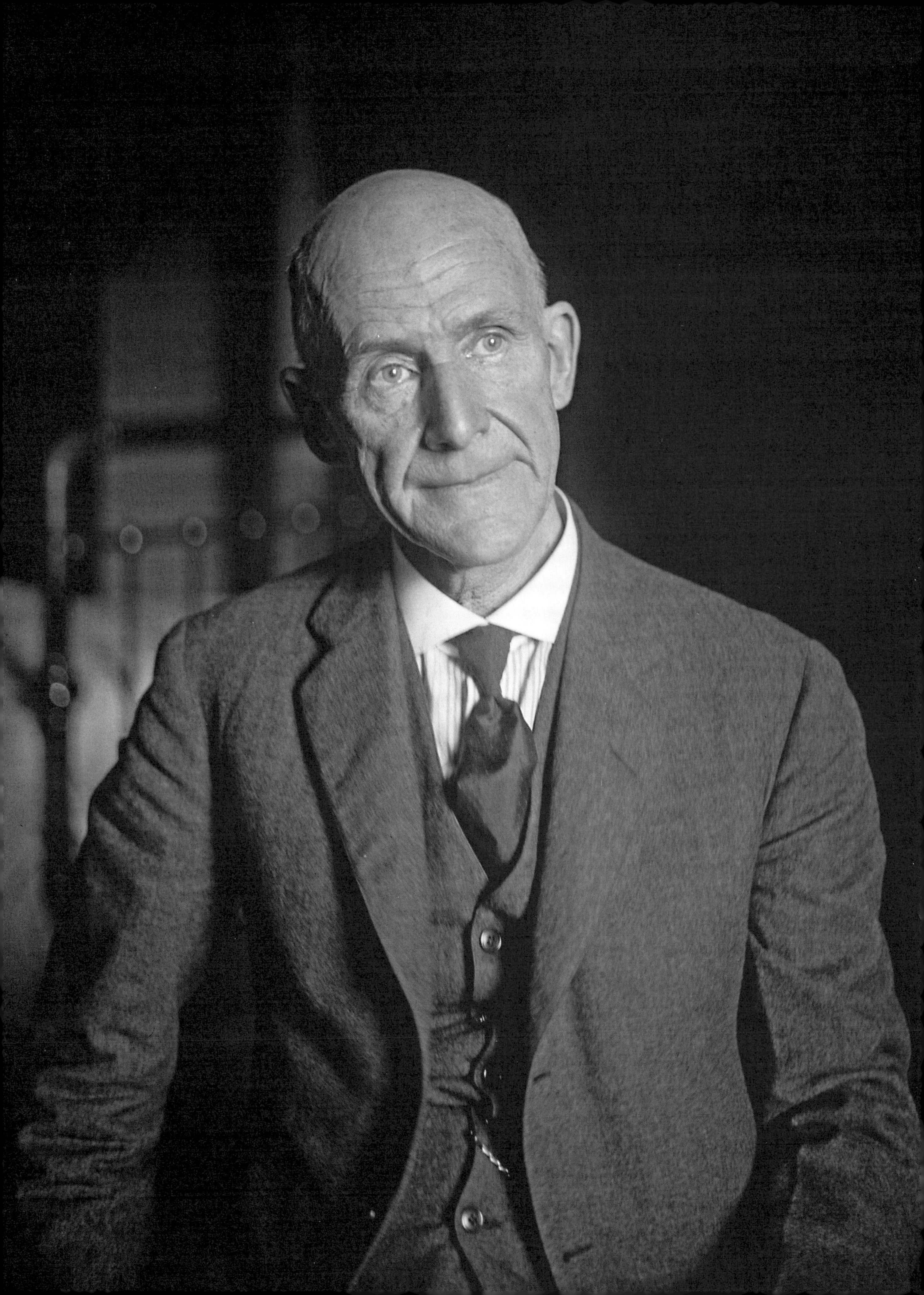

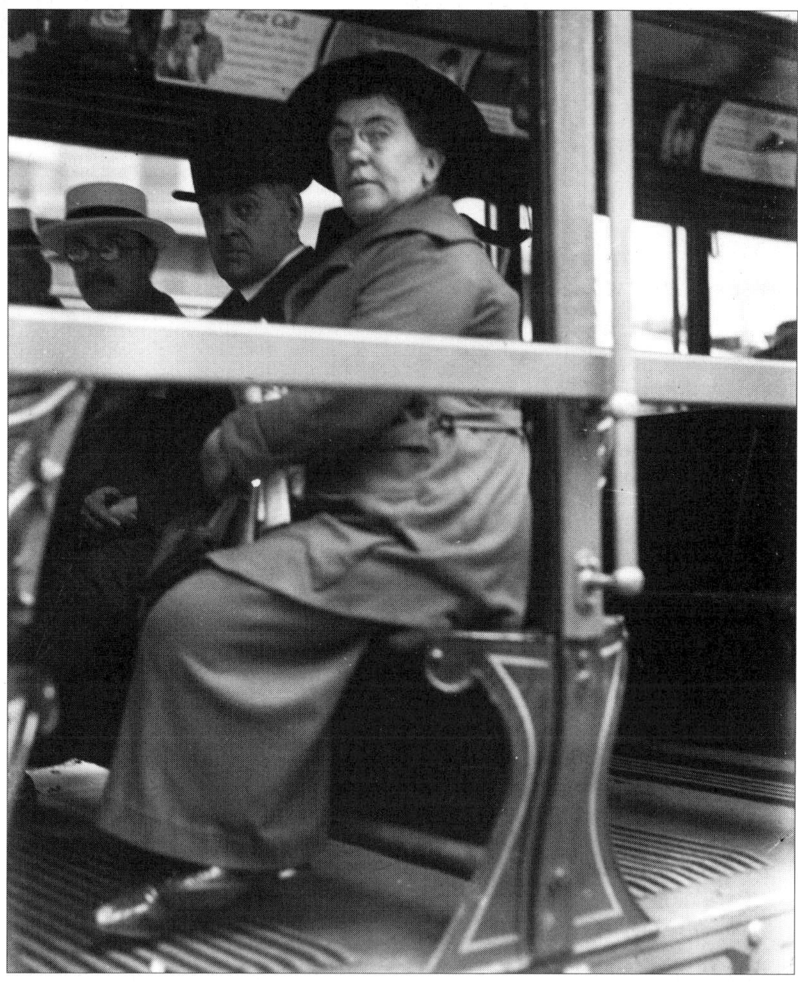

EMMA GOLDMAN (1869–1940)

Known for her eloquent lectures and biting wit, anarchist Emma Goldman belonged to a group of intellectuals and revolutionaries that embraced feminism, sexual freedom, socialism, and the labor movement. She published an anarchist magazine called *Mother Earth,* which focused on politics and literature. An American who was born during the Czar's cruel reign in Russia, Goldman became an ardent supporter of the Russian revolution. But when deported to Russia in 1919 during the Red Scare, she was horrified to discover the Bolshevik regime a corrupt and tyrannical dictatorship. Later she lived in England, Canada, and France, and traveled to Spain during the Civil War in the 1930s to support the anti-Fascist cause.

EUGENE DEBS (1855–1926)

In his youth Eugene Debs was a leader of the Brotherhood of Locomotive Firemen. Later he helped found the Socialist Party of America (1901) and the Industrial Workers of the World (1905). Sent to Federal prison following the Pullman Strike of 1894, Debs read the works of Karl Marx while incarcerated in Woodstock, Illinois, and became a socialist. Debs ran for President of the United States on the Socialist Party ticket five times starting in 1900. His final campaign was conducted from prison in 1920 following his conviction under the Espionage Act of 1917 for campaigning against the draft in World War I and fomenting opposition to the U.S. government. Although he was not successful in those elections, his ideas gave rise to the industrial union movement and spurred social and economic reform.

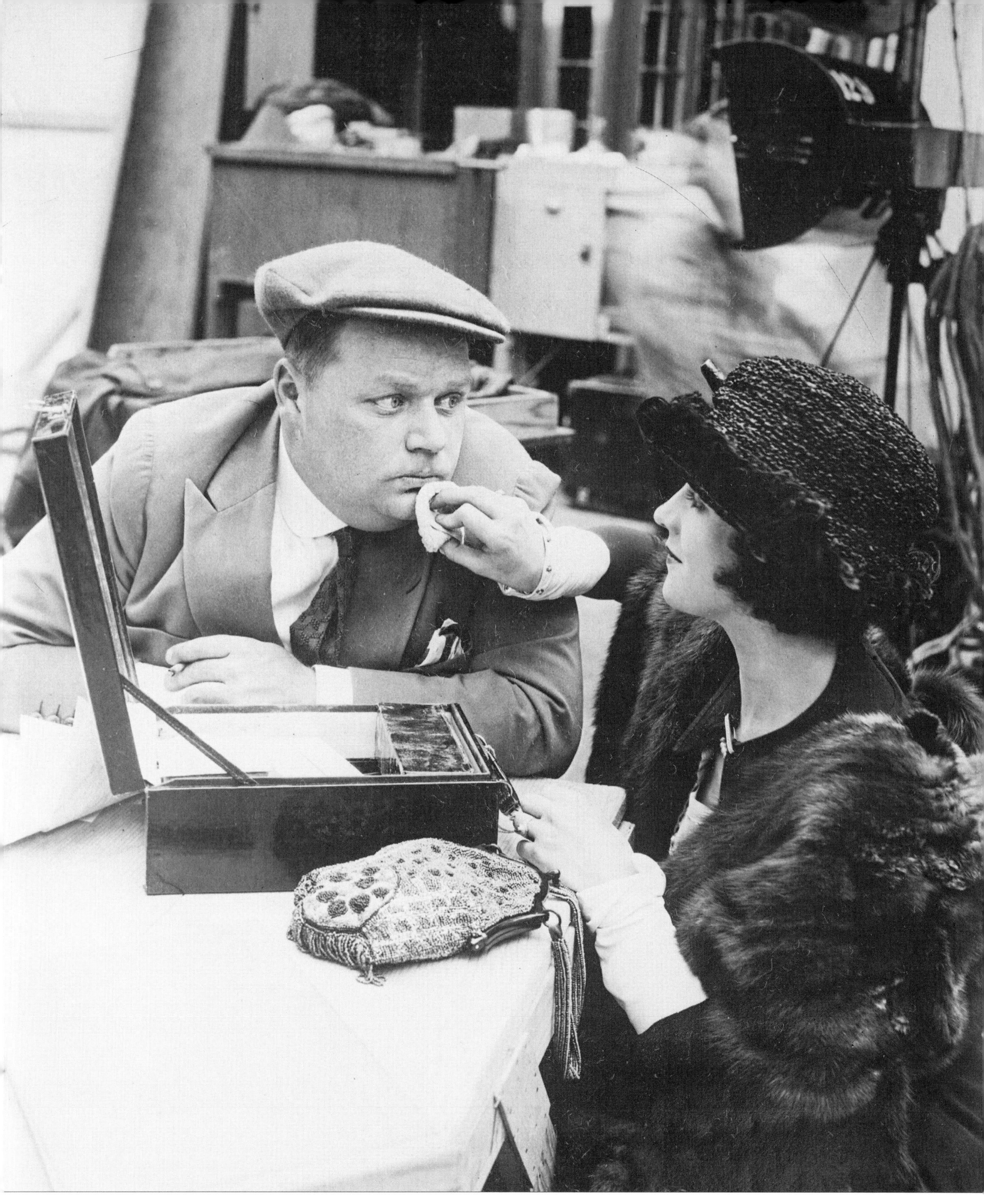

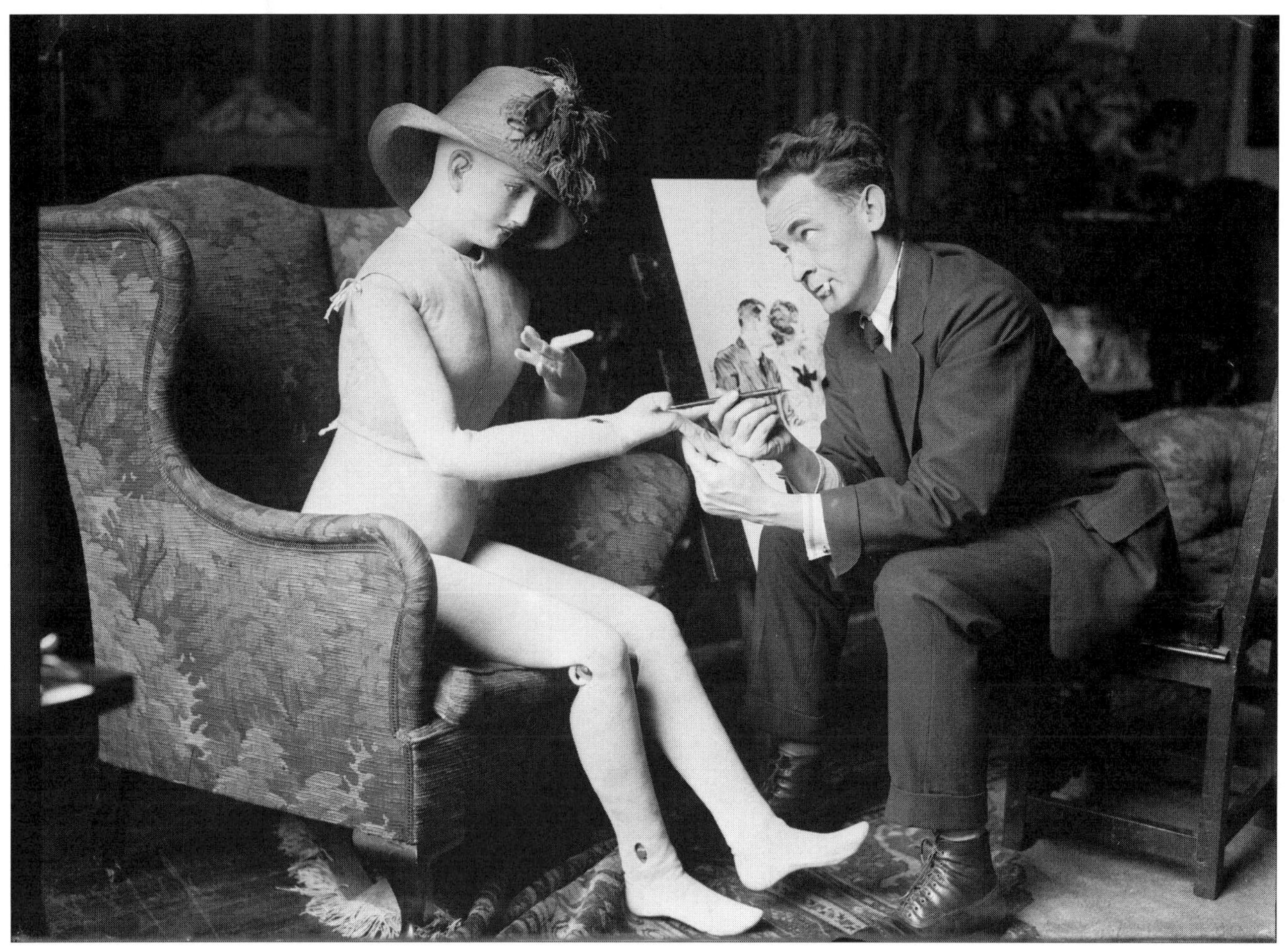

JAMES MONTGOMERY FLAGG (1877–1960)

James Montgomery Flagg was an acclaimed painter and illustrator. His work appeared in a variety of popular magazines including *St. Nicholas*, *Judge*, and *Life*. During World War I, Flagg designed forty-five military posters, including his most famous—an image of Uncle Sam pointing at the viewer with the caption, "I Want You for U. S. Army."

ROSCOE CONKLING "FATTY" ARBUCKLE (1887–1933)

Fatty Arbuckle was a silent filmmaker, comedian, director, and screenwriter. Large in size but light on his feet, he used slapstick and sight gags in his entertaining pictures. Arbuckle was a mentor to actors Buster Keaton and Charlie Chaplin. In 1921, Arbuckle was accused of murdering young actress Virginia Rappe during a private party in the St. Francis Hotel in San Francisco. Although he was eventually acquitted in court, the scandal completely ruined Arbuckle's acting career. In 1933, while attempting a comeback as an actor, he died of a heart attack at the age of forty-six.

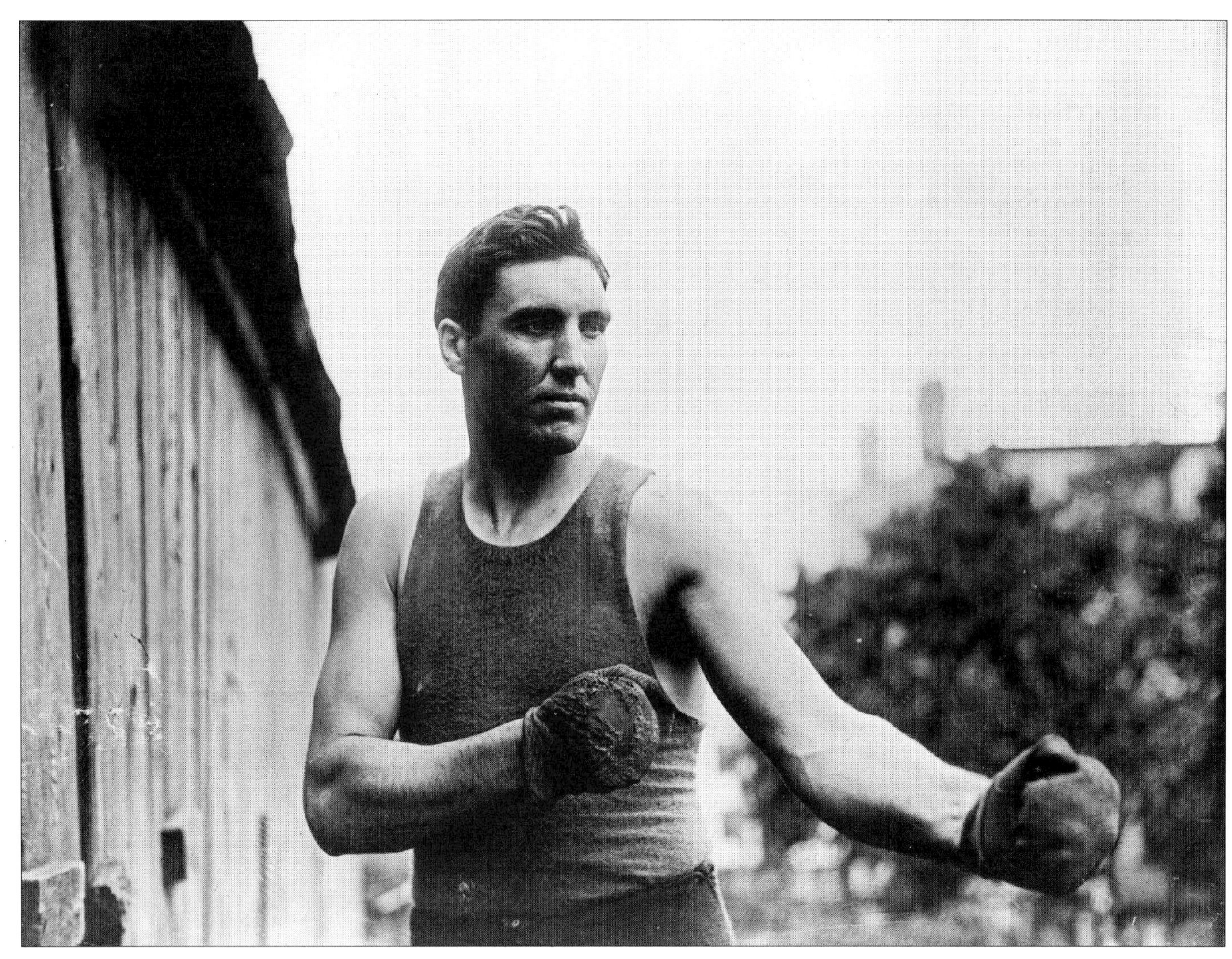

JESS WILLARD (1881–1968)

The powerful Jess Willard was a heavyweight champion of the world. He stood over six-and-a-half-feet tall and weighed 245 pounds. On April 5, 1915, in Havana, Cuba, he knocked out champion Jack Johnson to win the heavyweight title. Following the fight, Willard was heralded as "The Great White Hope" for defeating his African American opponent. In 1919, at age thirty-seven, on a third round technical knockout, Willard lost his title to Jack Dempsey.

JOHNNY WEISSMULLER (1904–1984)

Johnny Weissmuller was an Olympic swimming champion who had a second career playing the role of Tarzan in the movies. He won five U.S. Olympic gold medals and set sixty-seven world records in the 1920s—all before he was twenty-five years old. He never lost a race as an amateur swimmer. Weissmuller went to Hollywood in 1932 and became a box office hit in *Tarzan the Ape Man*. He made his last Tarzan film, *Tarzan and the Mermaids* (1948) at the age of forty-four.

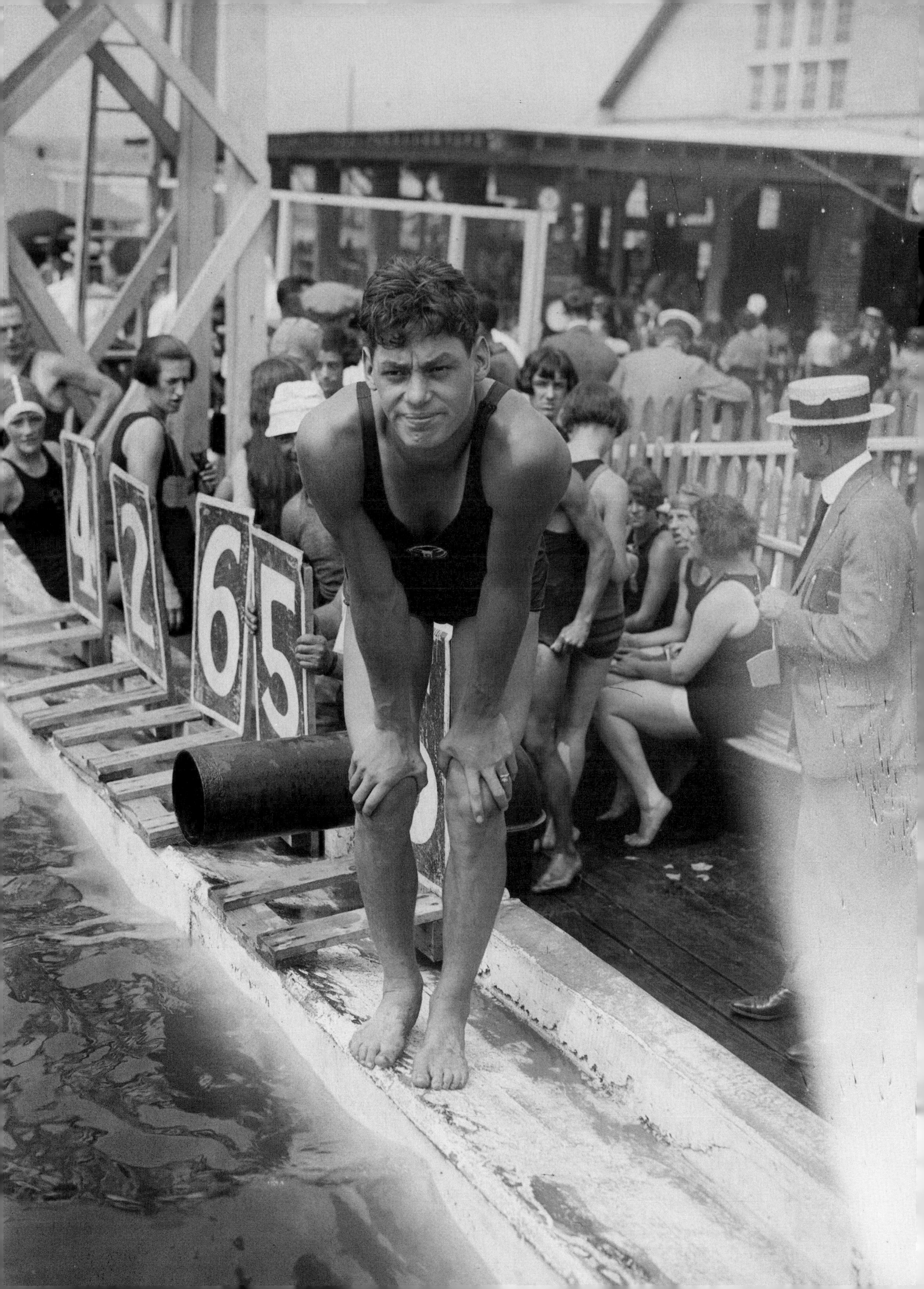
4
2
6
5

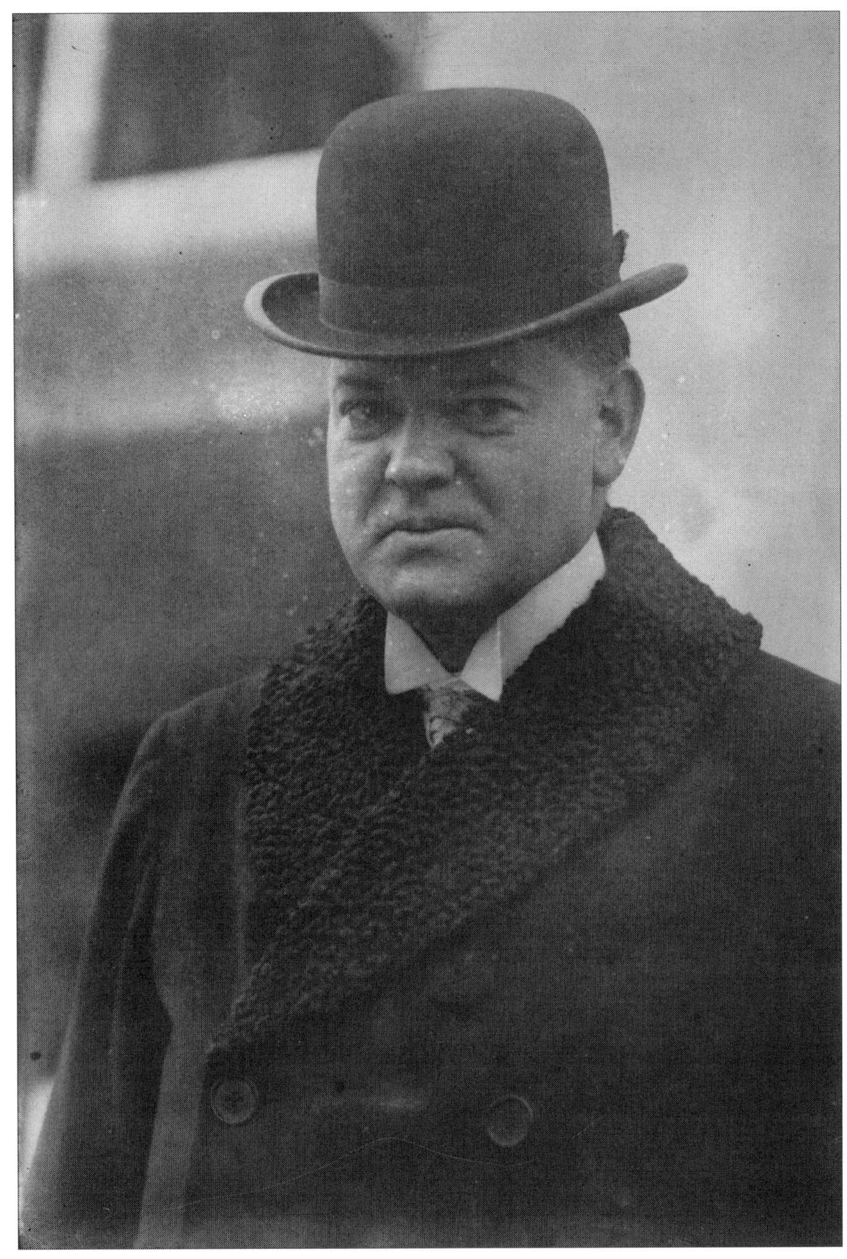

HERBERT HOOVER (1874–1964)

Herbert Hoover was the thirty-first president of the United States. His term (1929–1933) was devastated by the October 1929 stock market crash, which led the country into the Great Depression. Hoover was not able to win public confidence from a nation that largely blamed him for mortgage foreclosures, failed banks, unemployment, and widespread poverty. He was badly defeated by Franklin Roosevelt in the 1932 election, losing in all but six of the forty-eight states.

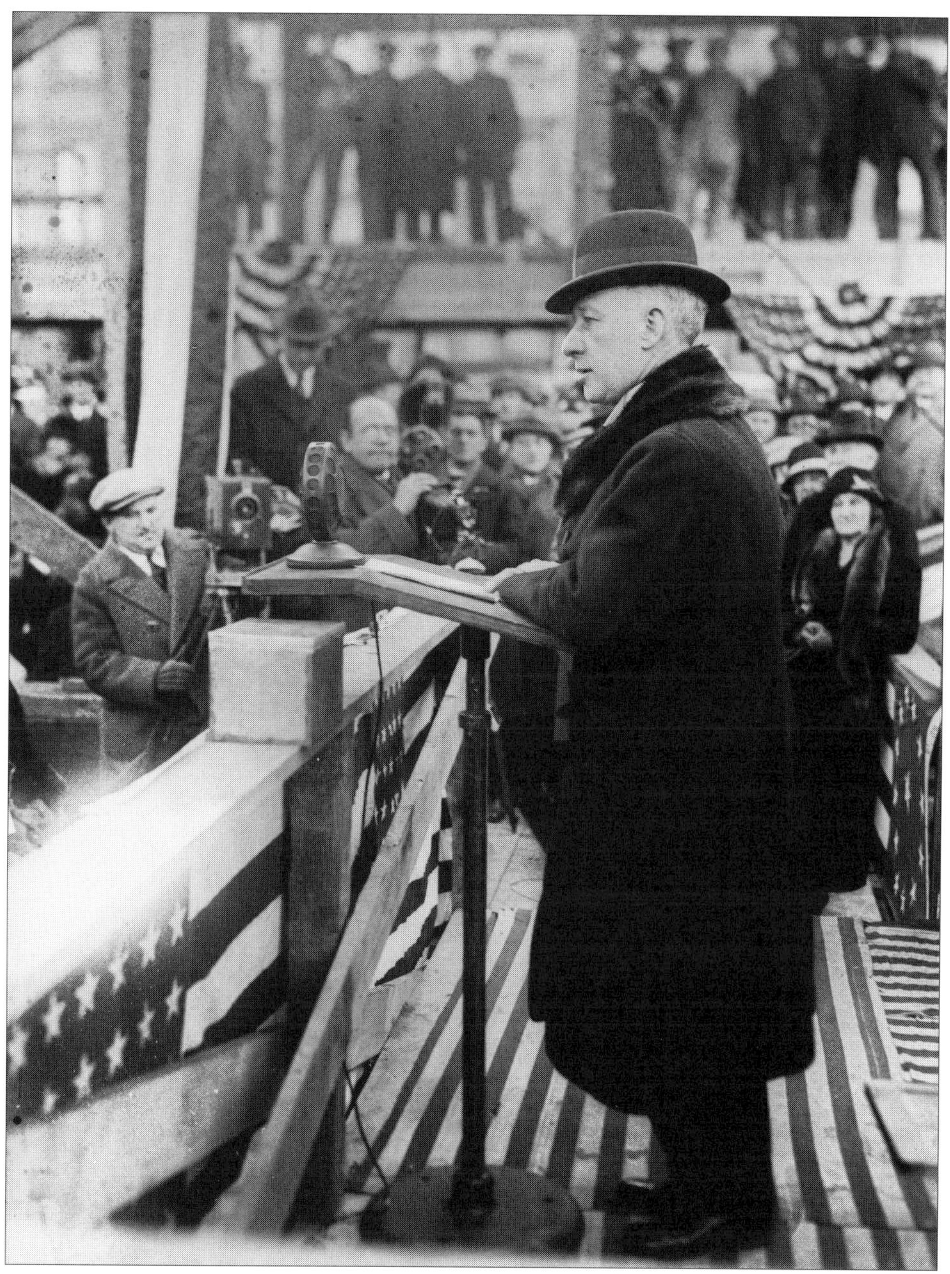

AL SMITH (1873–1944)

Al Smith was elected to four two-year terms as governor of New York State between 1918 and 1926, and was the Democratic presidential candidate in 1928. He was the first Roman Catholic and first Irish-American to run for president. Smith brought Catholics to the polls in large numbers but lost to Herbert Hoover decisively, winning only Massachusetts, Rhode Island, and six southern states (his running mate was a popular Democrat from Arkansas) and losing the overall popular vote by a huge margin, 58.2 to 40.8 percent, although he carried the ten most populous cities in the United States at that time. After leaving public office, Smith was involved with the organization that built the Empire State Building.

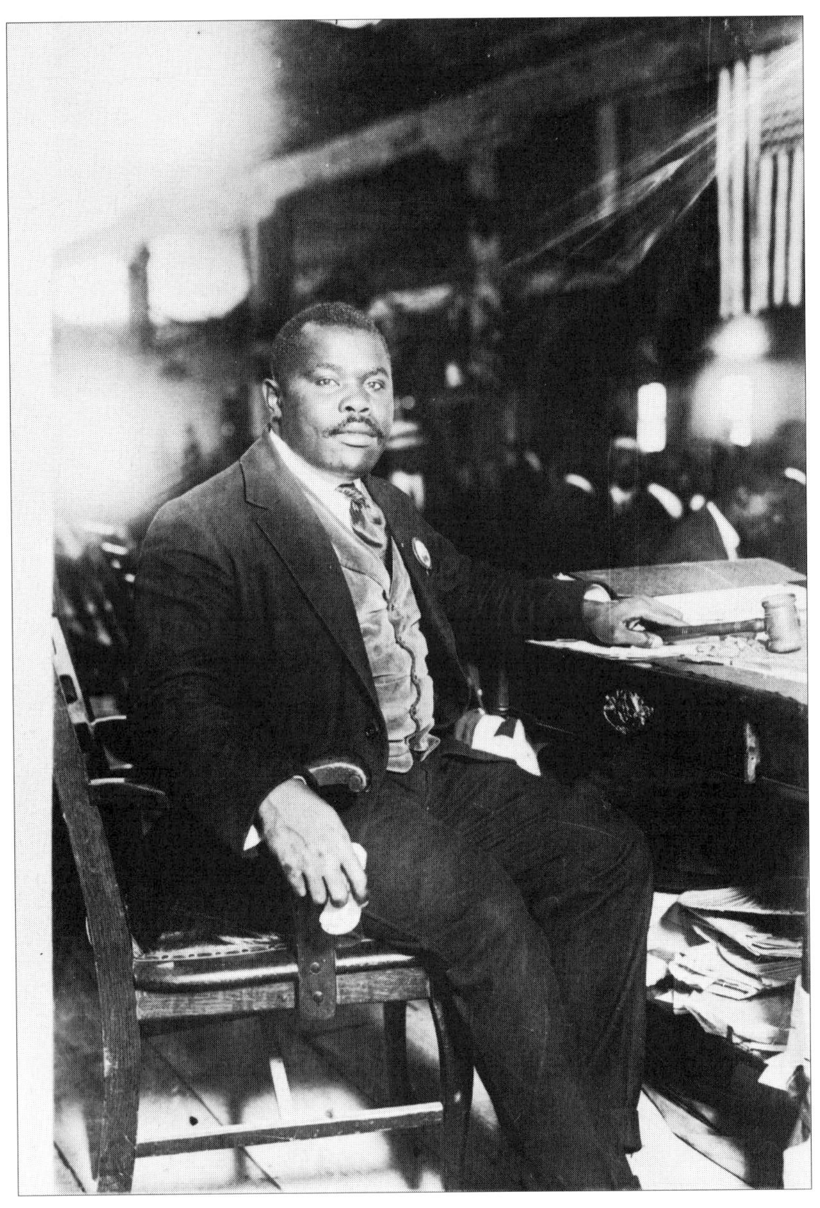

MARCUS GARVEY (1887–1940)

A native of Jamaica, Marcus Garvey founded the Universal Negro Improvement Association soon after immigrating to Harlem in 1916. Garvey was a Black Nationalist who believed that Africa was the ancestral and spiritual home for people of African descent. At a time of racial discrimination and economic hardship after World War I, Garvey built a small empire of devoted members who celebrated their race.

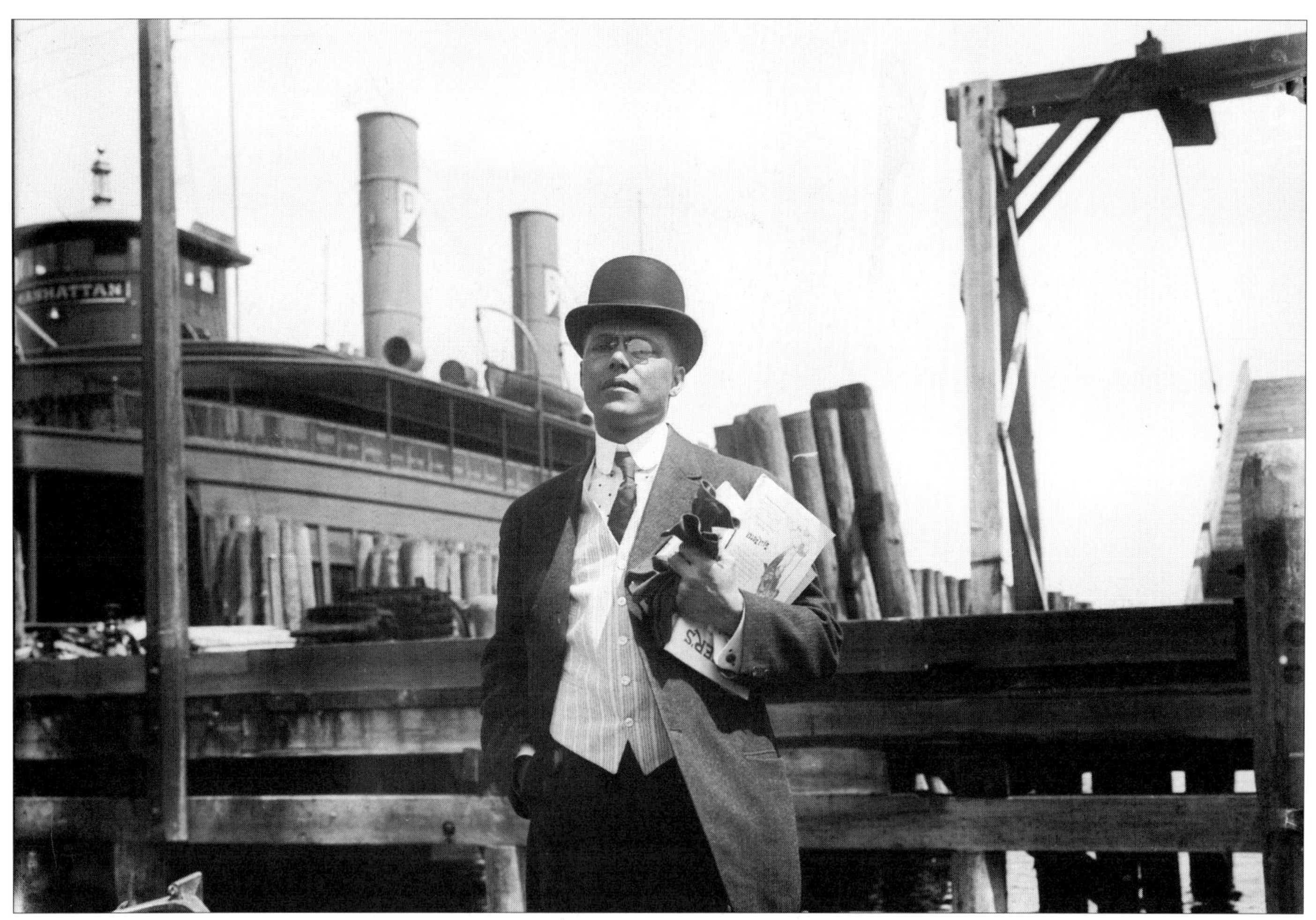

EMMETT SCOTT (1873–1957)

Emmett Scott was an African American author, editor, and civic leader. In 1897 he became private secretary to Booker T. Washington, which opened up other opportunities for him. In 1902 he was appointed secretary of the National Negro Business League. When photographed by the Bain News Service, Scott was serving as a member of the American Commission to Liberia, an appointment he received in 1909 from President William H. Taft.

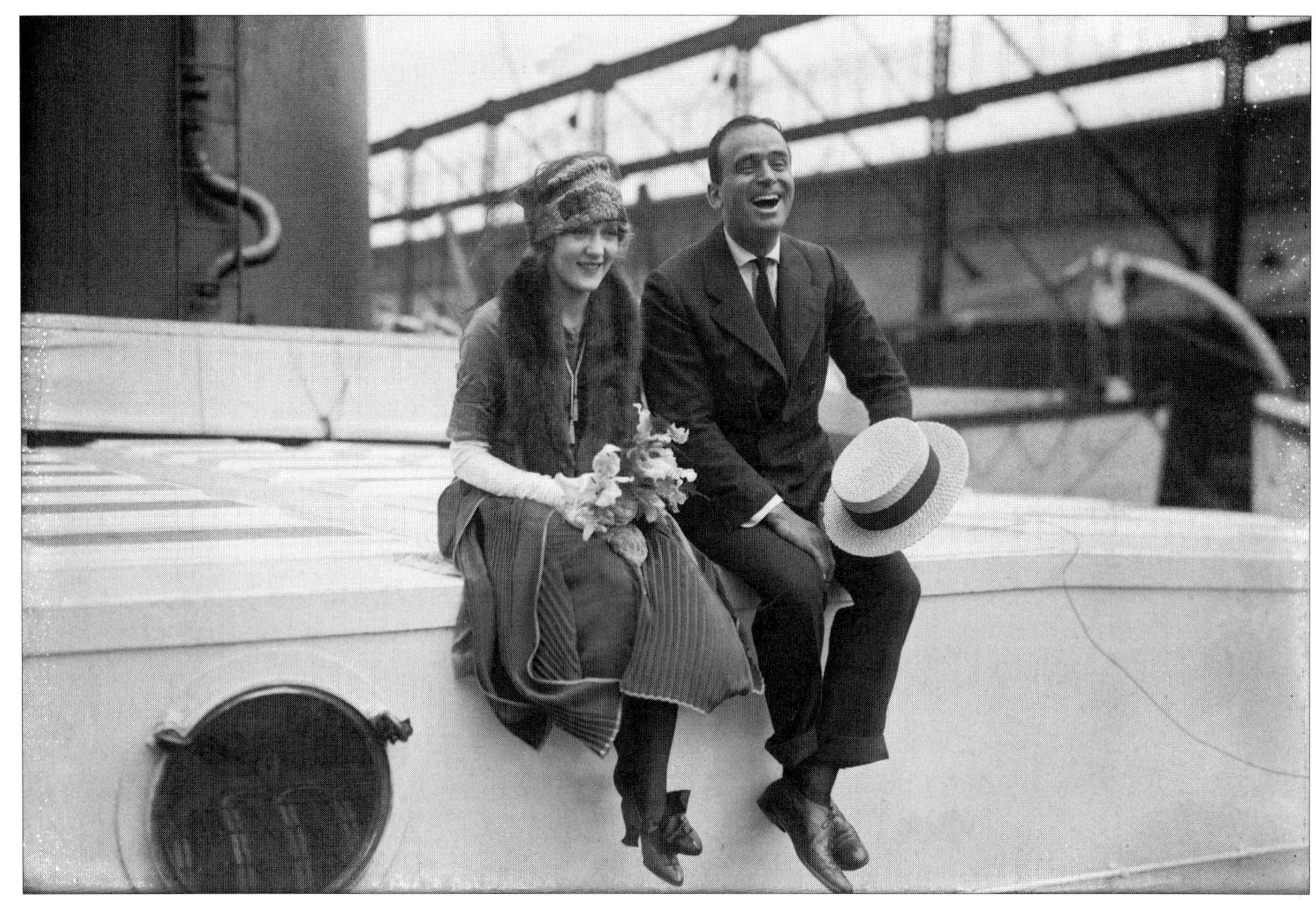

MARY PICKFORD (1893–1979) AND DOUGLAS FAIRBANKS (1883–1939)

Mary Pickford and Douglas Fairbanks—legends of the silent film era—married in 1920. Called "America's Sweetheart" by her fans, Pickford was the highest paid woman in Hollywood. Fairbanks was celebrated for his swashbuckling films, such as *The Mark of Zorro* (1920), and became a successful screenwriter, director, and producer. Both of their acting careers waned as the "talkies" took over. They divorced in 1936.

EDDIE CANTOR (1892–1964)

Eddie Cantor was a vaudeville performer, comedian, singer, actor, and songwriter who was well-known to Broadway, radio, and early television audiences. His radio shows revealed amusing anecdotes about his wife Ida and five children and earned him a huge following. Cantor earned the nickname "Banjo Eyes" for his wide eye-rolling song-and-dance routines. His Broadway career spanned the *Ziegfeld Follies* of 1917 through *Banjo Eyes* in 1941. His film career began with silent features in the 1920s and concluded with a cameo role in *The Eddie Cantor Story* in 1953.

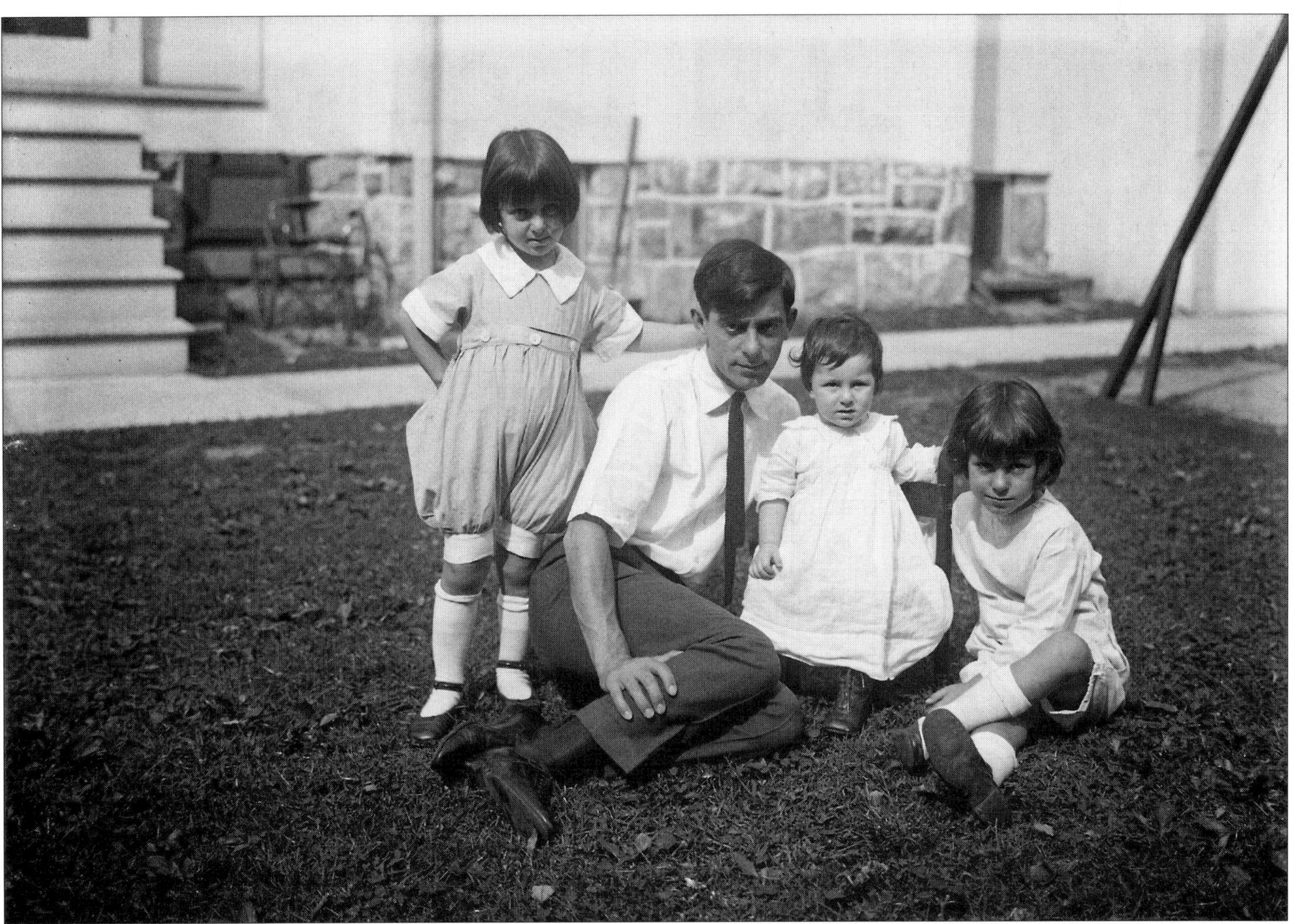

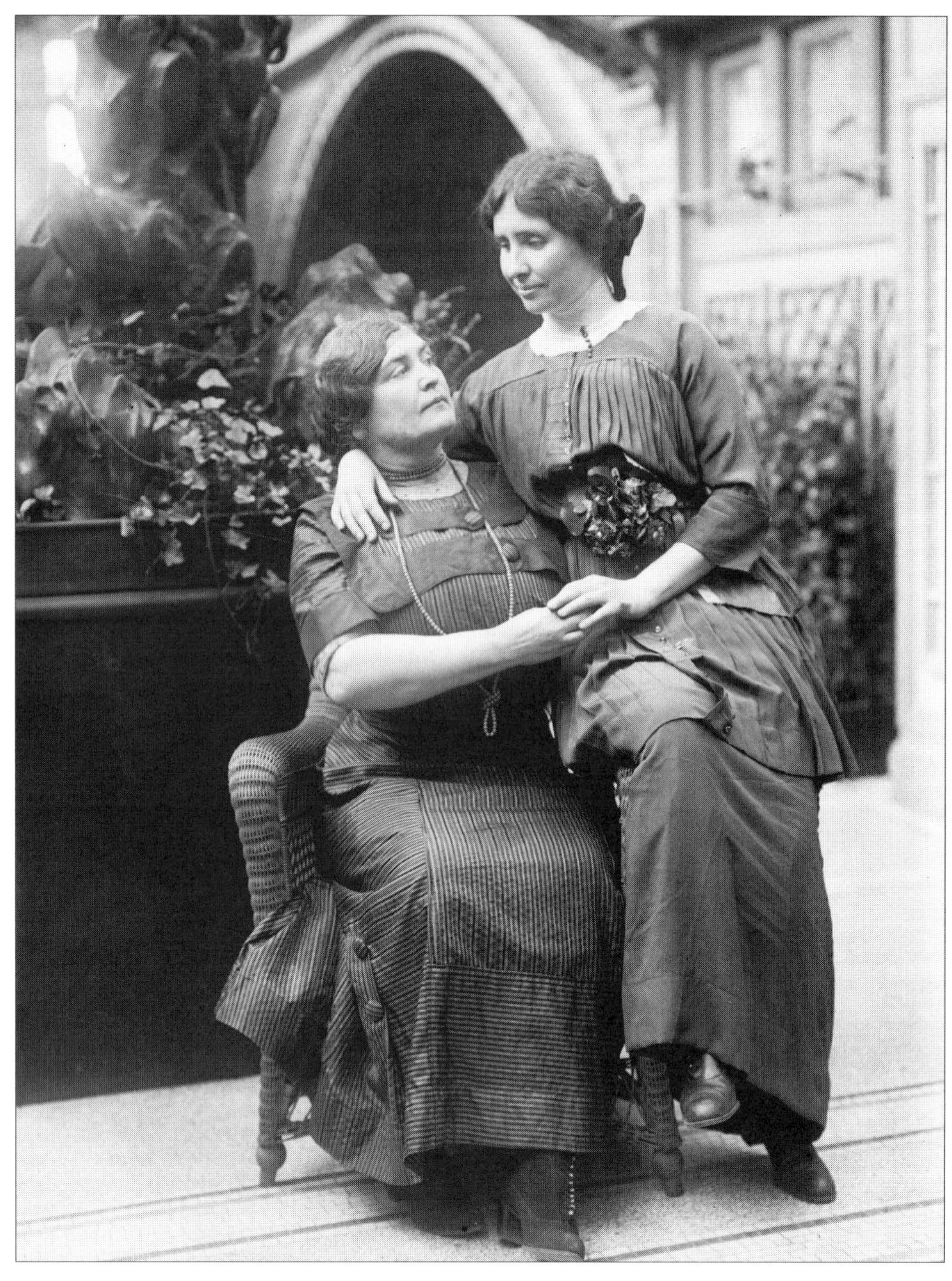

HELEN KELLER (1880–1968) AND ANNE SULLIVAN MACY (1866–1936)

Helen Keller, seen here with her teacher and dearest companion Anne Sullivan Macy *(seated),* was an author, activist, and the first deaf-blind person to graduate from college. As a young woman, Anne became Helen's link to the outside world, teaching her to communicate though sign language. Her success with Helen is immortalized in the play *The Miracle Worker* (1959) by William Gibson, which is based on Keller's autobiography, *The Story of My Life*. The play ran on Broadway for over 700 performances. Keller also campaigned for women's suffrage, workers' rights, and spoke out against war.

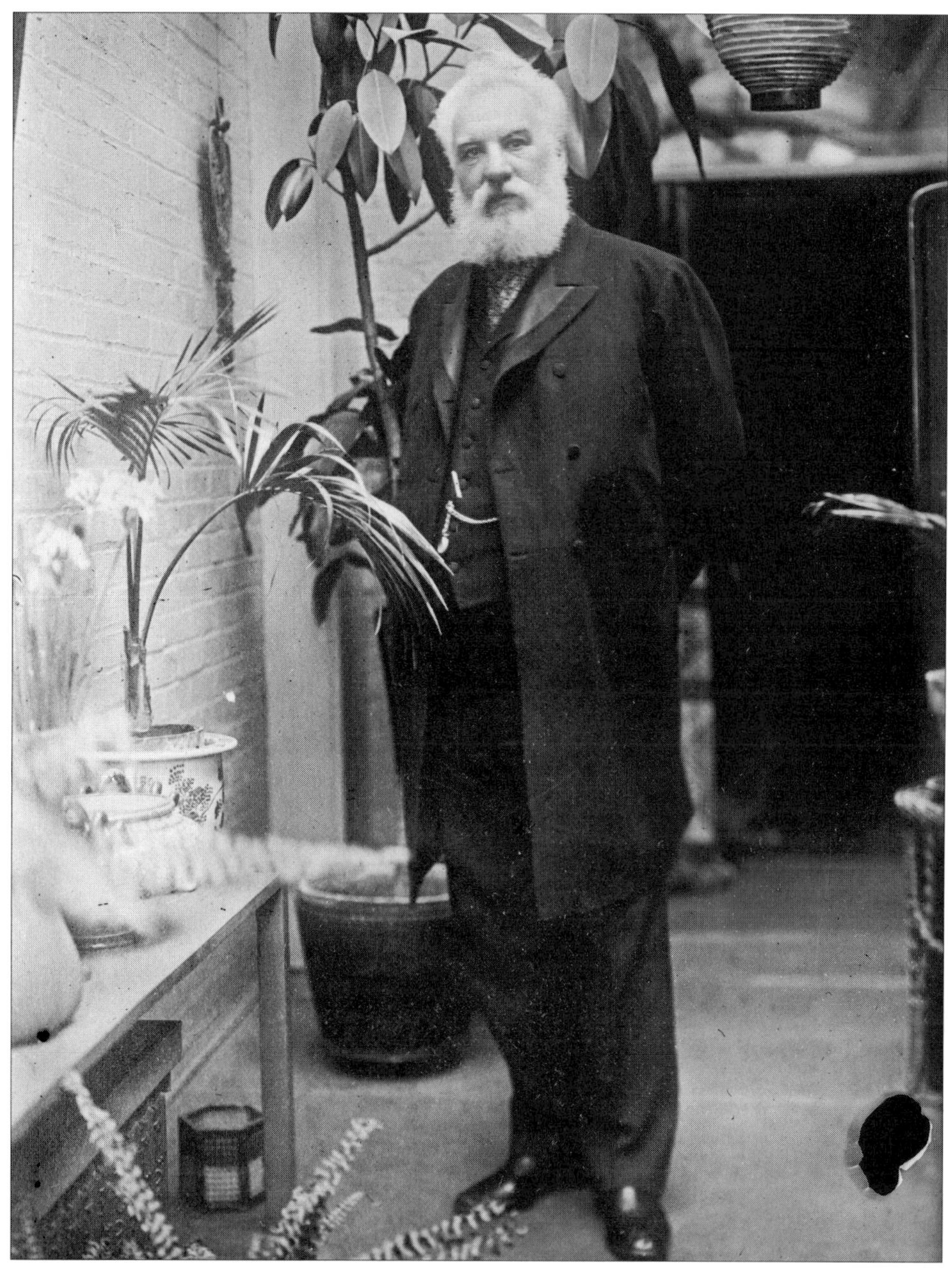

ALEXANDER GRAHAM BELL (1847–1922)

Alexander Graham Bell was a scientist and innovator who is credited with inventing the telephone. Both Bell's mother and wife were deaf and this had an enormous impact on his field of research. His experimentation with hearing devices won him the first U.S. patent for the telephone in 1876. A few days after his patent was issued, Bell succeeded in getting his telephone to work, speaking the famous sentence to his assistant in another room: "Mr. Watson—Come here—I want to see you." It is said that Bell thought the telephone a distraction and intrusion and did not have one in his study.

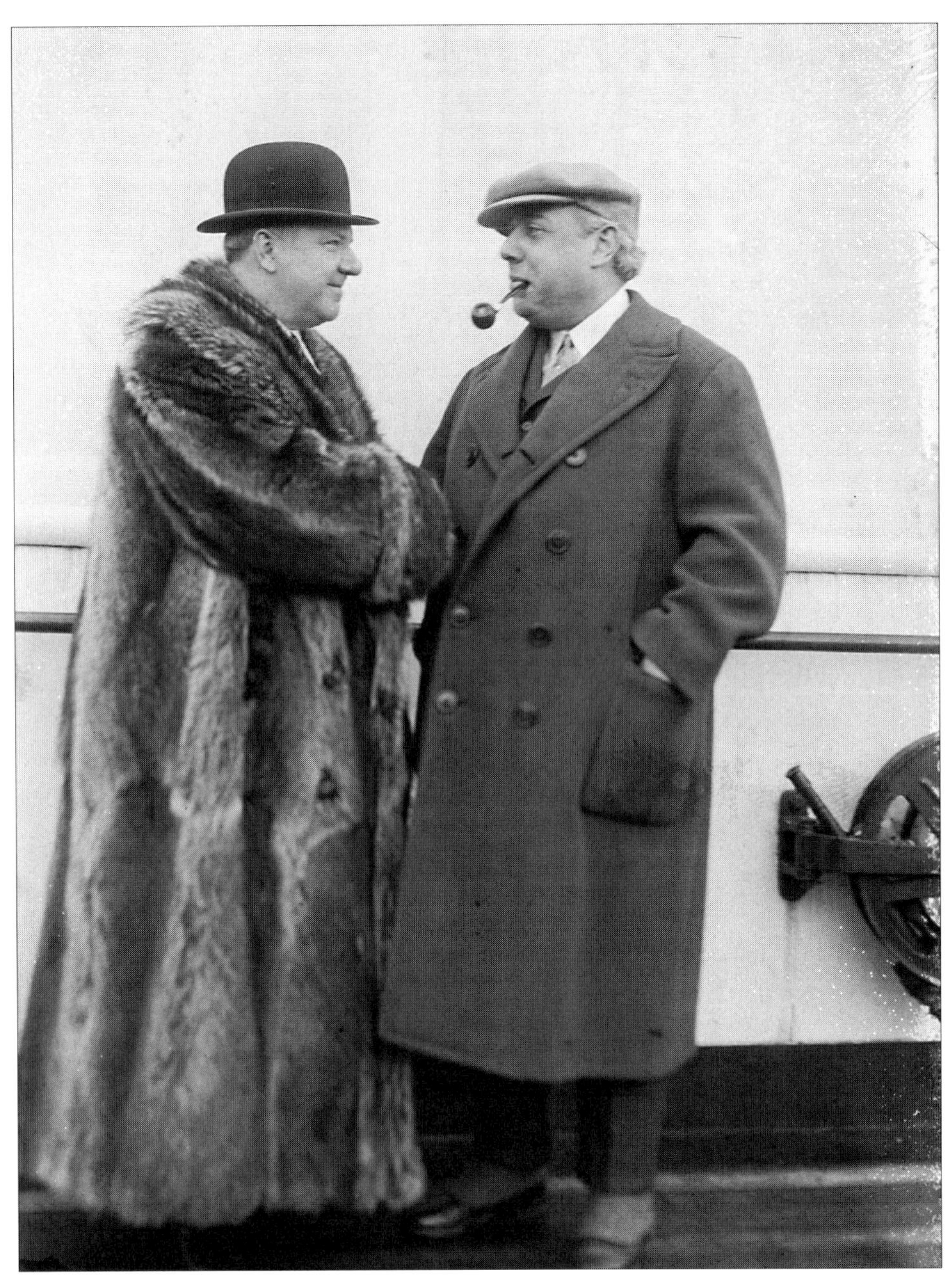

W. C. FIELDS (1880–1946) AND PHILIP GOODMAN (C. 1886–1941)

W. C. Fields was a comic actor who assumed the persona of harmless drunk, a child hater, and a dog hater. He is also remembered for his priceless quips. Fields started his career as a juggler in vaudeville and then starred in the *Ziegfeld Follies* revues. By 1934, he was a major screen star. Fields kept a flask of martinis with him on the set, which he called his "lemonade." When a prankster filled it with actual lemonade, Fields yelled, "Who put lemonade in my lemonade!" Philip Goodman was a theatrical producer.

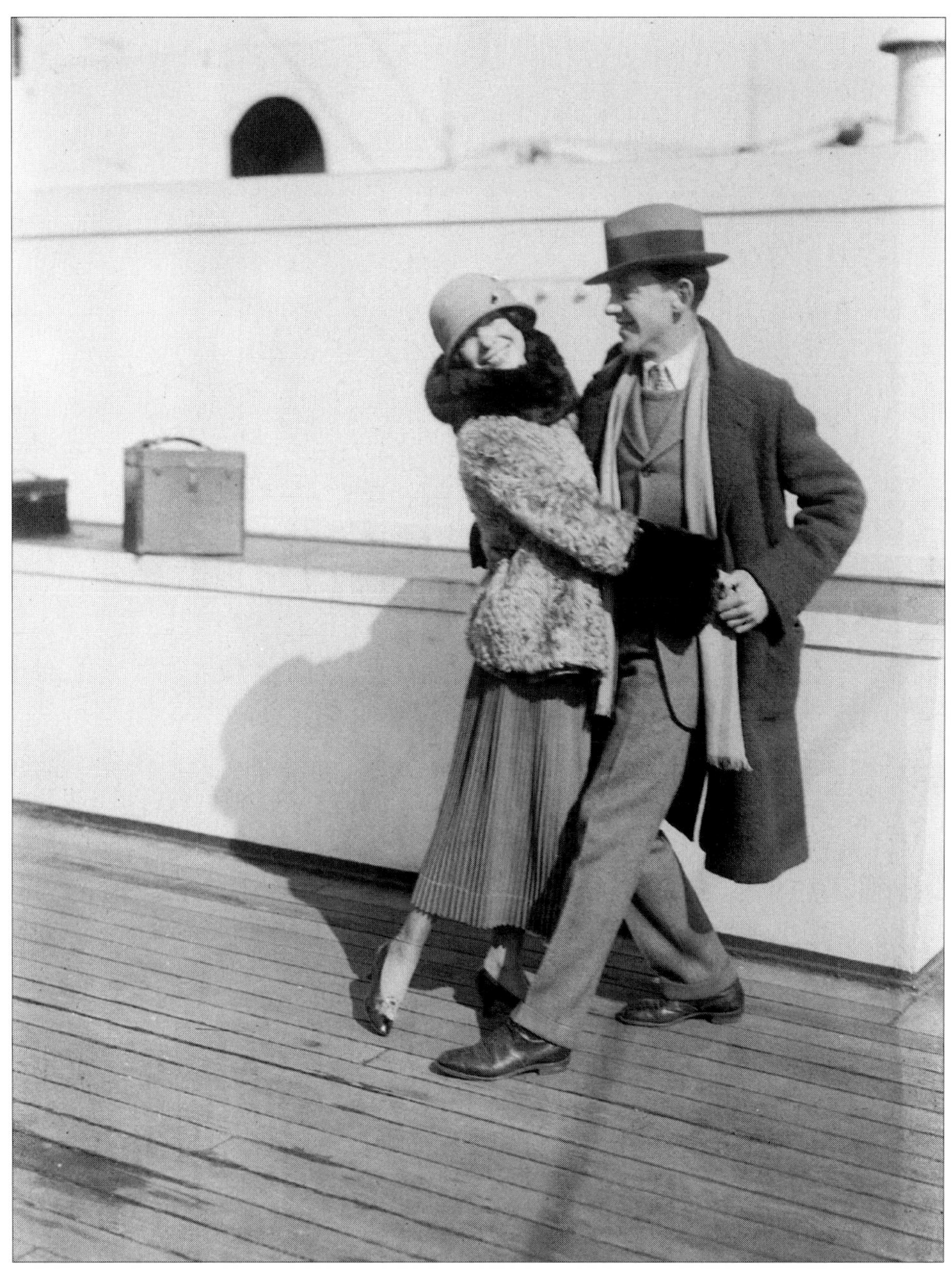

FRED ASTAIRE (1899–1987) AND ADELE ASTAIRE (1896–1981)

Although Ginger Rogers is generally considered his greatest partner, Fred Astaire started his dancing career with his sister, Adele. The brother and sister act performed in vaudeville and then on stages throughout the United States and abroad. When Adele married in 1932, she retired from dancing. Fred went on to star on stage and in film and is considered one of the great dancers of the twentieth century.

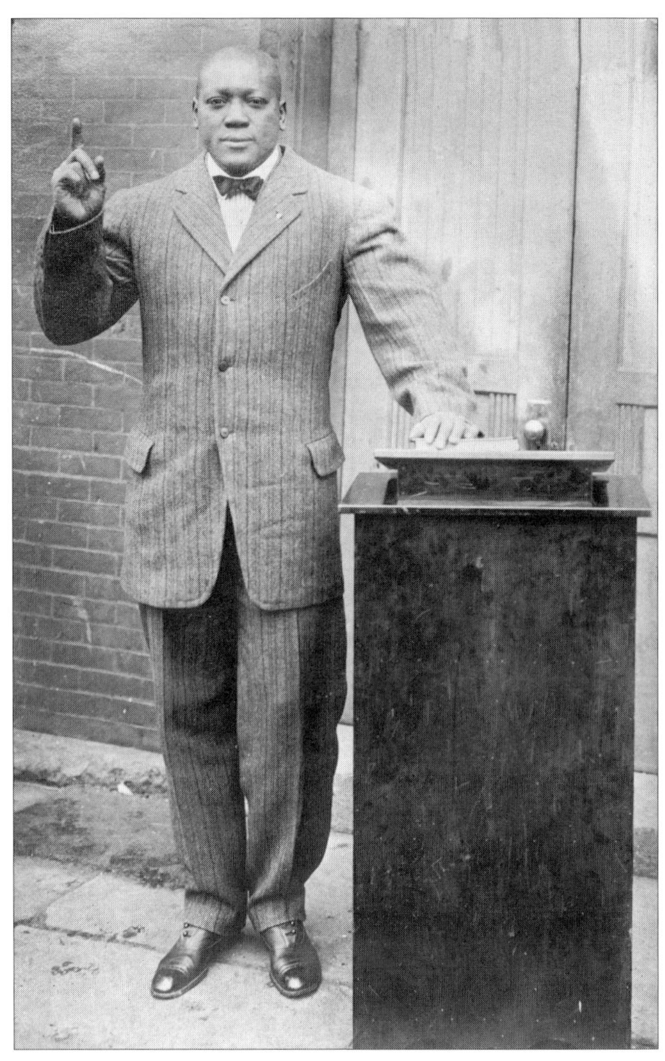

JACK JOHNSON (1878–1946)

The first African American to become a heavyweight champion of the world, Jack Johnson dominated boxing from 1908 to 1915. Born in Texas, Johnson grew up during a time when racism prohibited him from seeking any kind of title. But he refused to play by the rules set by the white establishment. He won the heavyweight championship in 1908 by beating Canadian Tommy Burns in Sydney, Australia. Johnson's defeat of "The Great White Hope"—Jim Jeffries—in 1910, sparked race riots across the country. Johnson eventually lost his title to Jess Willard in 1915. The occasion for this photo, Johnson standing at a pulpit, is not known.

JACK "MANASSA MAULER" DEMPSEY (1895–1983)

American boxer Jack Dempsey held the world heavyweight title from 1919 to 1926. On July 4, 1919, he and world heavyweight champion, Jess Willard, met at Toledo, Ohio. Willard was the favorite, but the first round of the fight proved to be one of the most brutal in boxing history. Dempsey knocked Willard down seven times and broke his cheekbone, jaw, some teeth, and a few ribs. After successfully defending his title several times, including against Georges Carpentier in 1921, Dempsey finally lost the heavyweight title to underdog Gene Tunney in 1926. A year later Tunney defeated Dempsey again, this time in the legendary "long count" fight in Chicago, after which Dempsey retired from the ring.

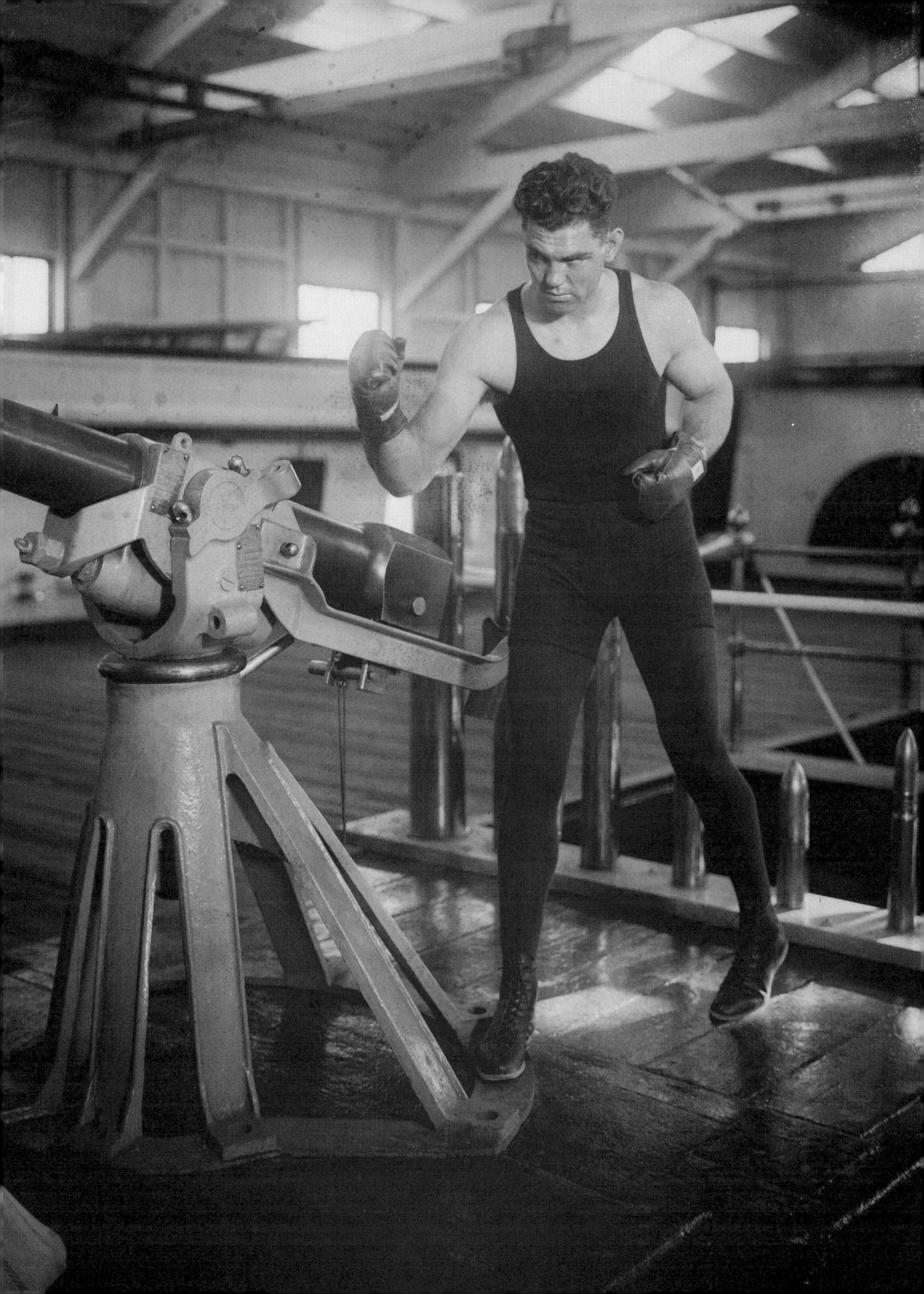

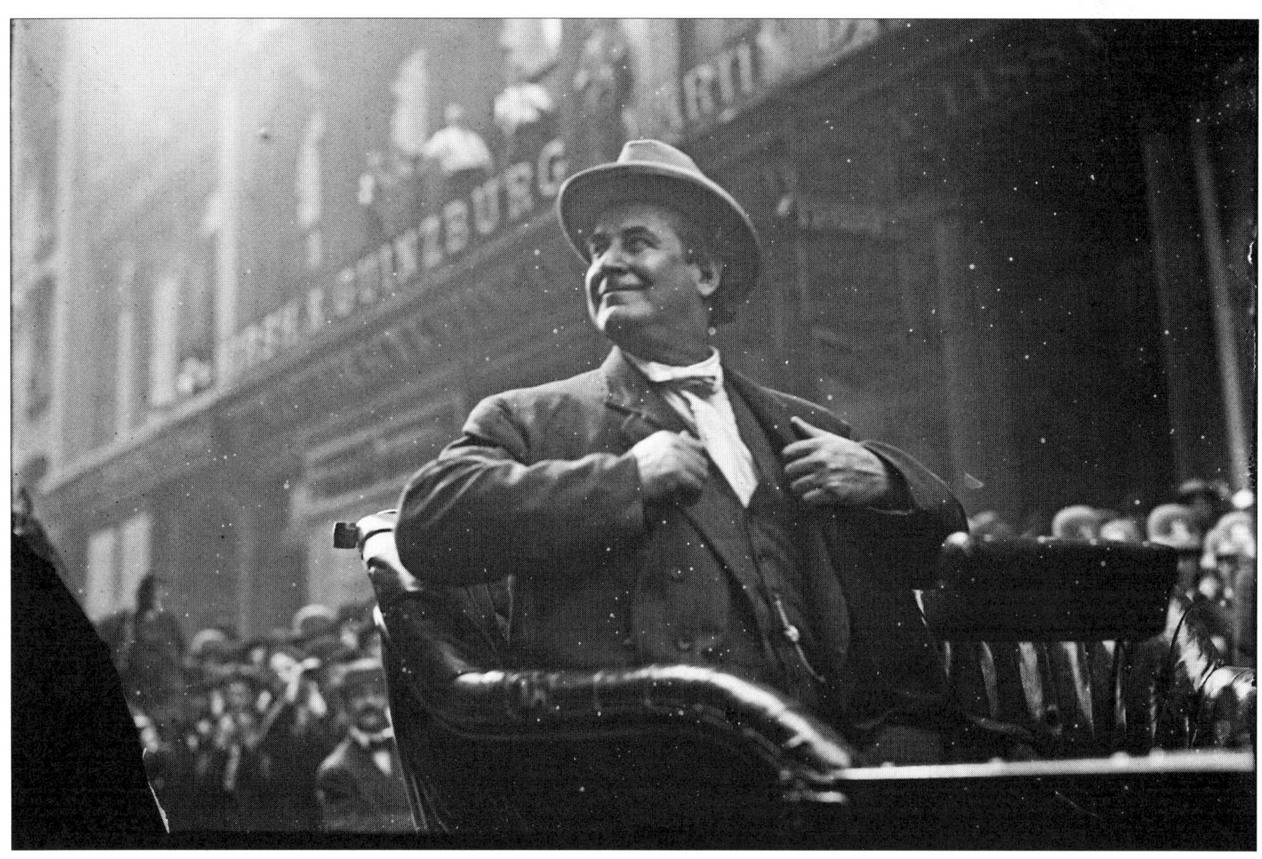

WILLIAM JENNINGS BRYAN (1860–1925)

A better orator than politician, William Jennings Bryan became a lawyer and served two terms in Congress. Nominated for president at the 1896 Democratic convention, Bryan traveled the country seeking support for his candidacy, but lost to Republican William McKinley. Bryan ran again for president and lost two more times, in 1900 and 1908. He later supported women's suffrage and prohibition and served as associate counsel at the Scopes "Monkey Trial" of 1925, where he sided with those opposed to teaching Darwin's theory of evolution.

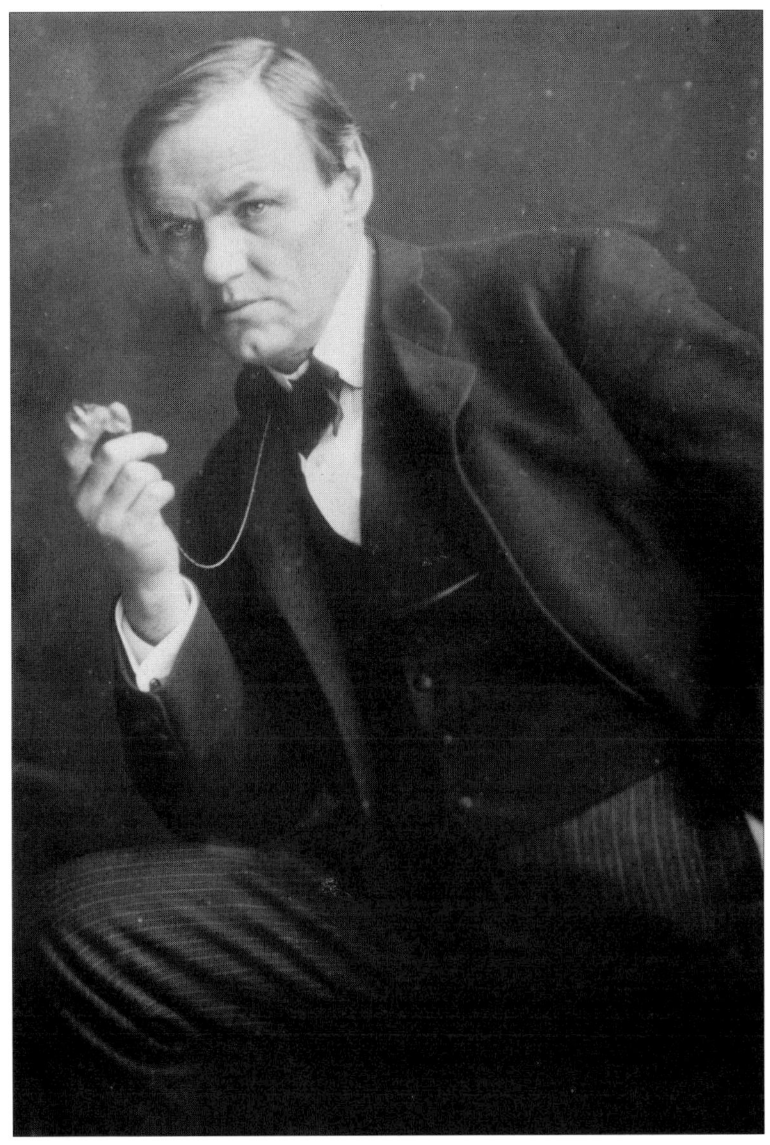

CLARENCE DARROW (1857–1938)

American lawyer Clarence Darrow gained fame as the defense attorney in several memorable trials including the 1925 "Monkey Trial." He defended Tennessee high school teacher John T. Scopes against charges of violating Tennessee law by denying the biblical account of creation and teaching the Darwinian theory of evolution. Darrow's opponent in this high-profile trial was the three-time failed Democratic presidential candidate William Jennings Bryan. Despite Darrow's efforts, in which he easily bested Bryan as a debater, Scopes was convicted of teaching evolution and fined $100, but the verdict was later overturned on a technicality. The trial raised public consciousness about the ongoing conflict between proponents of the theory of evolution and religious fundamentalism.

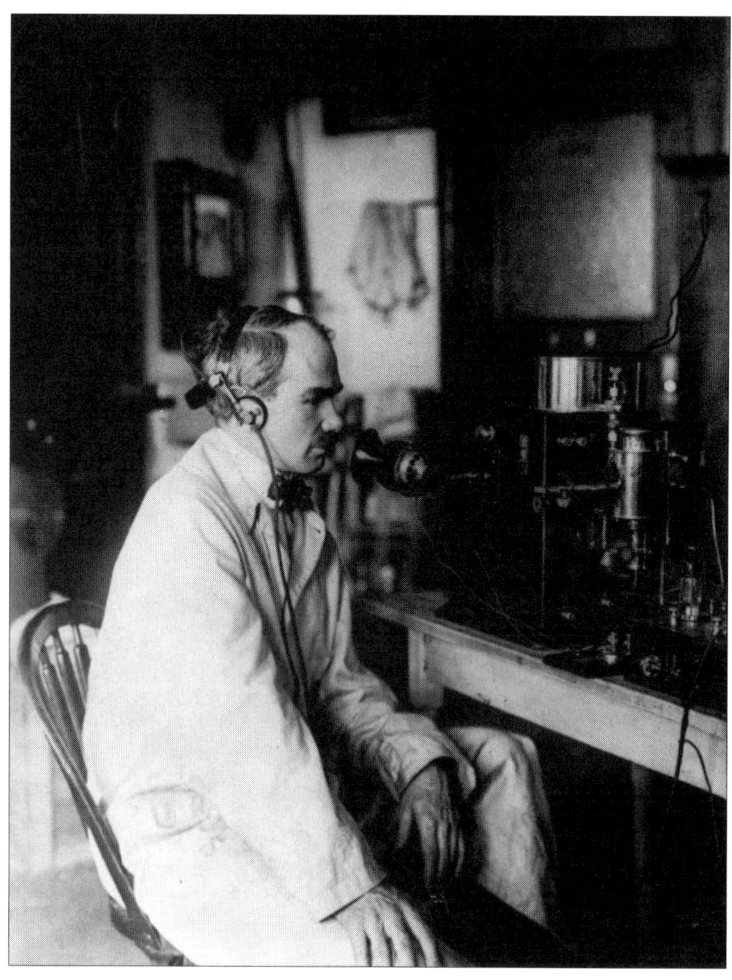

LEE DE FOREST (1873–1961)

In 1906 Lee De Forest invented the Audion triode vacuum tube, which could greatly amplify weak electrical signals. It became the basis of all subsequent electrical sound systems until the invention of the transistor in 1947. It was first used to detect radio waves, and later helped amplify long distance telephones. In 1910 De Forest was among those responsible for the birth of public radio broadcasting when he conducted experimental broadcasts from New York's Metropolitan Opera House, including a performance by Enrico Caruso. In 1916, he broadcast the first radio reports of a presidential election. When he was the guest celebrity on an episode of the popular television show *This is Your Life* (1957), he was introduced as "the father of radio and the grandfather of television."

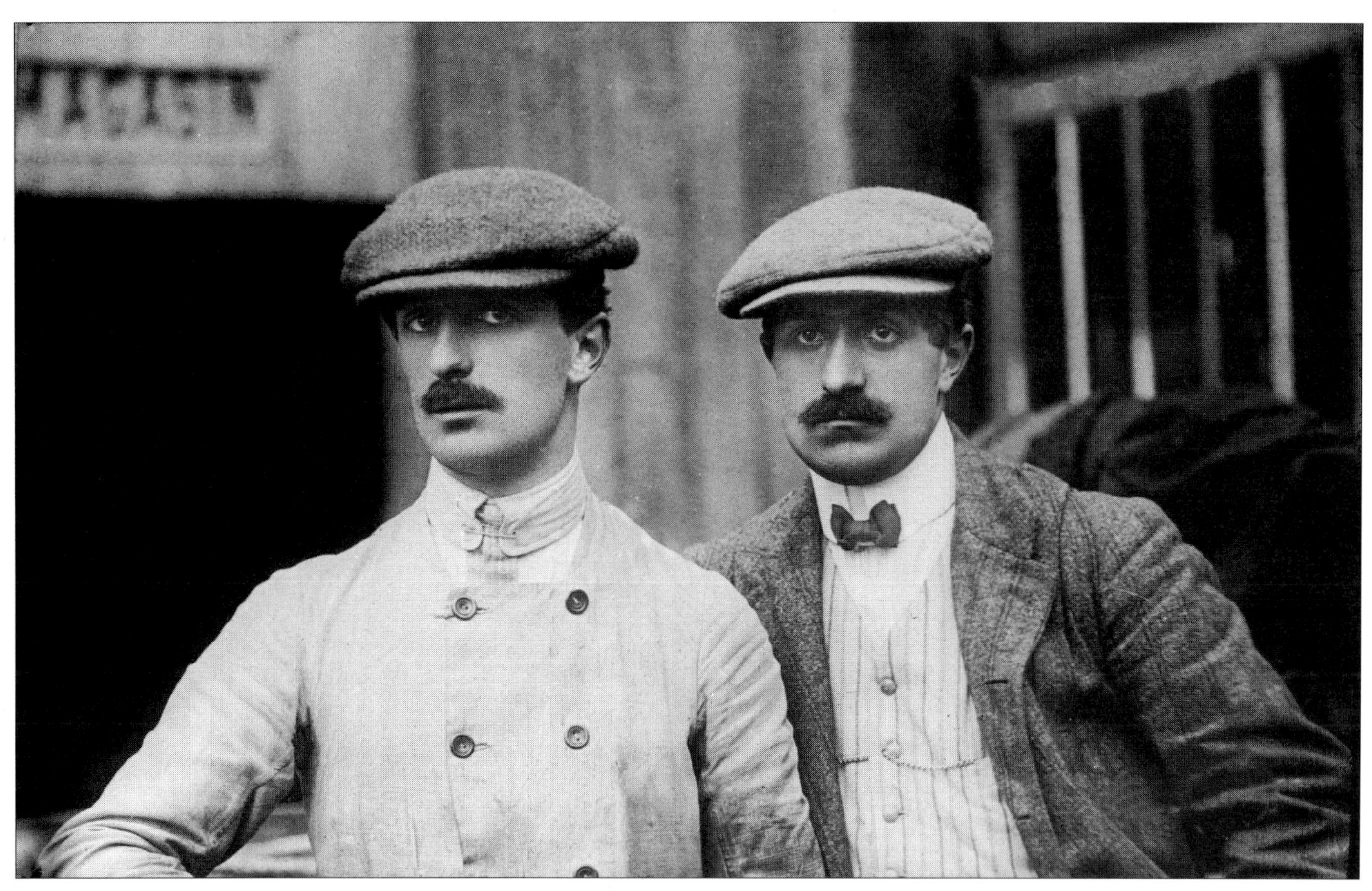

GABRIEL VOISIN (1880–1973) AND CHARLES VOISIN (1882–1912)

Gabriel Voisin and his brother Charles created Europe's first successful heavier-than-air flying machines. Henri Farman, a French aviation pioneer—and one of their first customers—helped popularize Voisin planes with his record-breaking flights. In 1908 the modified Voisin biplane became the first airplane on the European continent to succeed in landing where it had taken off after flying a pre-assigned one-kilometer circuit. Voisin planes were widely used during World War I for spotting and bombing enemy aircraft. After the war, Gabriel devoted his efforts to the field of luxury automobiles.

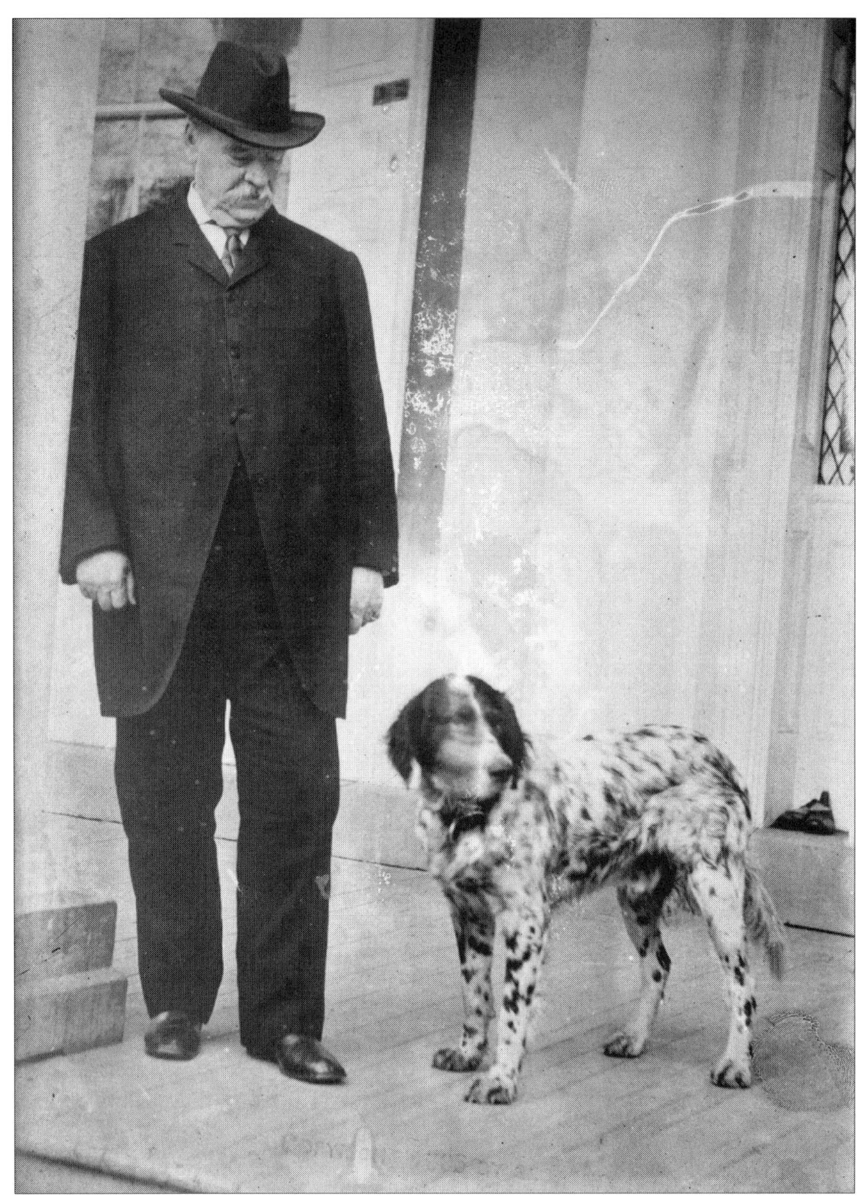

GROVER CLEVELAND (1837–1908)

Grover Cleveland, seen here with his dog in 1905, was both the twenty-second and twenty-fourth president of the United States. Cleveland is the only president to serve two non-consecutive terms (1885–1889 and 1893–1897). He was also the only Democrat elected to the presidency in the era of Republian political domination that lasted from 1860 to 1912. A reformer, Cleveland worked against corruption and patronage.

CALVIN COOLIDGE (1872–1933)

Calvin Coolidge, the thirtieth president of the United States, was a Republican lawyer from Vermont. He entered politics in Massachusetts before becoming his party's choice as vice president. He succeeded to the office of president on Warren Harding's death in 1923, and was elected in his own right in 1924, defeating John W. Davis. A dedicated small government conservative, Coolidge was a man of few words, who was jokingly called "Silent Cal." On hearing of Coolidge's death, the witty writer Dorothy Parker remarked, "How can they tell?"

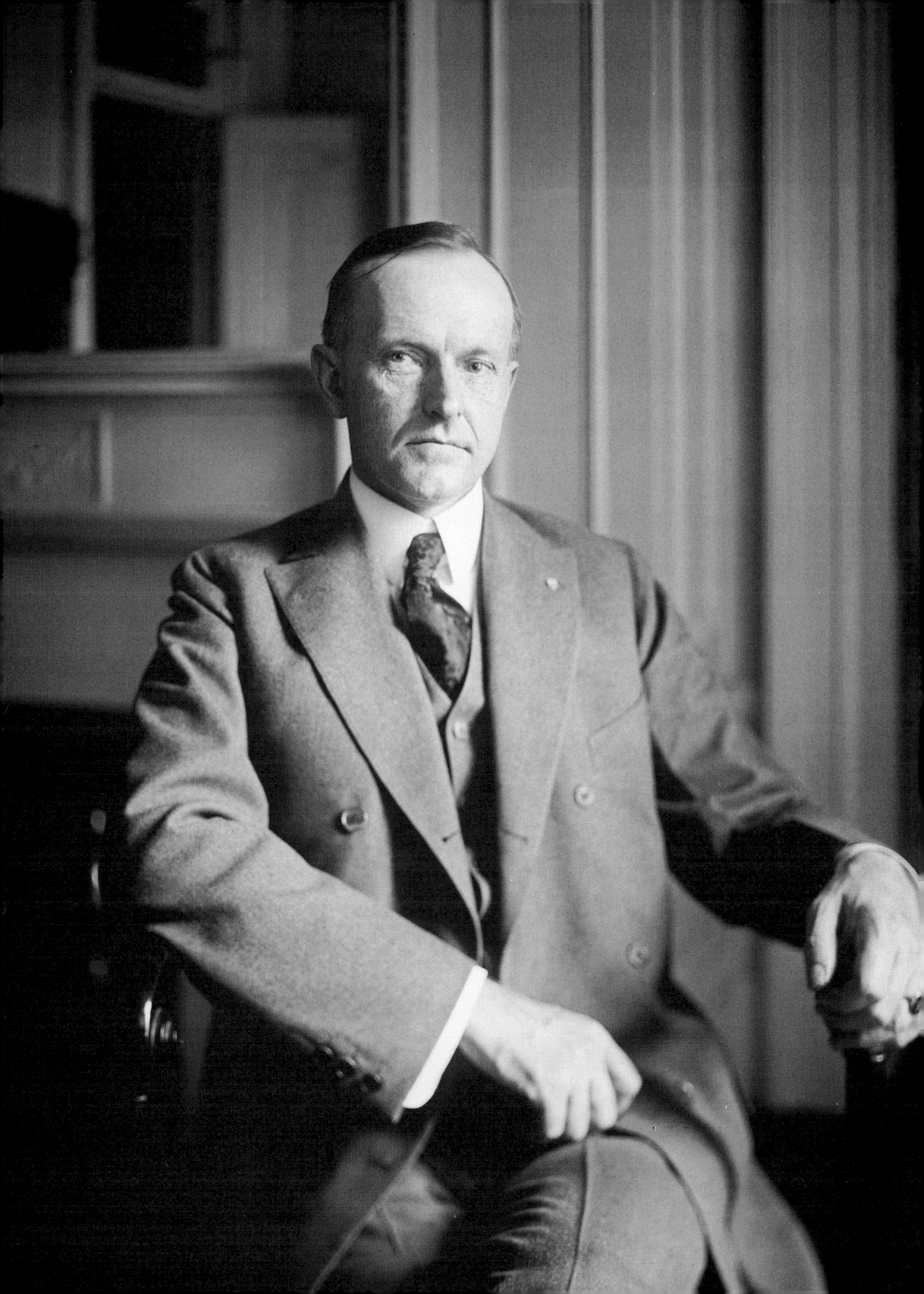

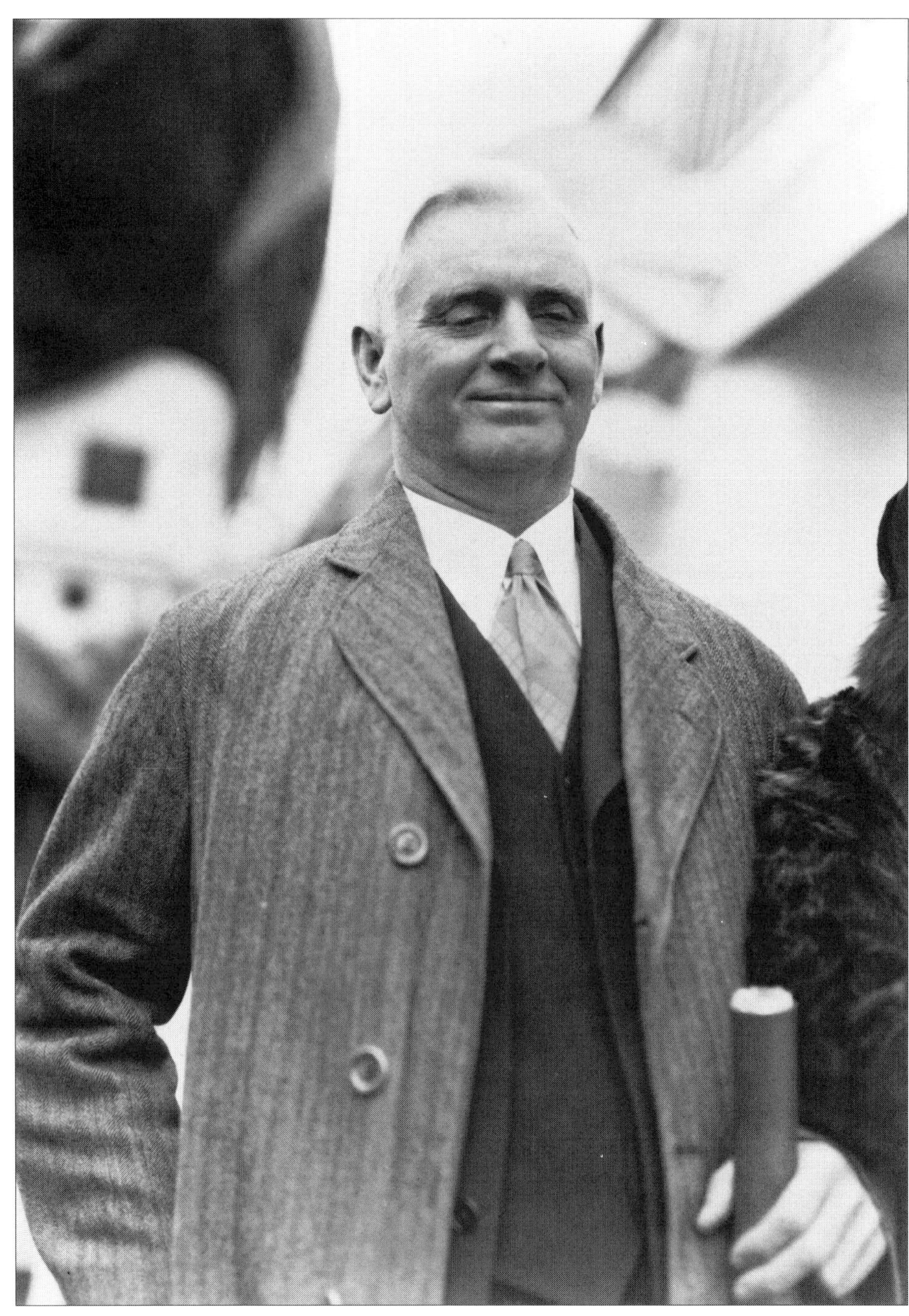

THOMAS PRYOR GORE (1870–1949)

Thomas Pryor Gore lost sight in both eyes as a boy, but never let his blindness interfere with his aspirations. In 1907 the Populist Democrat was elected one of Oklahoma's first two senators and was reelected to the Senate for full six-year terms in 1908 and 1914. Although he lost the 1920 election, he served one more term from 1931 to 1937. Gore was the grandfather of well-known American author Gore Vidal.

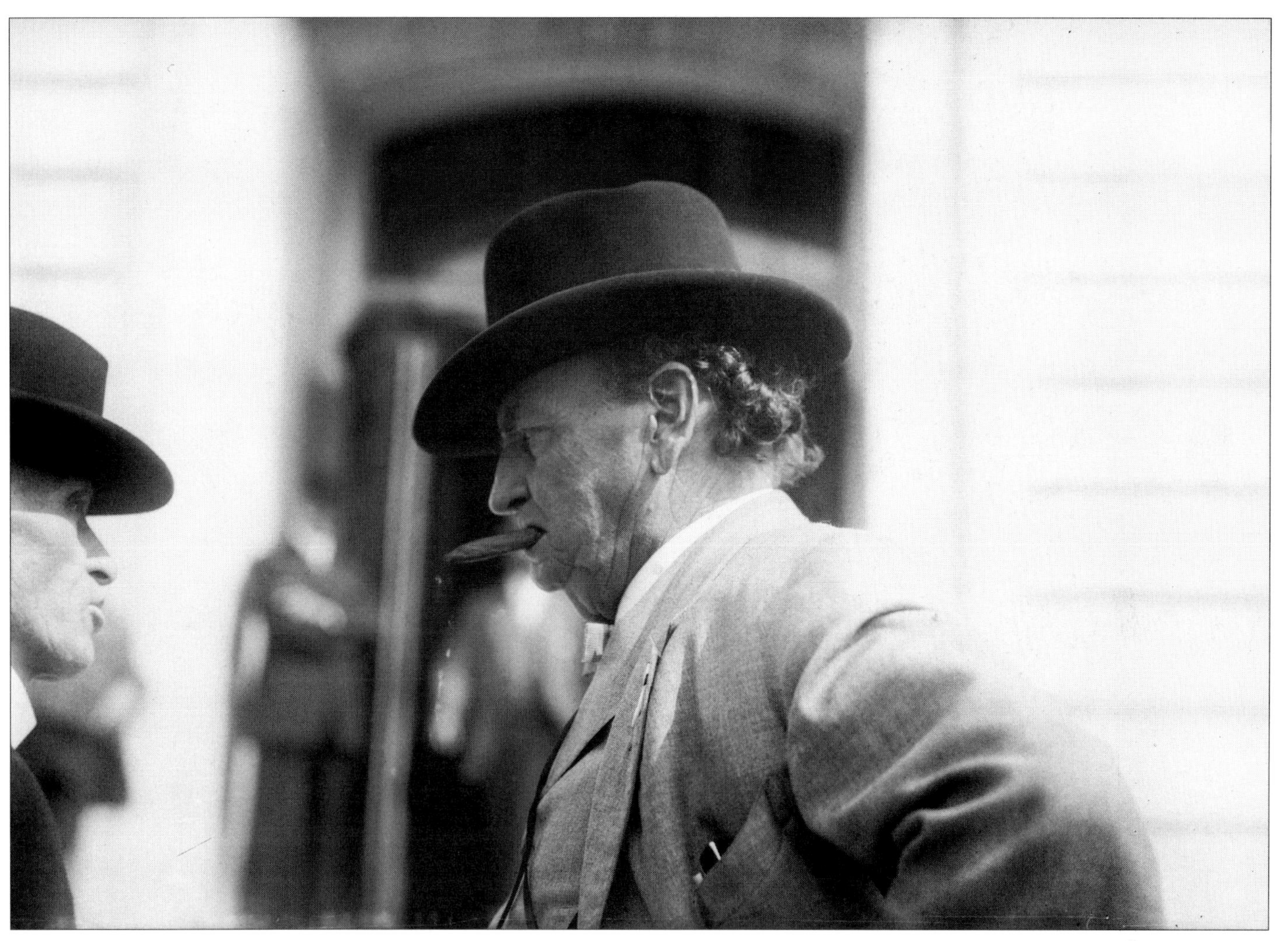

JOHN HOLLIS BANKHEAD (1842–1920)

John Hollis Bankhead was a U.S. Senator from the state of Alabama. He was in the Confederate Army, Alabama Infantry, during the Civil War. Bankhead served in the Senate from June 18, 1907 to his death on March 1, 1920. U.S. Senator John H. Bankhead II and Speaker of the House William Brockman Bankhead were his sons and actress Tallulah Bankhead was his granddaughter.

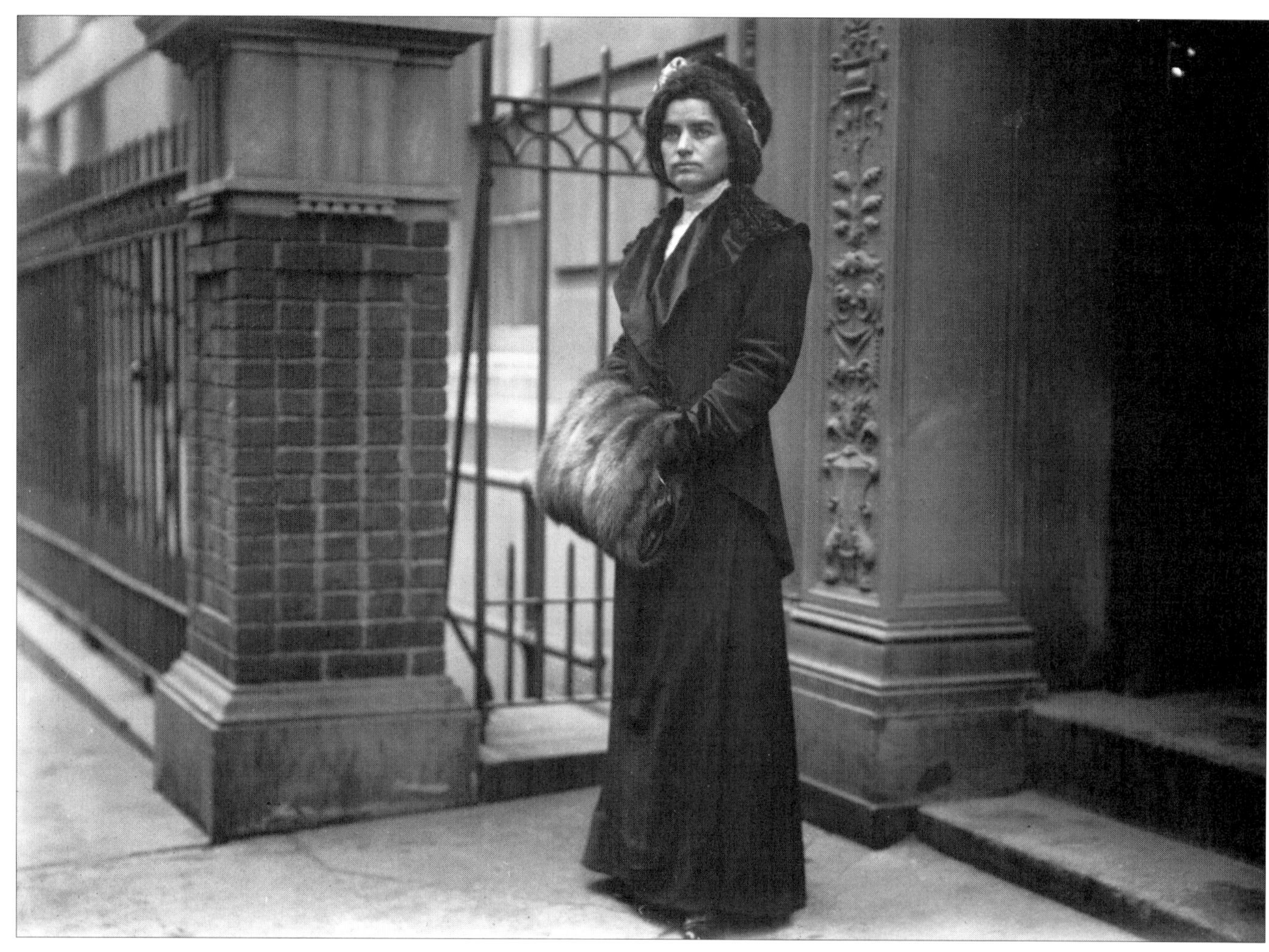

CATHERINE ANN "KATE" BARNARD (1875–1930)

Kate Barnard was the first woman elected to a state office in Oklahoma. In 1906, in Oklahoma's first general election, Barnard, a Democrat, was elected Commissioner of Oklahoma Charities and Corrections based on her prior work as a public advocate in those areas, even though women could not vote in that election. Barnard supported laws for compulsory education and fought for a ban on child labor. Her work on behalf of Native American children ultimately caused her to lose favor with prominent officials and the state legislature withdrew funding for her position.

MARY HOBART (1851–1940)

Mary Hobart was born in Boston and in 1884 graduated from the Woman's Medical College of the New York Infirmary. Dr. Elizabeth Blackwell, the first woman in the United States to graduate from medical school, founded that institution. Hobart later worked at the New England Hospital, the second hospital in the United States run by women for women.

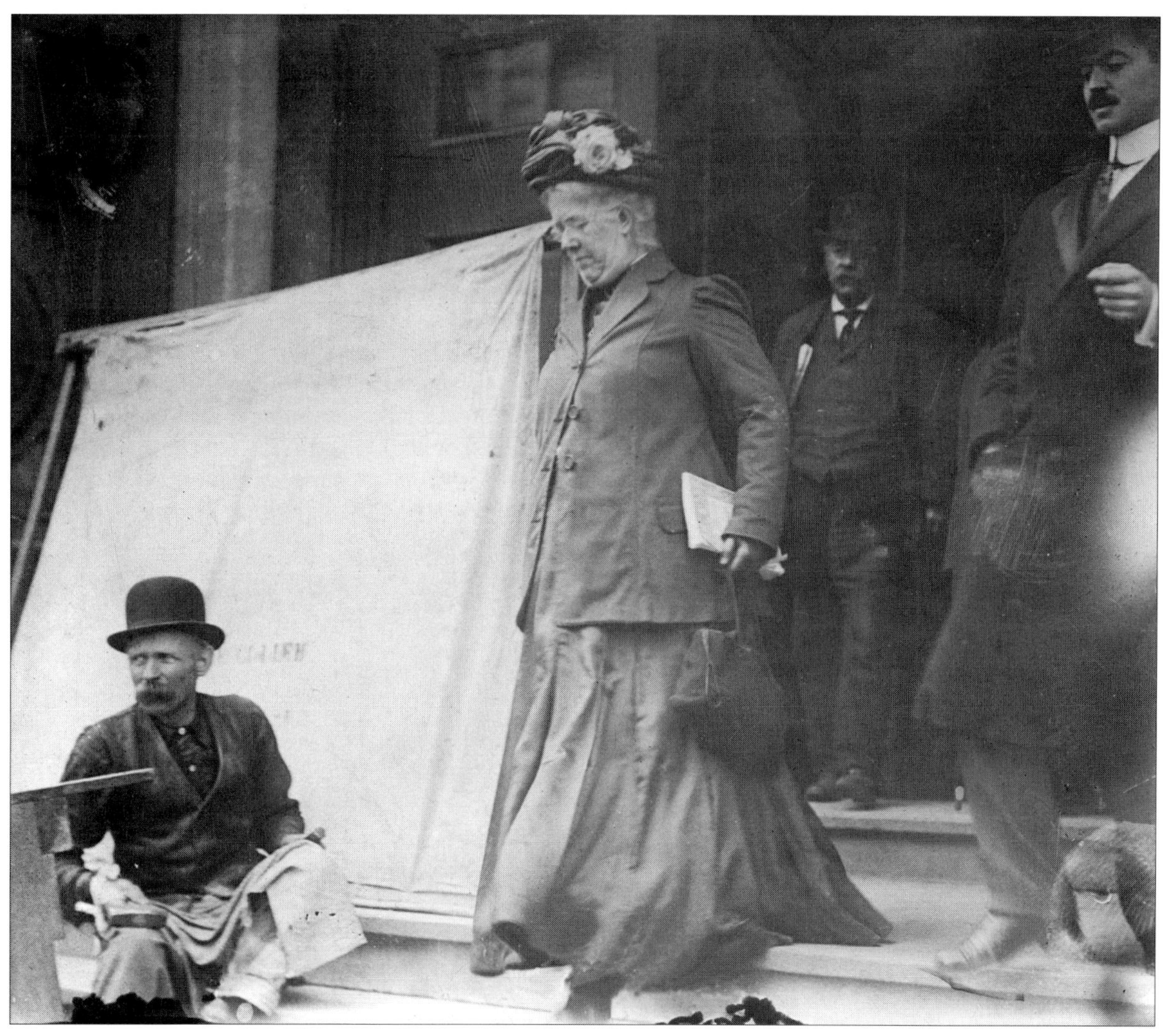

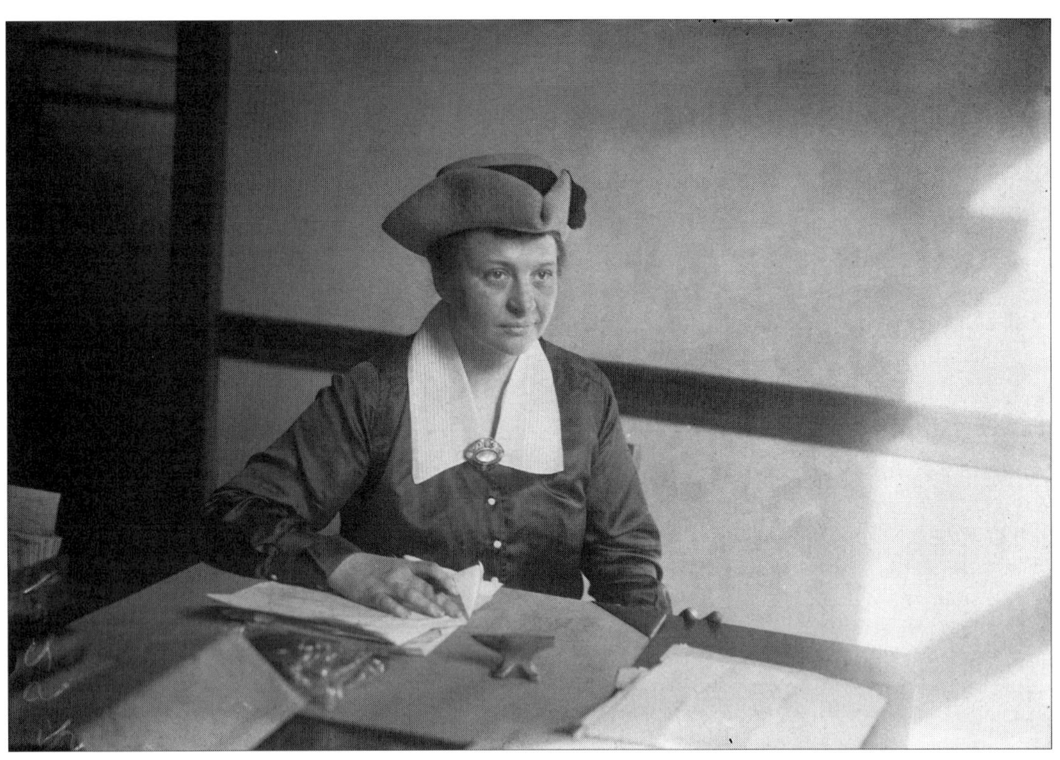

FRANCES PERKINS (1882–1965)

In 1911 Frances Perkins watched in horror as female factory workers jumped to their deaths during the Triangle Shirtwaist Factory fire in New York City, which claimed 148 lives. Already an advocate for women and children laborers, she became even more committed to the labor movement. In 1929 Franklin Roosevelt, then New York governor, appointed her industrial commissioner for the state. As president, Roosevelt again called on Perkins, who became the Secretary of Labor in 1933. She was the first female cabinet member in U.S. history and served for the duration of Roosevelt's presidency. While Secretary of Labor she was also chairwoman of the Presidents Committee on Economic Security. In that role she played a vital part in the passage of the 1935 Social Security Act.

JEANNETTE RANKIN (1880–1973)

Jeannette Rankin of Montana was elected on November 7, 1916 to the United States House of Representatives. She was the first female member of the U.S. Congress. During Rankin's first term in Congress (1917–1919), many women in the United States did not have the right to vote (the Nineteenth Amendment which gave all women the vote was not ratified until 1920). A lifelong pacifist, Rankin voted against the entry of the United States into both World War I and World War II. Losing popularity following her protest vote on entering the Second World War she declined to seek reelection. Toward the end of her life she actively protested against the Vietnam War.

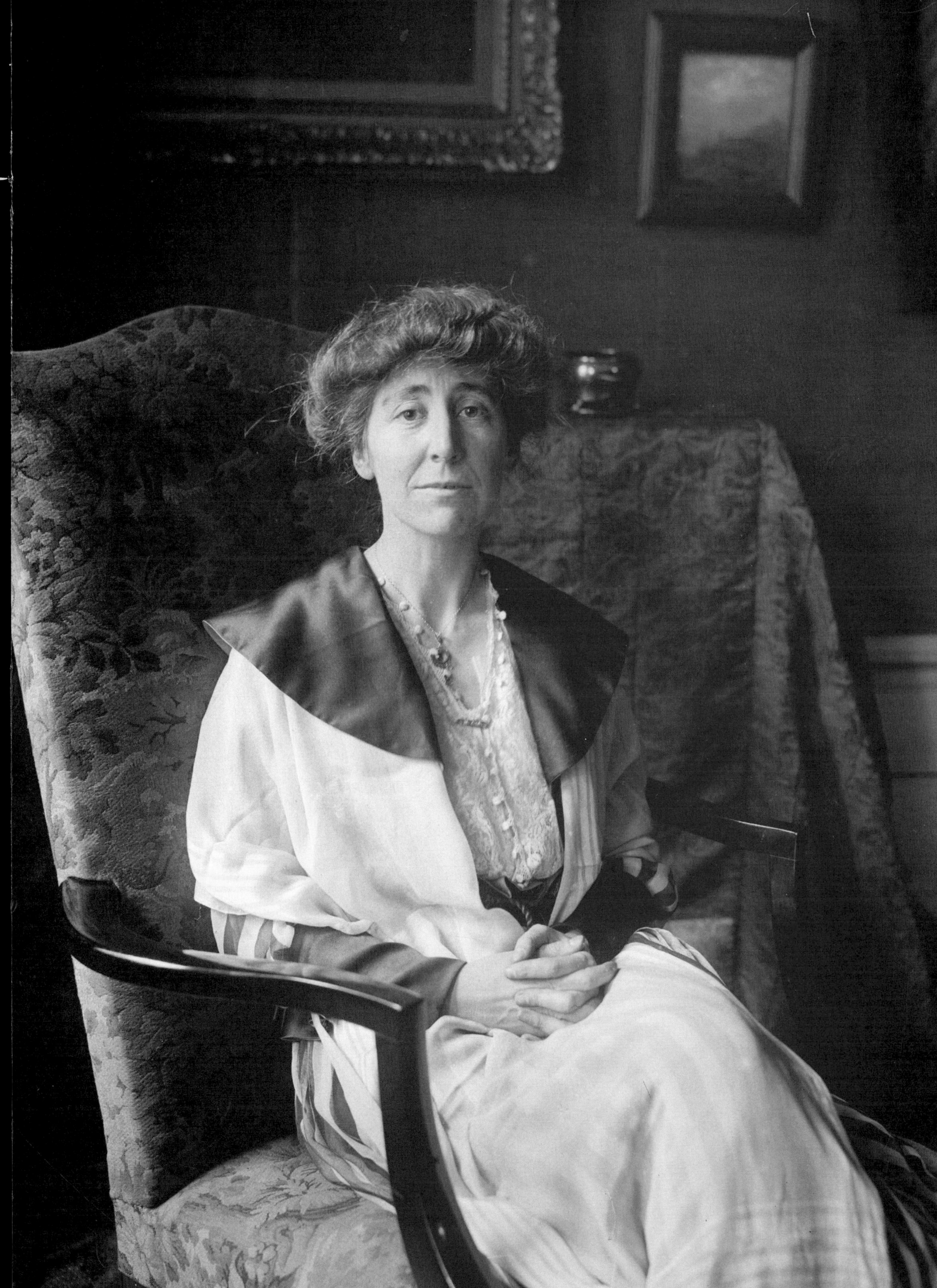

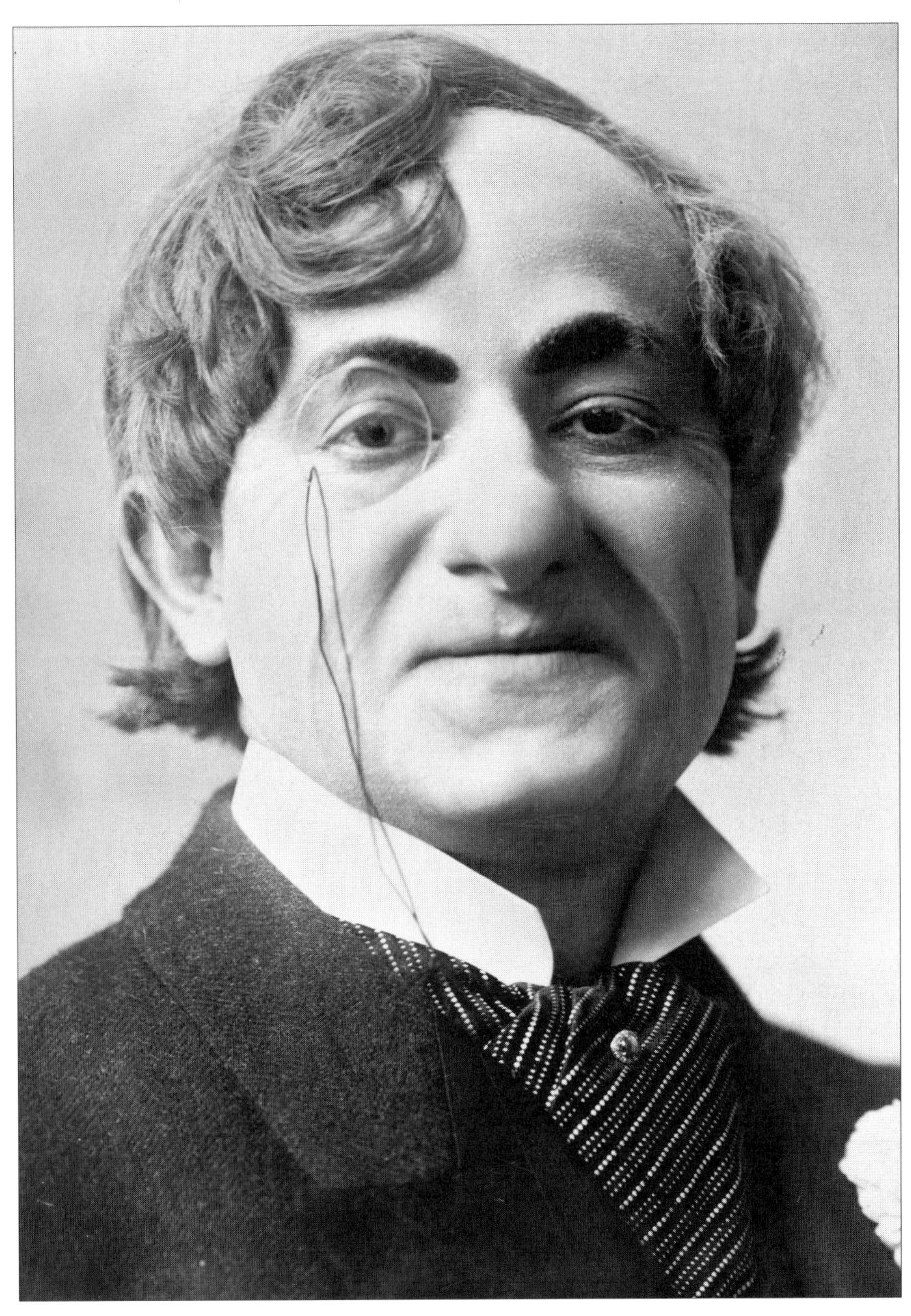

SAM BERNARD (1863–1927)

English actor Sam Bernard began his career in vaudeville but later performed on stage and screen. He is seen here as Herman Schultz in *The Girl and the Wizard,* which opened at the Casino Theater in New York in 1909. The *New York Times* declared it a musical comedy of "high rank" and added: "The irrepressible Bernard foolishness was plentiful, especially in a screaming imitation of a stage manager trying to educate a couple of bad actors."

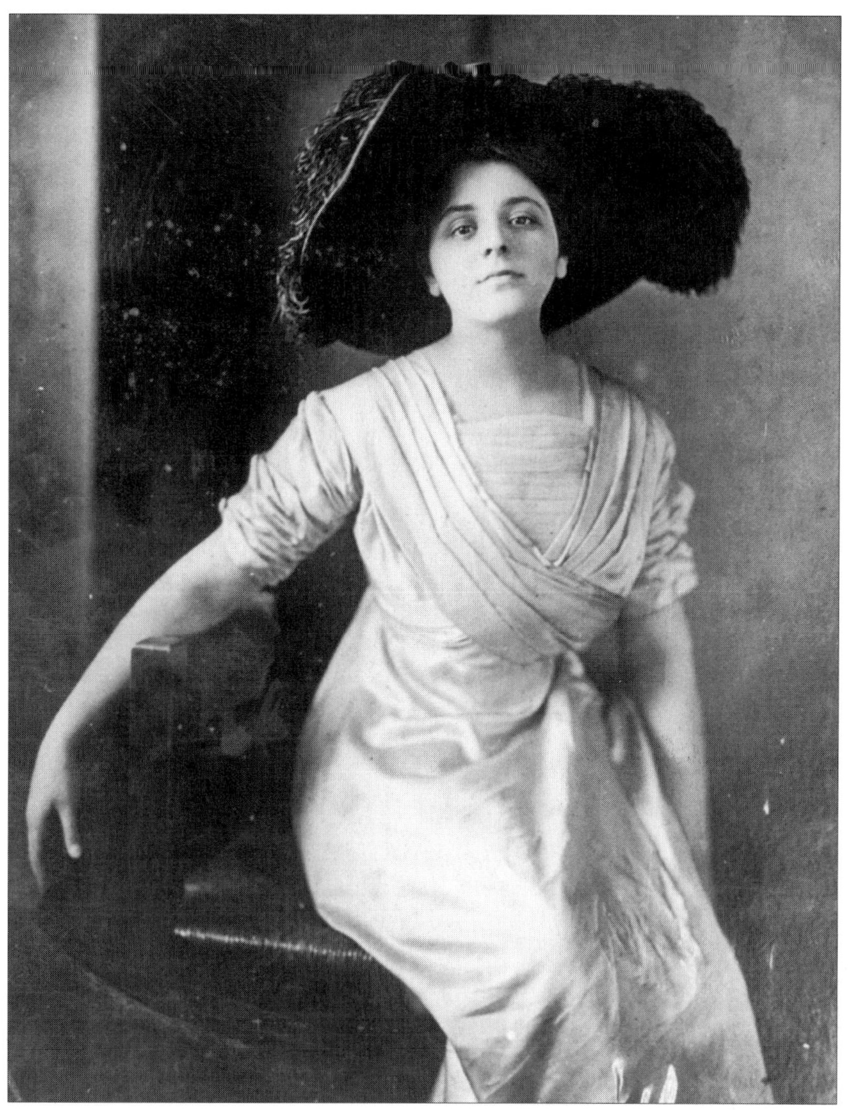

FRIDOLYN GIMBEL (1891–N.D.)

Fridolyn Gimbel was the daughter of the Gimbel family, whose department store chain lasted from 1887 to 1999. Gimbels was once the largest department store chain in America. One of the most successful businesses run by nineteenth-century Jewish immigrants, Gimbels was the primary rival of Macy's department store.

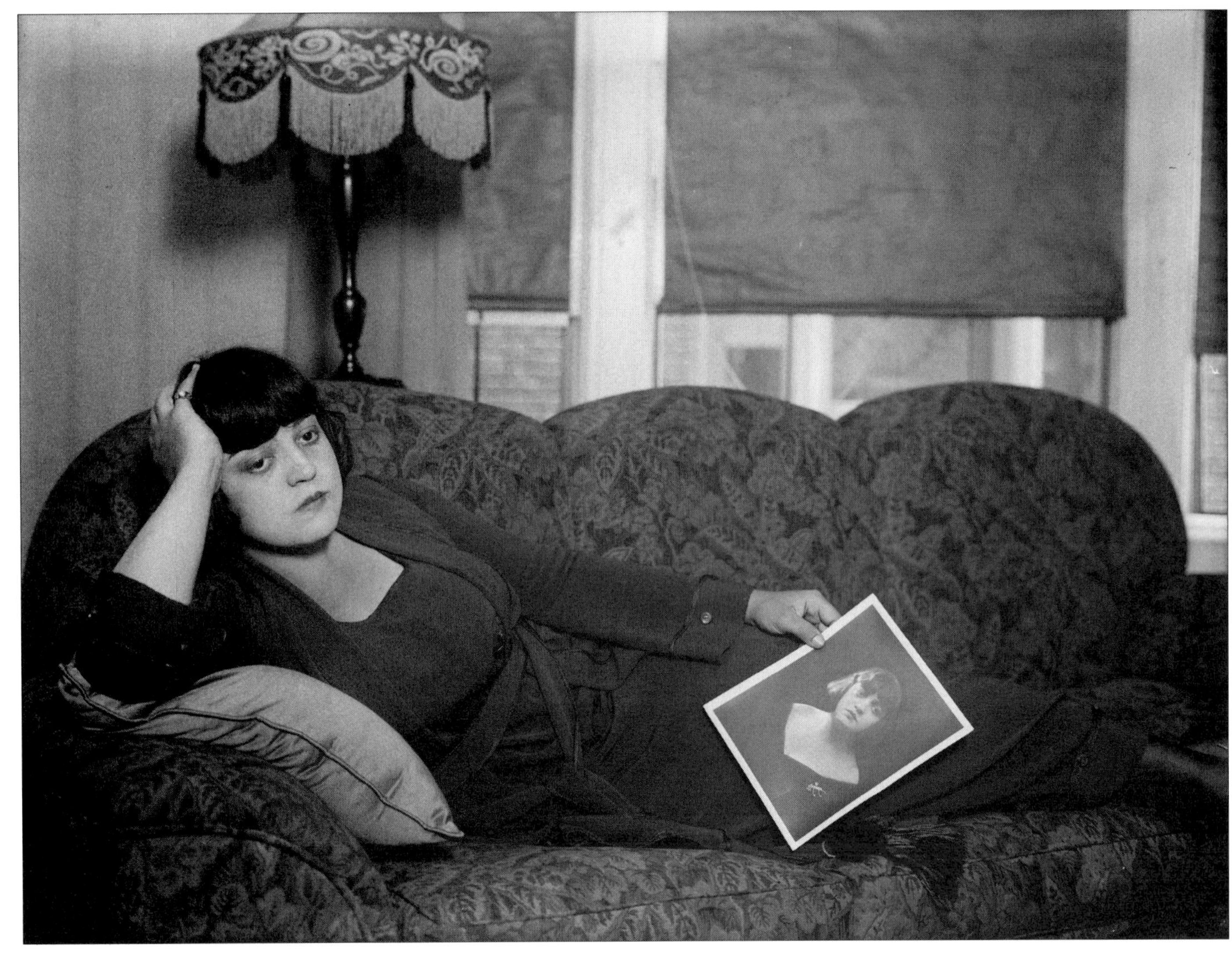

ROSA PONSELLE (1897–1981)

Rosa Ponselle was an American operatic soprano. Her parents were Italian immigrants from Naples. She made her Metropolitan Opera debut on November 15, 1918, as Leonora in Verdi's *La forza del destino*, opposite Enrico Caruso, and scored a tremendous success with both the public and the critics. Many considered her greatest achievement the title role in Bellini's *Norma*.

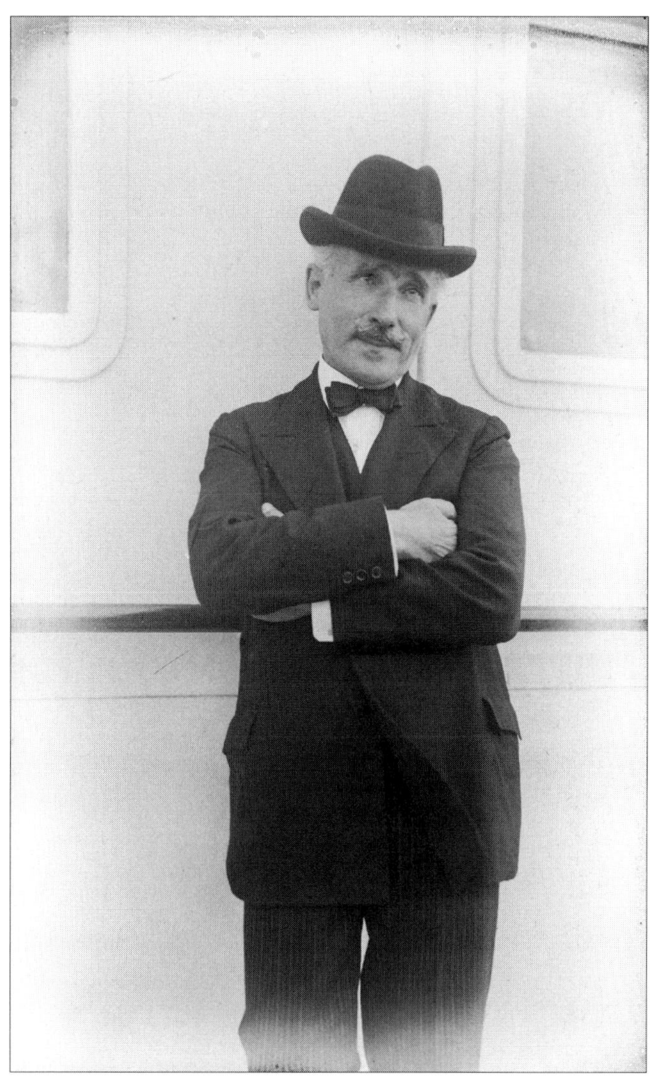

ARTURO TOSCANINI (1867–1957)

Arturo Toscanini is considered by critics, musicians, and fans of classical music to have been one of the greatest conductors of all time. He was renowned for intensity, perfectionism, and his phenomenal ear. Toscanini conducted in Europe, South America, and at the Metropolitan Opera in New York, the New York Philharmonic, and for the NBC Symphony Orchestra on radio. The NBC Symphony Orchestra was created for Toscanini at the time he left his native Italy because of conflicts with the fascist Mussolini regime. The orchestra lasted until his retirement in 1954. During his long career, Toscanini conducted the world premieres of many operas, four of which have become part of the standard operatic repertoire: *Pagliacci, La bohéme, La Fanciulla del West,* and *Turandot.*

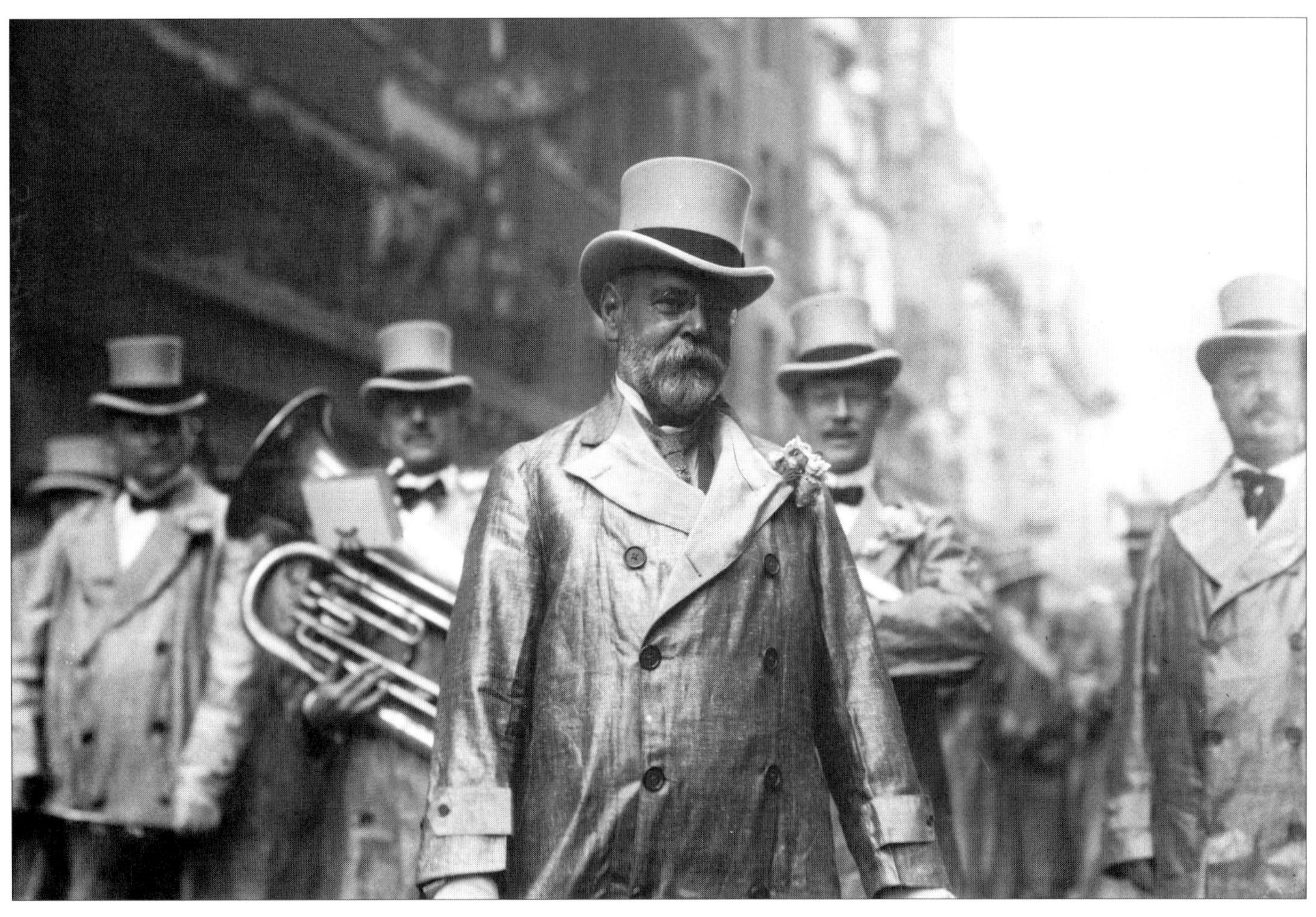

JOHN PHILIP SOUSA (1854–1932)

John Philip Sousa was crowned the "March King" for his rousing and patriotic musical compositions. He served in the U.S. Marine Corps from 1868 to 1875 as an apprentice musician and headed the Marine Band. Later, he formed his own group, the Sousa Band, which gave more than 15,000 concerts, with Sousa often conducting in military uniform. *Stars and Stripes Forever,* composed in 1896, is one of his best-known marches and was declared by act of Congress the National March of the United States.

HARRY HOUDINI (1874–1926)

Harry Houdini was born Ehrich Weiss in Budapest, Hungary. In 1878 his family immigrated to America and settled in Appleton, Wisconsin, where his father was the rabbi of a reform congregation. He adopted the stage name Houdini in homage to the great French magician, Jean Eugène Robert-Houdin. From 1907 and throughout the next decade, Houdini astounded American audiences, freeing himself from handcuffs, chains, ropes, and straitjackets, often while hanging from a rope in plain sight of spectators. He later turned his attention to debunking psychics and mediums.

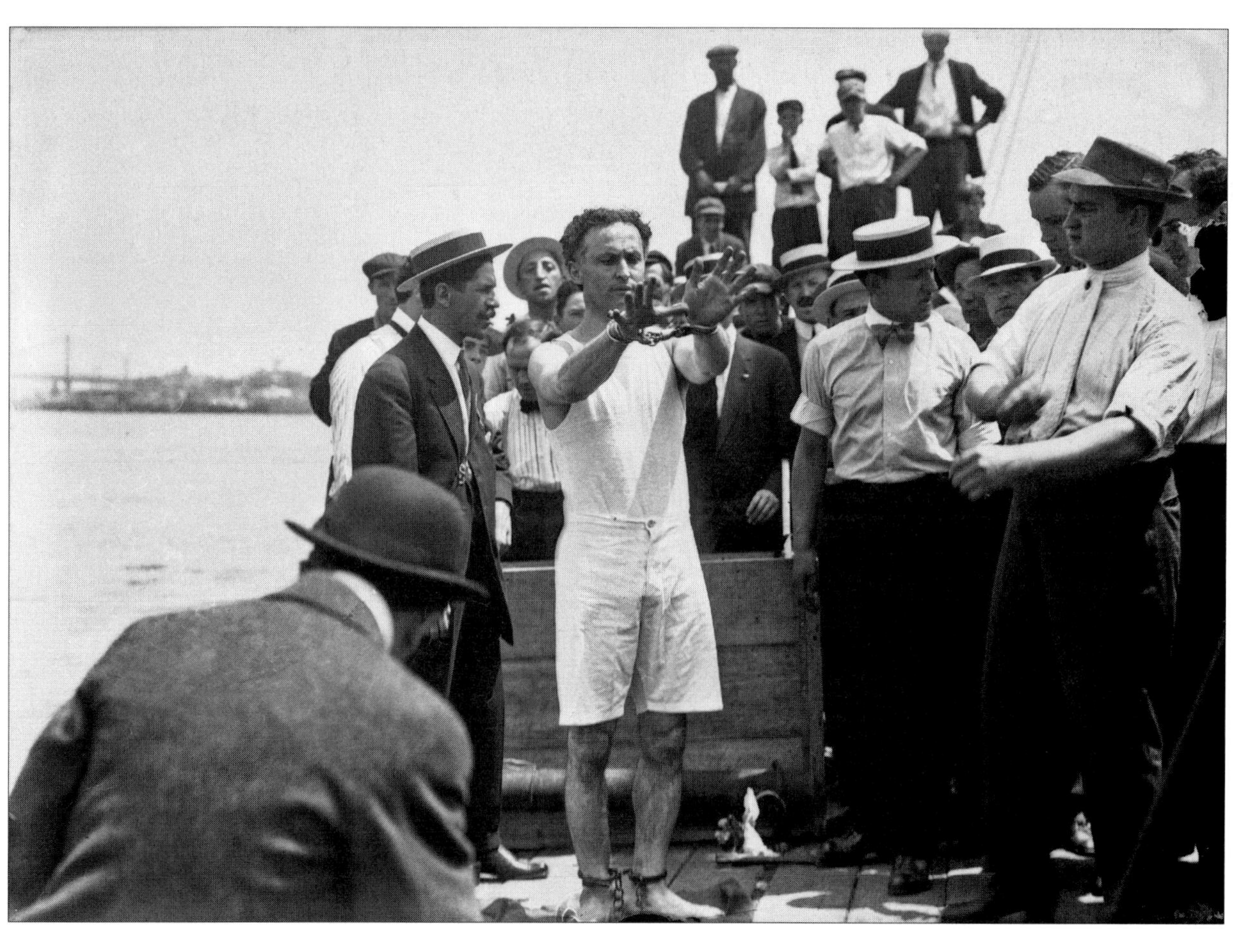

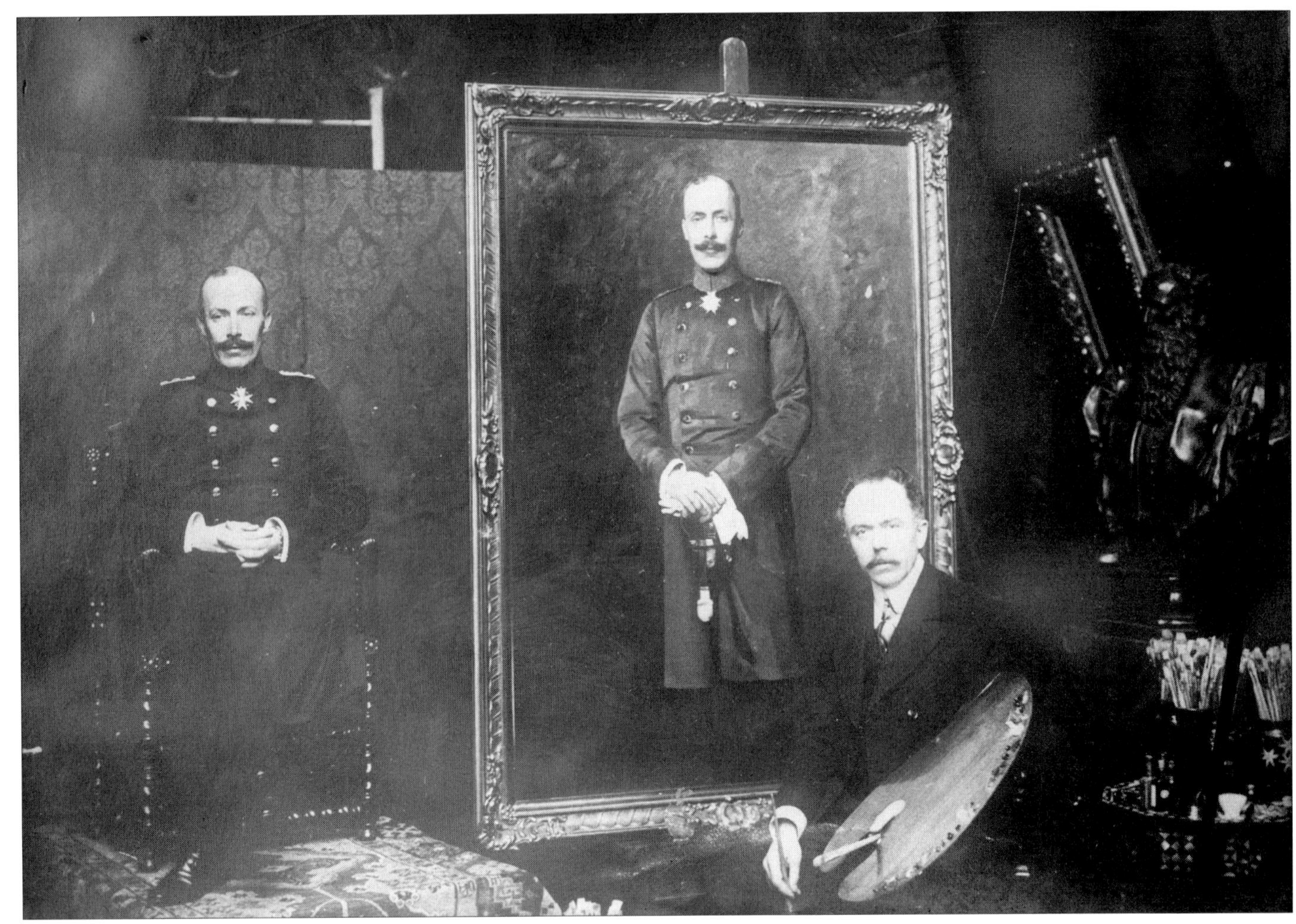

ALFRED SCHWARTZ (1867–1951) AND KING WILLIAM OF ALBANIA (1876–1945)

Alfred Schwartz, born in Berlin, was a portrait painter whose clients included dignitaries and heads of state, as well as society families and their children. Here, King William of Albania sits for the artist in his studio.

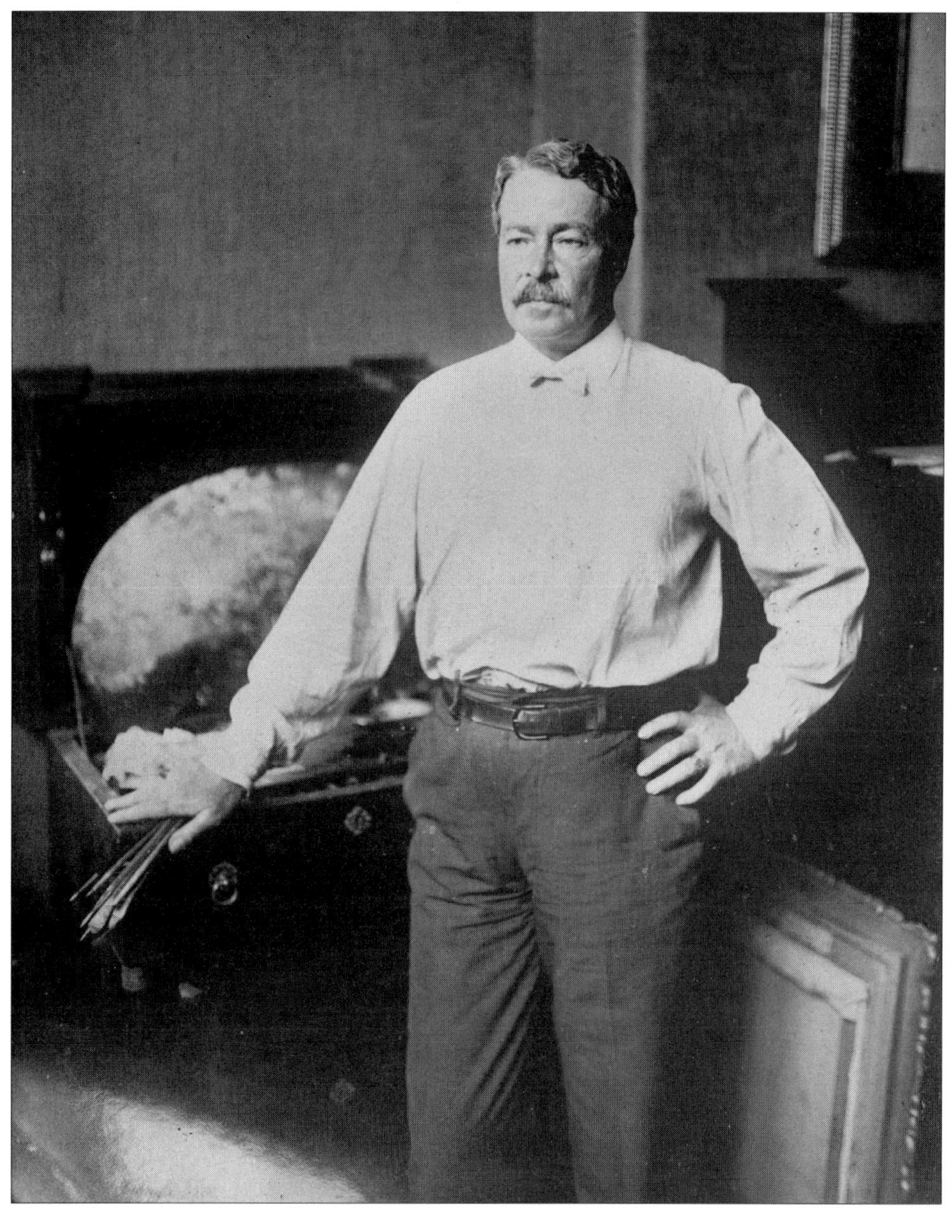

FREDERICK CHILDE HASSAM (1859–1935)

Frederick Childe Hassam, who later dropped his first name, was an American Impressionist painter best known for his images of the New England coast and his series of "flag" paintings. Hassam was a founder of a group of influential artists known as The Ten, which included J. Alden Weir, John Henry Twachtman, and others. The Ten resigned from the Society of American Artists in protest, thinking it to be too much about business and too little about art. They were proponents of Impressionism, which became mainstream by the time of the New York Armory Show in 1913. Hassam exhibited six paintings at the Armory Show.

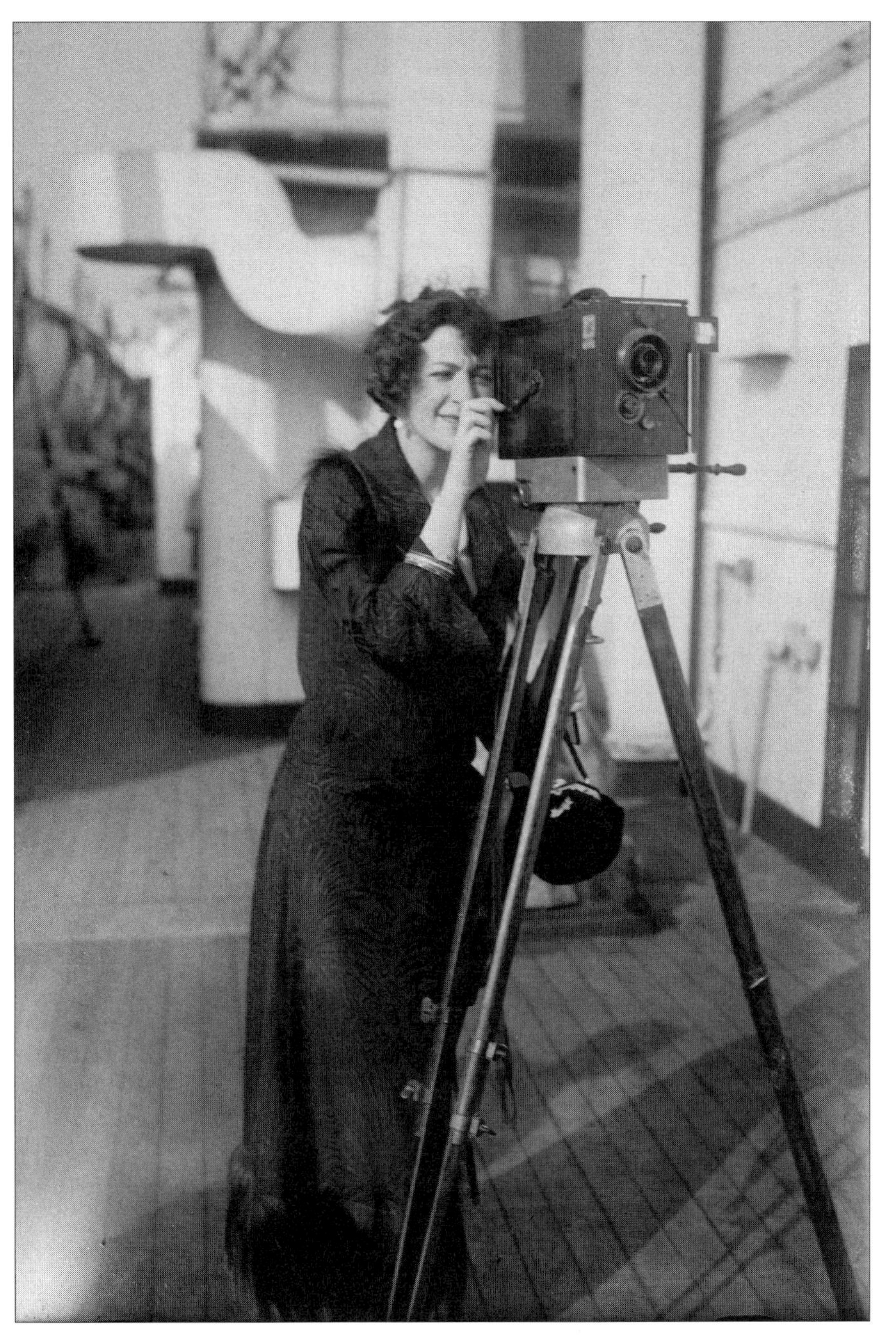

FANNY BRICE (1891–1951)

A queen of comedy and satire, Fanny Brice was a New York saloonkeeper's daughter who made it big in the *Ziegfeld Follies* starting in 1910 and continuing into the 1930s. She created the character Baby Snooks, an annoying but hilarious toddler who was a perennial favorite with audiences. Brice took Baby Snooks to radio in 1928. The 1964 Broadway musical *Funny Girl* starring Barbra Streisand was based on her life.

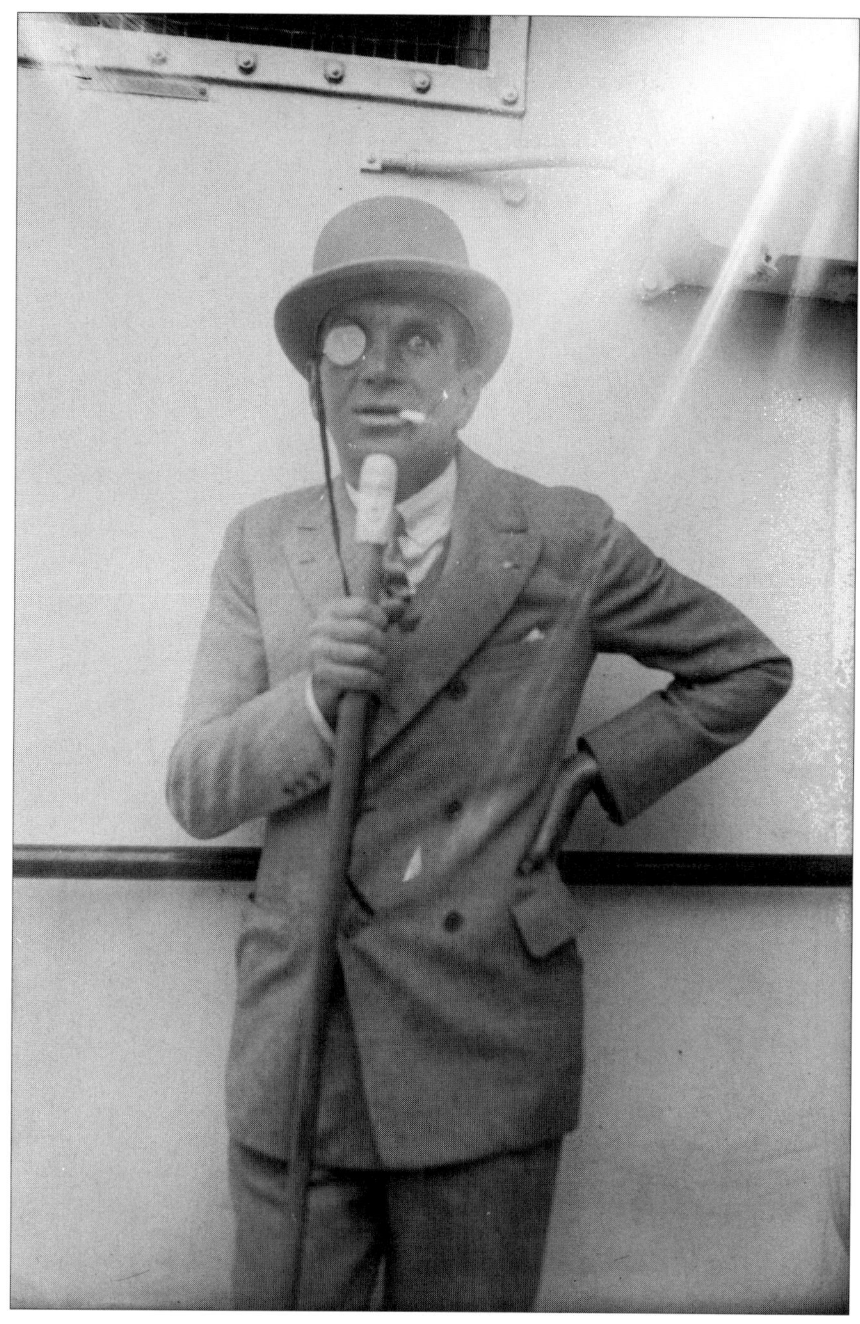

AL JOLSON (1886–1950)

Al Jolson, often referred to as "the world's greatest entertainer," coined the phrase, "You ain't heard nothin' yet." A Russian Jewish immigrant whose family fled oppression under the Czarist regime, he arrived in New York at the age of six in 1892. His career as a singer was launched in 1911 at the Winter Garden Theater where he sang Stephen Foster's songs in blackface. By 1920, he was the highest-paid entertainer in America, and starred in the film *The Jazz Singer* (1927), the first feature-length talking picture, in which he performed six songs. Jolson established an enduring tradition as the first celebrity to entertain troops overseas during World War II.

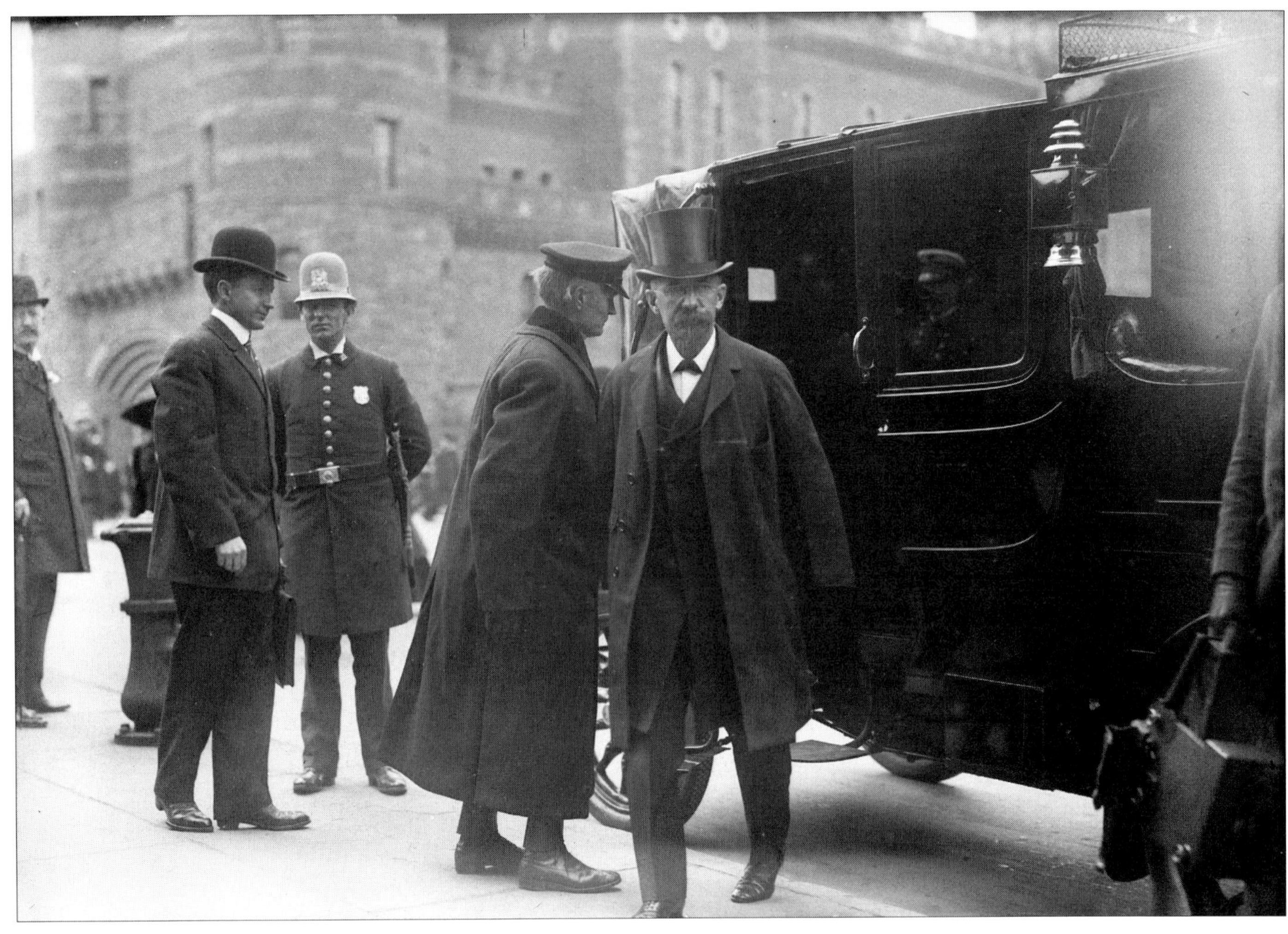

E. H. HARRIMAN (1848–1909)

E. H. Harriman was an American railroad executive. He started working as an errand boy at age fourteen, became a member of the New York Stock Exchange at age twenty-two, and owned his first railroad in his thirties. Harriman eventually became president of both the Union Pacific and the Southern Pacific Railroads. In 1899 Harriman financed a scientific expedition to Alaska to study flora, fauna, and Native cultures.

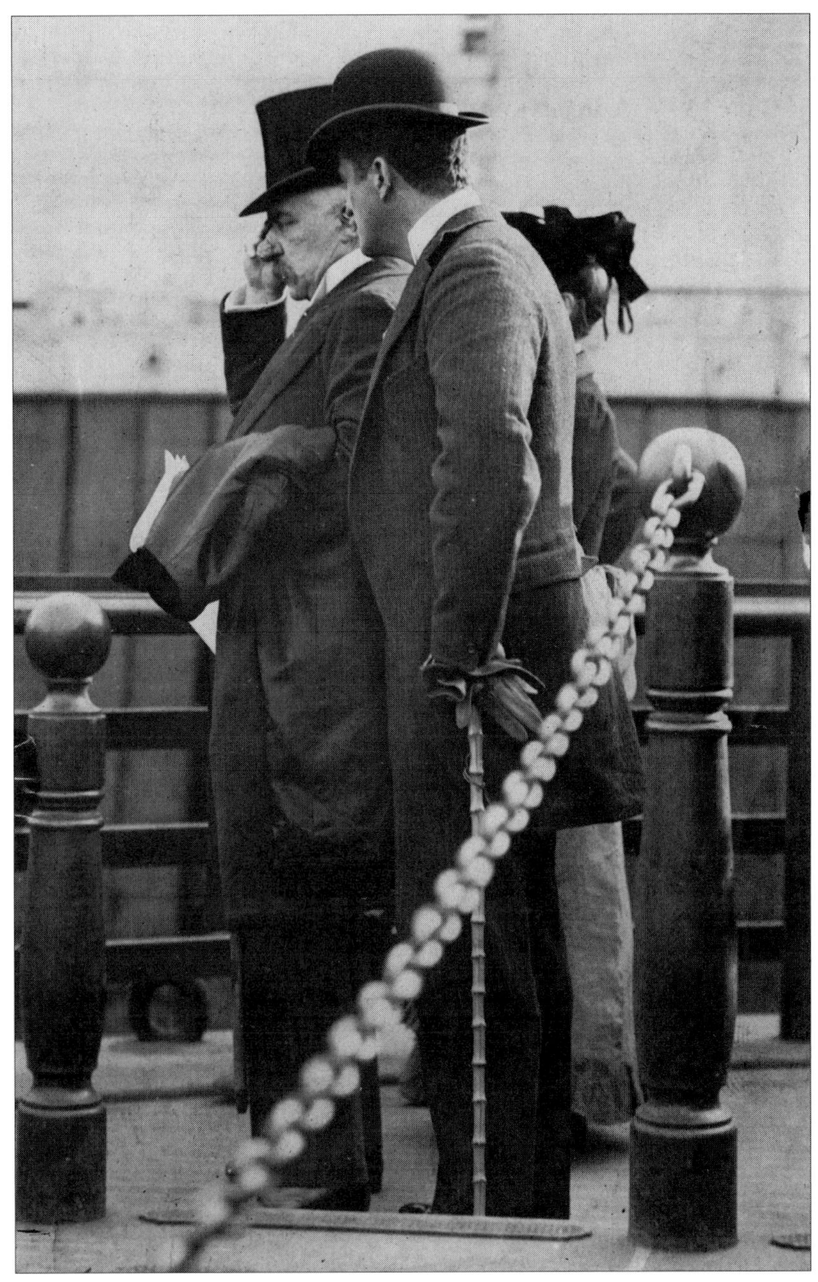

JOHN PIERPONT MORGAN (1837–1913) AND ROBERT BACON (1860–1919)

John Pierpont Morgan *(left),* seen here with business partner Robert Bacon in 1902, dominated American corporate finance in the early part of the twentieth century. He created both General Electric and the U.S. Steel Corporation. A patron of the arts, he bequeathed major parts of his collections to the Metropolitan Museum of Art in New York and the Wadsworth Atheneum in Hartford, Connecticut. His immense personal library, housed in a building next to his residence on 36th Street in New York, was preserved and transformed into a public institution by his son in 1924. Robert Bacon was a member of J. P. Morgan Company from 1895 to 1903. In 1905, President Theodore Roosevelt appointed Bacon Assistant Secretary of State. He became Secretary of State in 1909.

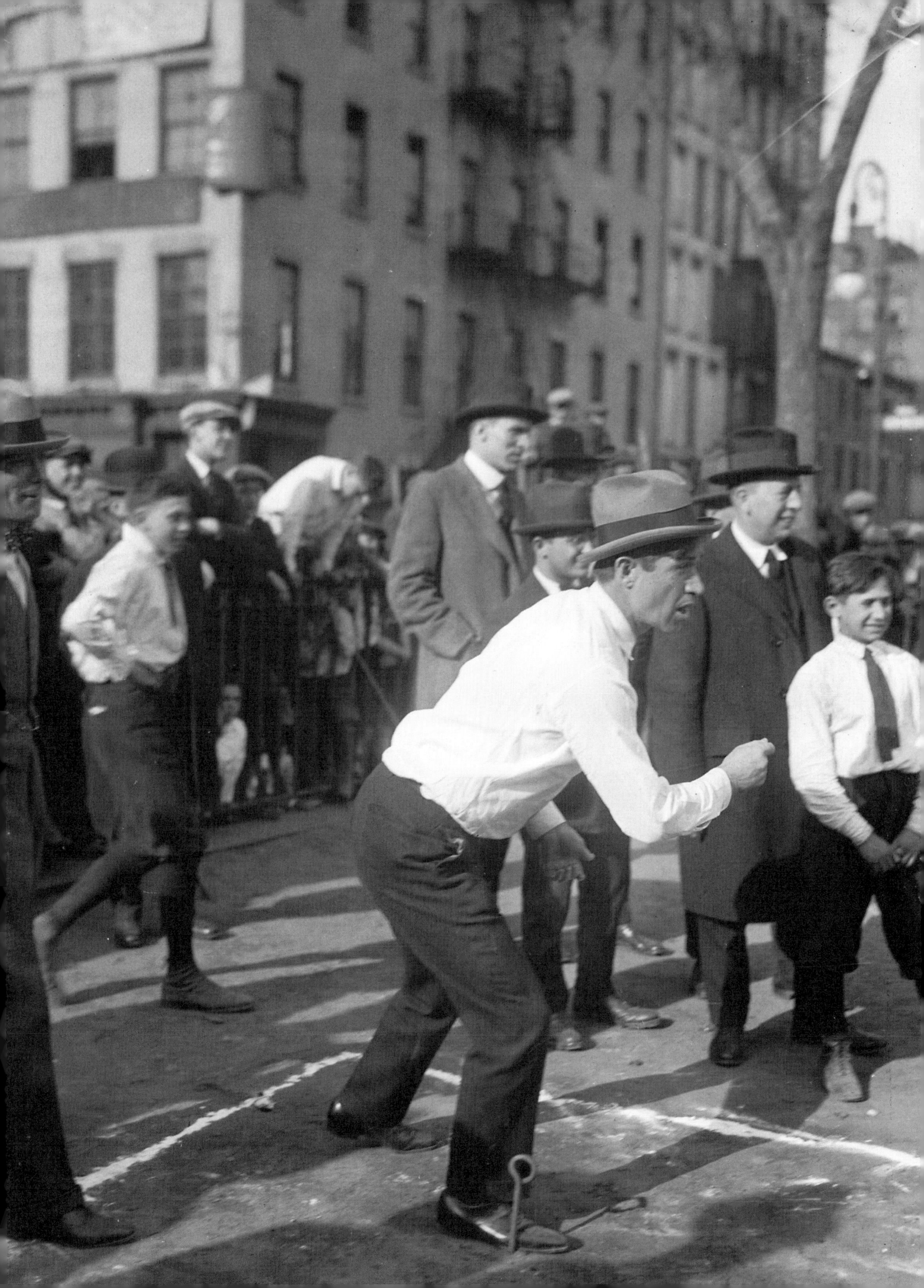

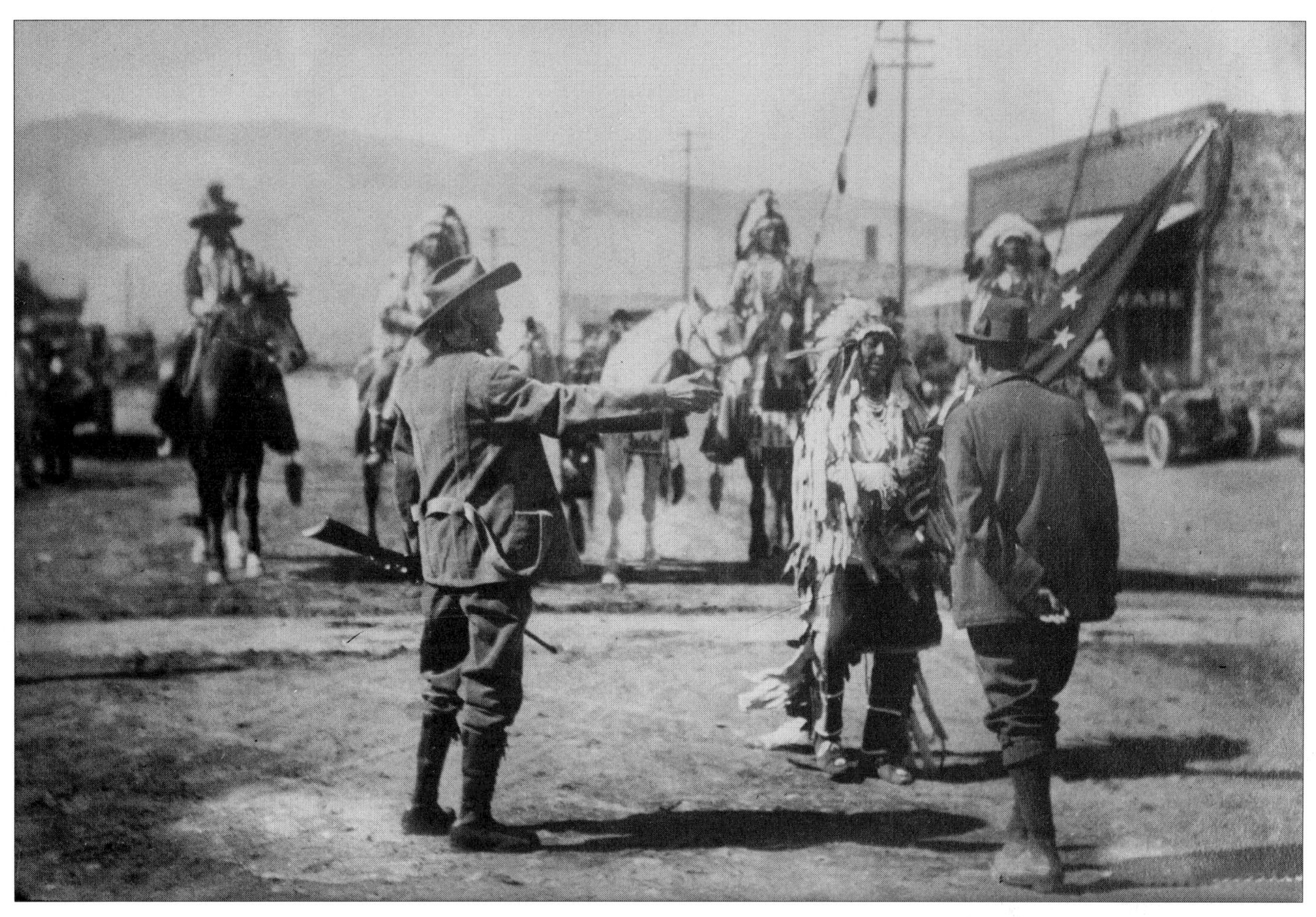

COLONEL WILLIAM F. "BUFFALO BILL" CODY (1846–1917) AND PRINCE ALBERT OF MONACO (1848–1922)

In 1913 Prince Albert of Monaco visited Wyoming at the invitation of artist A.A. Anderson. Anderson had befriended the prince while studying art in Paris and was also a friend of Colonel William F. Cody. Cody, widely known as Buffalo Bill, was a Pony Express rider, army scout, and Wild West show performer.

WILL ROGERS (1879–1935)

Will Rogers was born in Cherokee territory in Oklahoma. He was a cowboy, actor, vaudeville performer, comedian, social commentator, and radio personality. Rogers made seventy-one movies (fifty of them silent features) and wrote thousands of nationally syndicated newspaper columns. He died in a plane crash in 1935 while accompanying aviator Wiley Post on a flight to Point Barrow, Alaska. He was one of the most popular entertainers in the history of American show business and his death sparked what has been described as the greatest show of mourning since the assassination of Abraham Lincoln. Rogers' wry sense of humor lives on in innumerable quotes which still resonate today: "On account of being a democracy and run by the people, we are the only nation in the world that has to keep a government four years, no matter what it does."

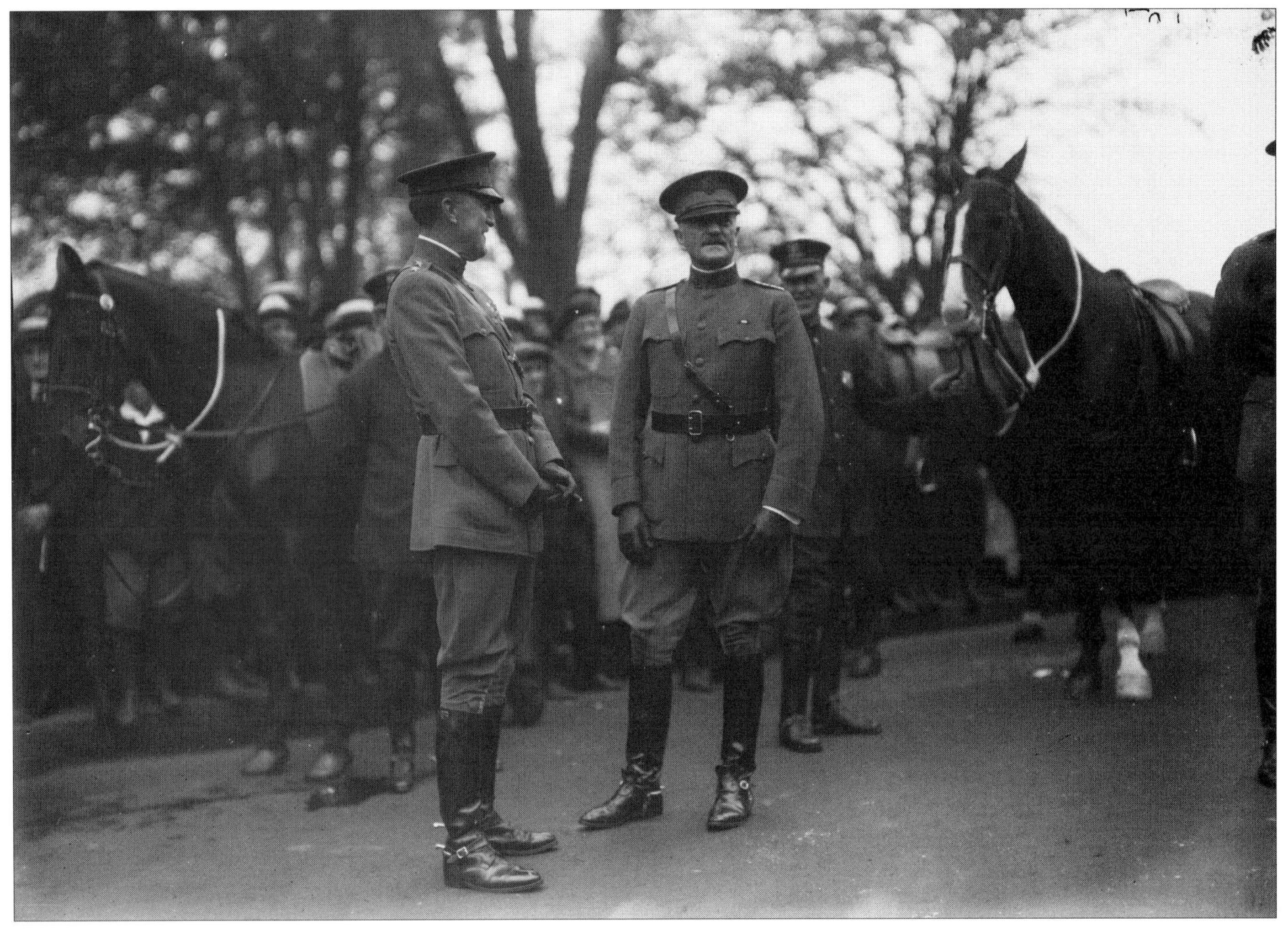

GENERAL JOHN JOSEPH PERSHING (1860–1948)

General John Joseph Pershing was the only officer to be promoted in his own lifetime to the highest rank ever held in the U.S. Army—General of the Armies. (George Washington was posthumously awarded that rank by an act of Congress in 1976.) Pershing graduated from West Point in 1886. His career spanned the Indian wars of the late nineteenth century, the Spanish-American War, and the Philippine-American War of the 1890s, action against Pancho Villa across the border in Mexico between 1916 and 1917, and reached it's peak in World War I, when he commanded the huge American expeditionary forces in Europe. He mentored a generation of officers who served in World War II, including George Patton, George Marshall, Dwight D. Eisenhower, and Omar Bradley.

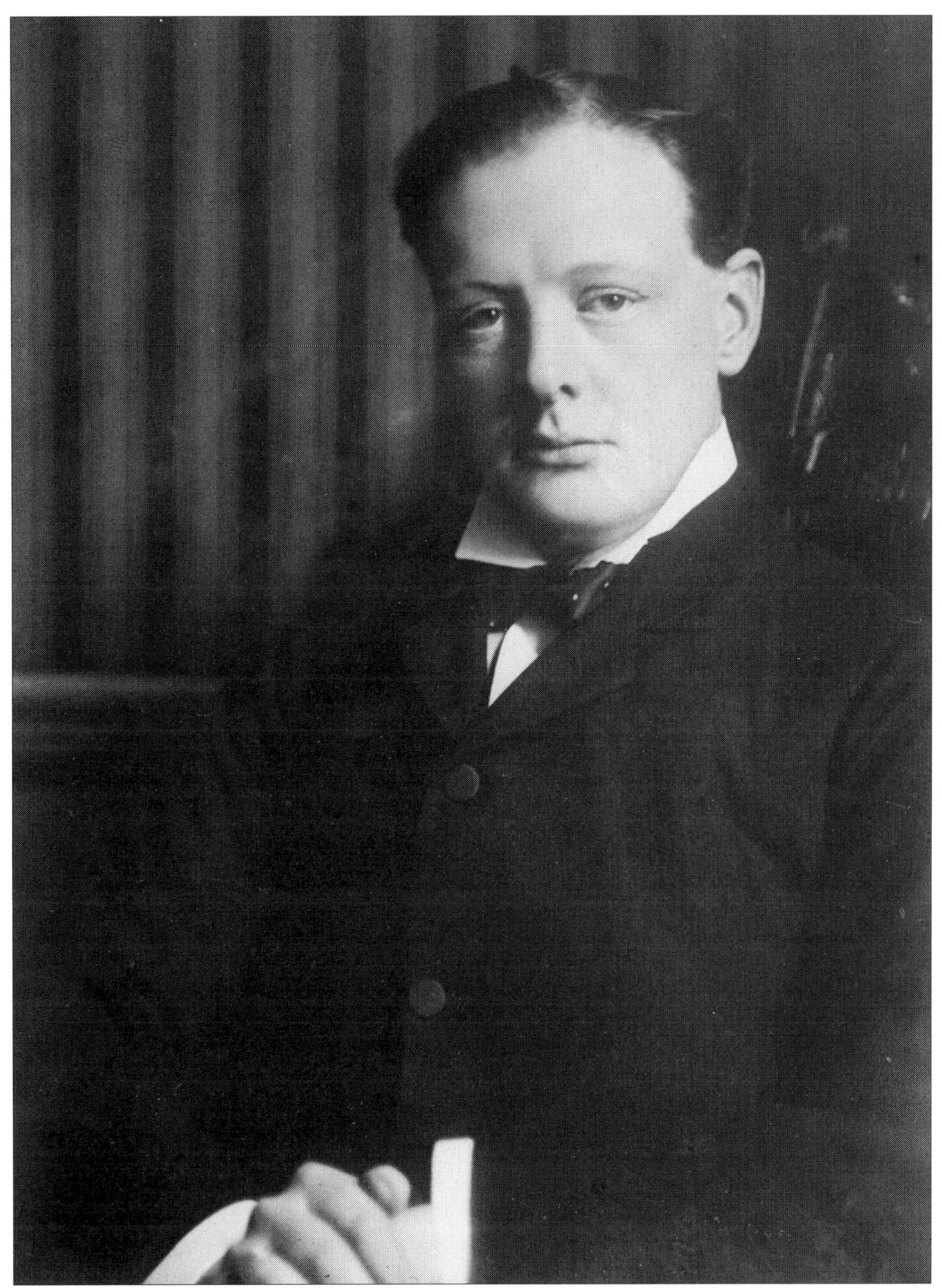

SIR WINSTON LEONARD SPENCER CHURCHILL (1874–1965)

Sir Winston Leonard Spencer Churchill was Prime Minister of England from 1940 to 1945, leading Britain and Europe to victory in World War II in partnership with America and President Roosevelt. He served as Prime Minister again from 1951 to 1955. Churchill was also an officer in the British Army, a historian, a Nobel Prize–winning author, and an accomplished amateur artist. This photograph was possibly taken while the young Churchill was on a lecture tour of the United States to promote one of his books on military history.

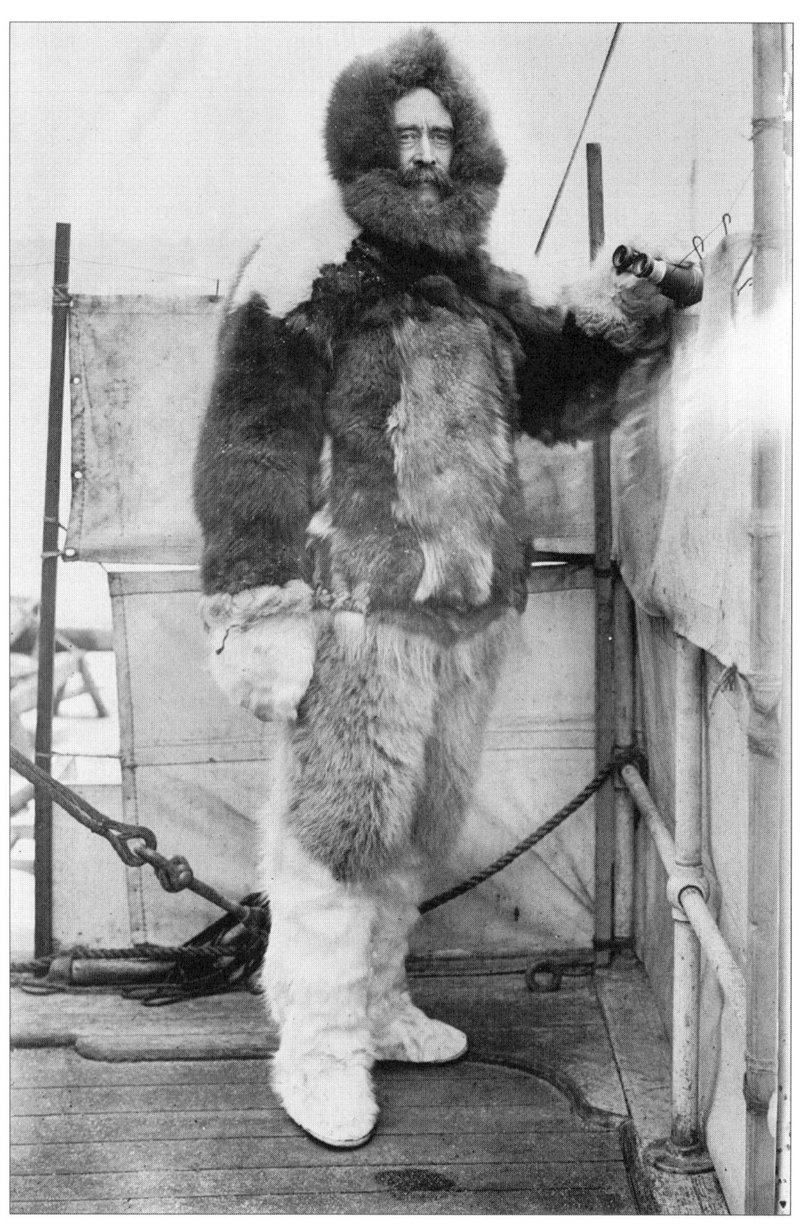

ROBERT EDWIN PEARY (1856–1920)

Robert Edwin Peary claimed to have been the first person to reach the geographic North Pole, a claim that is now widely doubted. Peary is seen here on his ship, the *Roosevelt,* dressed in native furs. The explorer studied Inuit survival techniques, built igloos, and relied on the Inuit as hunters and dog drivers on his expeditions. After several expeditions to the Arctic, starting in 1886, Peary claimed to have reached the geographic North Pole on April 6, 1909. If he didn't reach the North Pole, he and his five companions, Matthew Henson and four Inuit men, were certainly very close to it.

The *Roosevelt* was used in Peary's last two Arctic expeditions: 1905–1906, in which he probably reached 86° 30' latitude, and the final expedition of 1908–1909. There is no question that Peary risked his life traveling across the Arctic ice by dog sled and that his work advanced knowledge of Arctic survival techniques. The claims of Frederick Cook to have reached the North Pole a year earlier than Peary is also not widely accepted and is insufficiently supported by verifiable evidence.

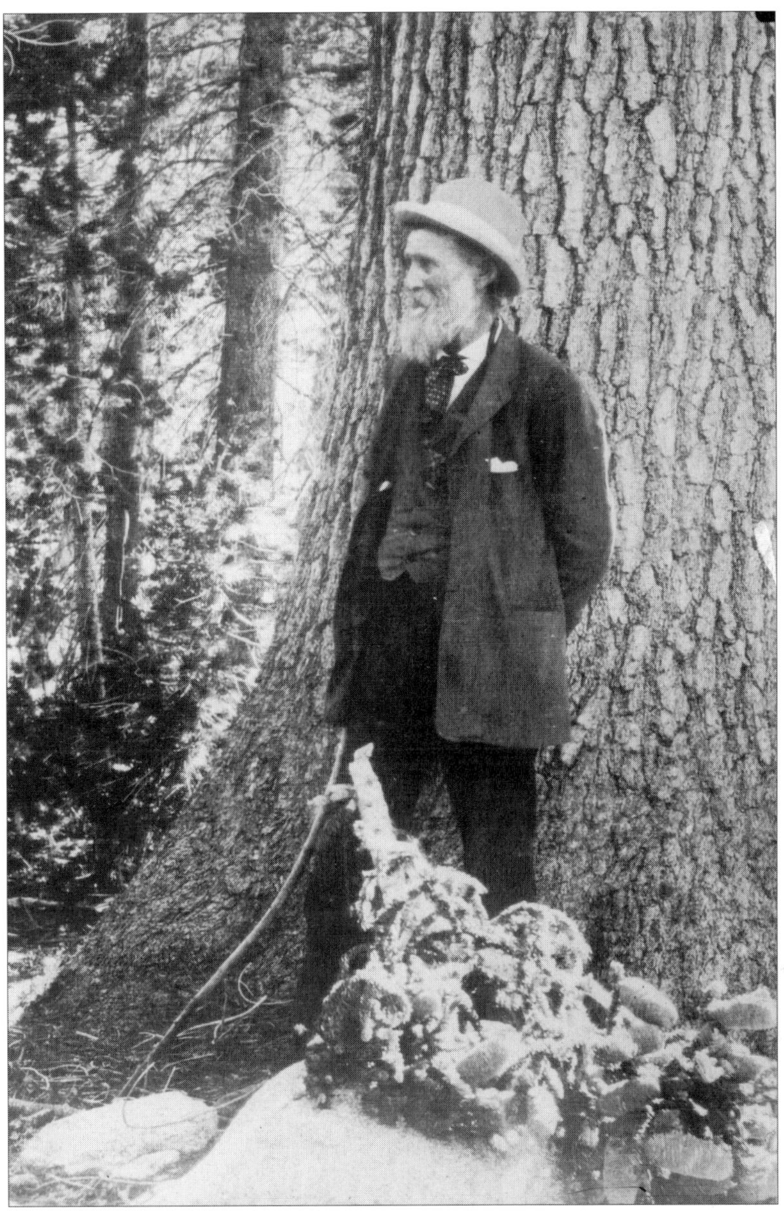

JOHN MUIR (1838–1914)

Scottish-born John Muir was an American naturalist, author, and early advocate of conservation of U.S. wilderness. His direct activism helped to save the Yosemite Valley, Sequoia National Park, and other wilderness areas. The Sierra Club, which he founded, is now one of the most important conservation organizations in the United States. Muir's writings and philosophy strongly influenced the formation of the modern environmental movement.

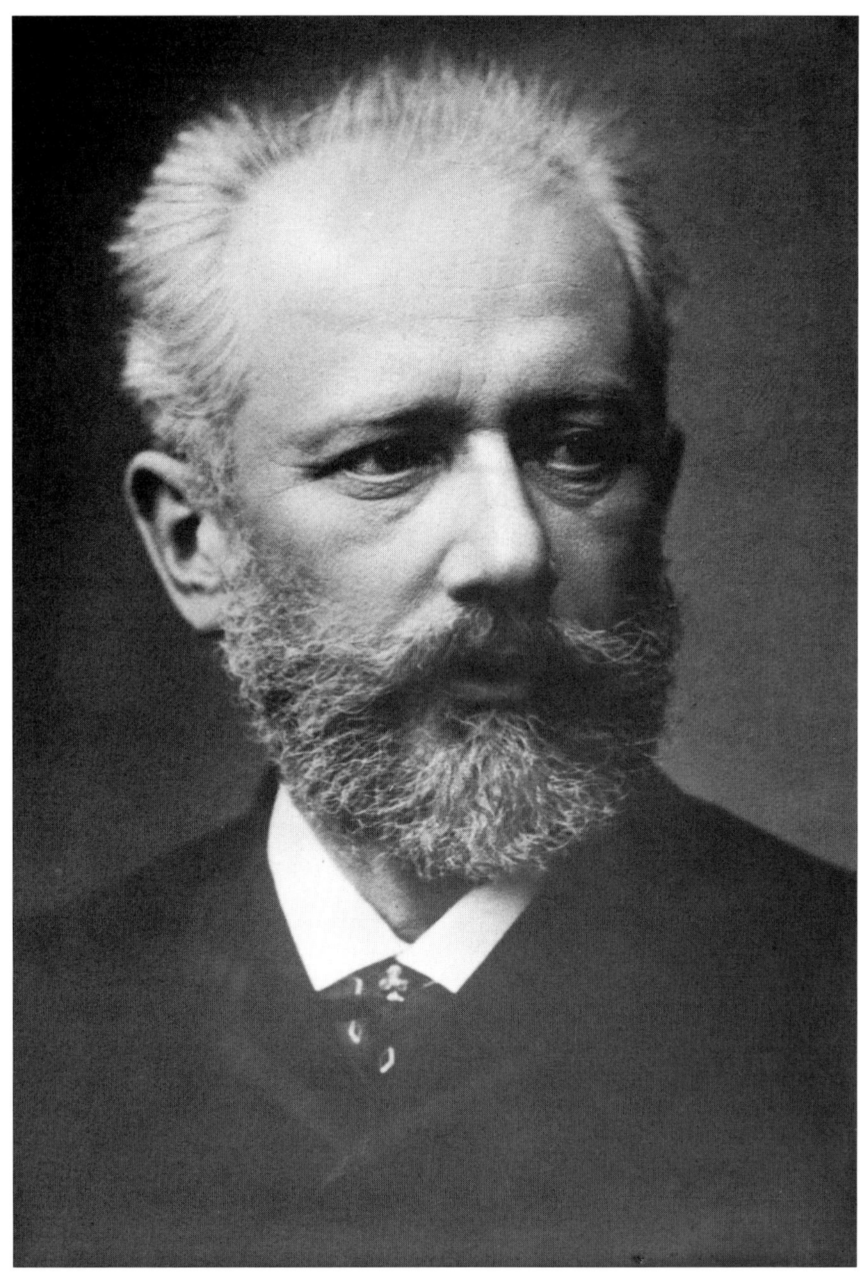

PETER (PYOTR) ILYICH TCHAIKOVSKY (1840–1893)

Russian composer Peter (Pyotr) Ilyich Tchaikovsky wrote some of the most-recognized melodies of classical music. Tchaikovsky's expressive orchestral pieces earned him fame beyond Russia and brought him to America on tour in 1891. His most famous works include the opera *Eugene Onegin*, the ballet *Swan Lake*, the overtures *Romeo and Juliet* and *1812 Overture* and his *Sixth Symphony,* known as *Pathétique*, all first performed between 1879 and 1893. His ballet *The Nutcracker* is a winter holiday favorite.

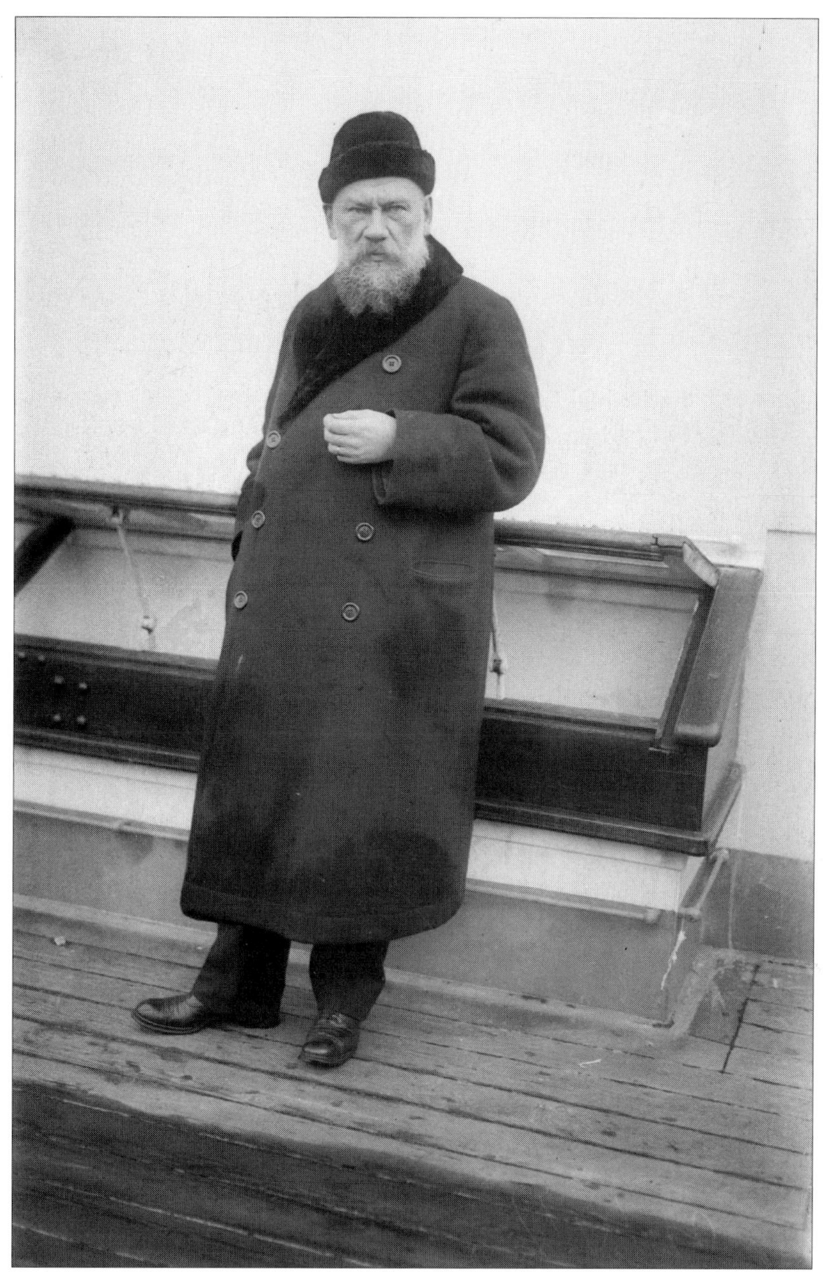

COUNT LEV NIKOLAYEVICH "LEO" TOLSTOY (1828–1910)

Leo Tolstoy was a Russian author widely regarded as one of the greatest of all novelists for his masterpieces *War and Peace*, originally published in parts from 1865 to 1869 and *Anna Karenina*, also first published in serial installments in a periodical, from 1873 to 1877. Late in his life he become a fervent Christian anarchist and pacifist.

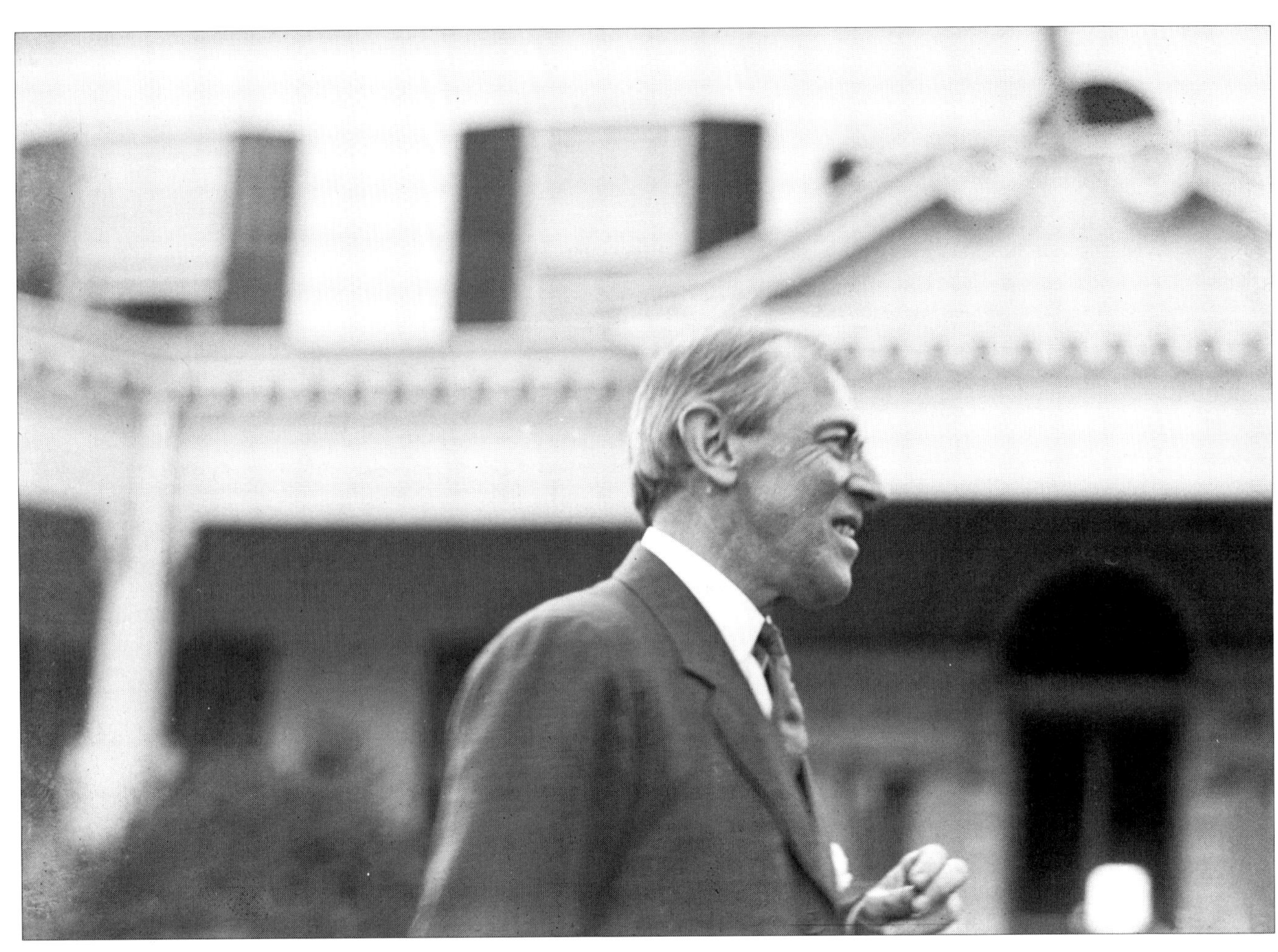

WOODROW WILSON (1856–1924)

Woodrow Wilson was the twenty-eighth president of the United States, serving from 1913 to 1921. Before conservative democrats urged him into politics, Wilson was a political science professor and later president of Princeton University from 1902 to 1910. Wilson's first term saw the passage of the Federal Reserve Act, lower tariffs along with the first graduated federal income tax, and the establishment of the Federal Trade Commission to combat unfair business practices. Wilson led America into World War I in 1918 and on to victory with allies France and England, but was unable to maneuver the Treaty of Versailles, including the covenant of the League of Nations, through the Republican Congress elected midway through his second term.

WILLIAM HOWARD TAFT (1857–1930)

A distinguished lawyer, William Howard Taft rose to the presidency through various administrative posts rather than by political prowess. The large, jovial twenty-seventh president was a federal circuit judge, civil administrator in the Philippines, and Secretary of War to Theodore Roosevelt before winning the election in 1908. Taft was among the first presidential candidates to stump for votes, traveling 18,000 miles on a 400-speech tour. Here he visits Cedar Falls, Iowa. A progressive Republican, Taft served only one term as president, losing his bid for reelection when his feud with Theodore Roosevelt divided the Republican vote and enabled Democrat Woodrow Wilson to win in 1912. Taft was later Chief Justice of the Supreme Court, the only ex-president to serve in that capacity and, a sign of changing times, was the last president to have facial hair.

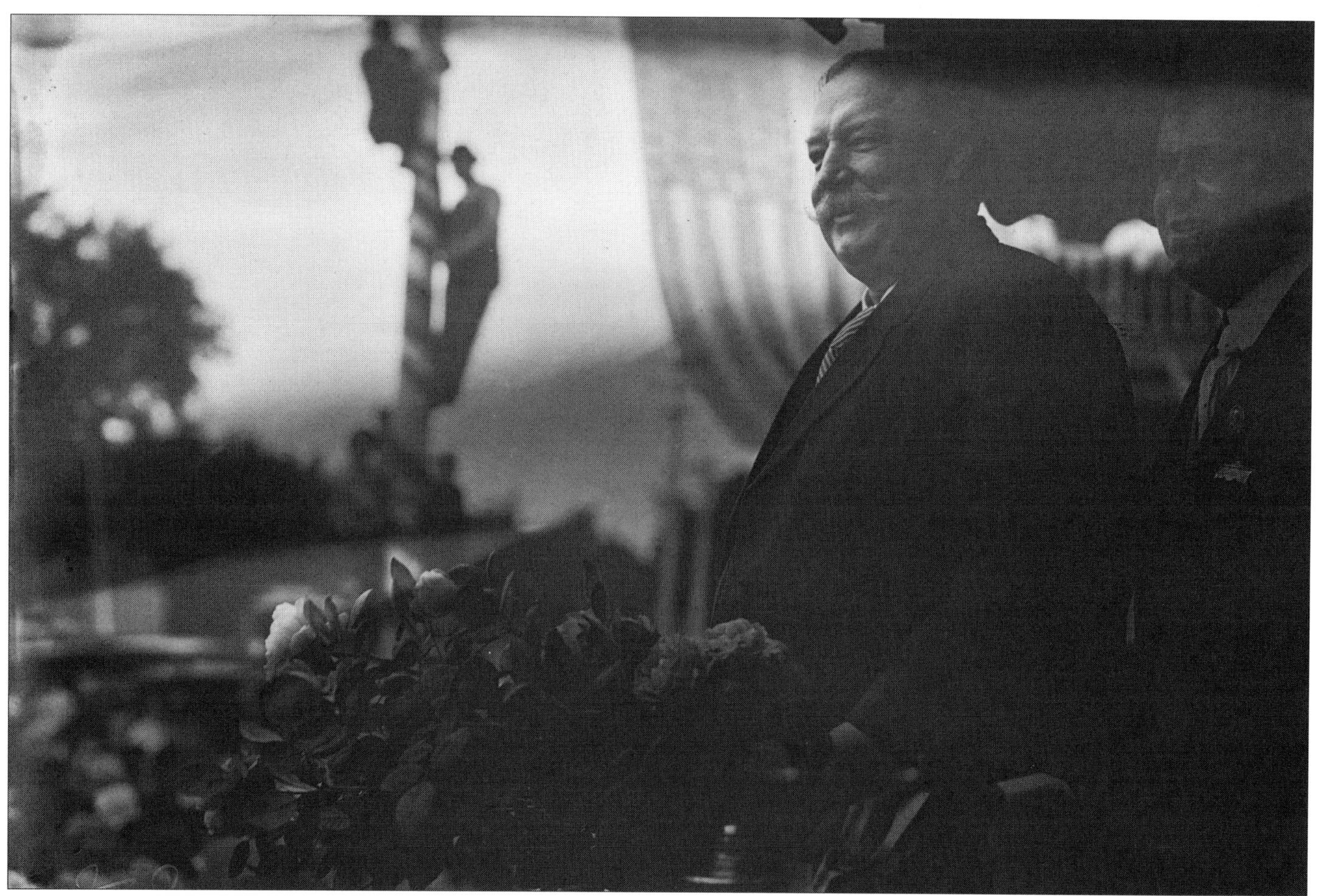

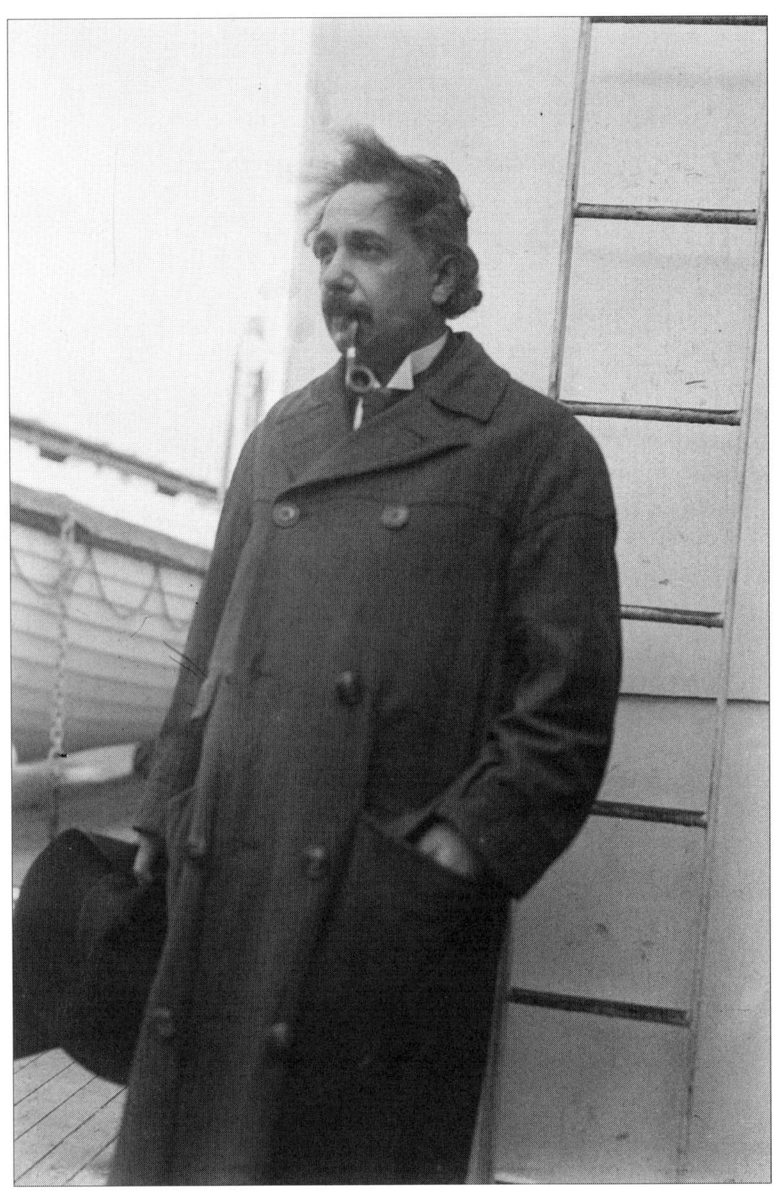

ALBERT EINSTEIN (1879–1955)

Albert Einstein was a German-born theoretical physicist whose name is synonymous with genius. He is best known for his theory of relativity and specifically mass-energy equivalence, $E = mc^2$. Einstein received the 1921 Nobel Prize in Physics. His extraordinary contributions led *Time* magazine to name him the "Person of the Century," in 1999.

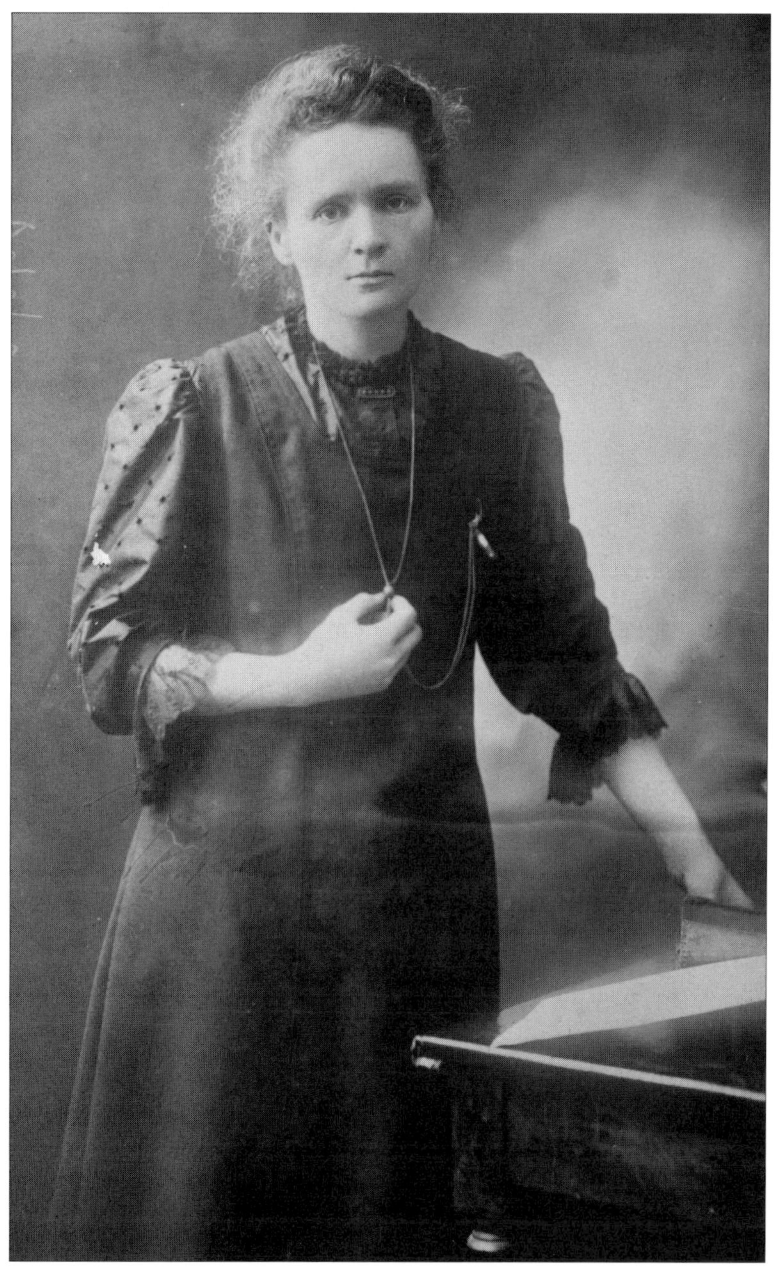

MARIE CURIE (1867–1934)

The only person to be awarded Nobel prizes in two different sciences, Marie Curie was a physicist, chemist, and pioneer in the field of radioactivity. Curie was born in Warsaw and lived there until she was twenty-four. In 1891 she followed her elder sister Bronisława to study in Paris, where she obtained her higher degrees and conducted her subsequent scientific work with her husband, Pierre, until his death in 1906. She is most famous for discovering the elements radium and polonium. In 1903 the Royal Swedish Academy of Sciences awarded Pierre Curie, Marie Curie, and Henri Becquerel the Nobel Prize in Physics, "in recognition of the extraordinary services they had rendered by their joint researches on the radiation phenomena discovered by Henri Becquerel." Eight years later, she received the Nobel Prize in Chemistry, "in recognition of her services to the advancement of chemistry by the discovery of the elements radium and polonium, by the isolation of radium and the study of the nature and compounds of this remarkable element."

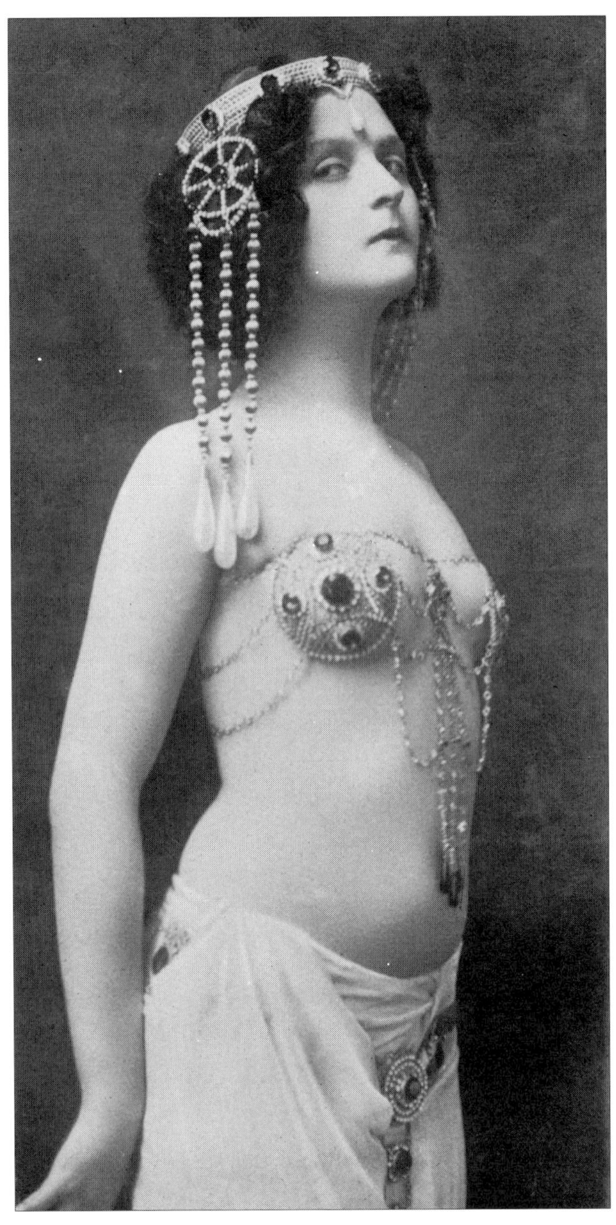

FRITZI SCHAFFER (N.D.)

Belly dancer Fritzi Schaffer performs as Salome (c. 1910). Salome was a tragedy written by Oscar Wilde in 1891. One of the memorable scenes from the play is of Salome performing the "Dance of the Seven Veils." In this photo, Ms. Schaffer is wearing one of the more revealing Salome costumes.

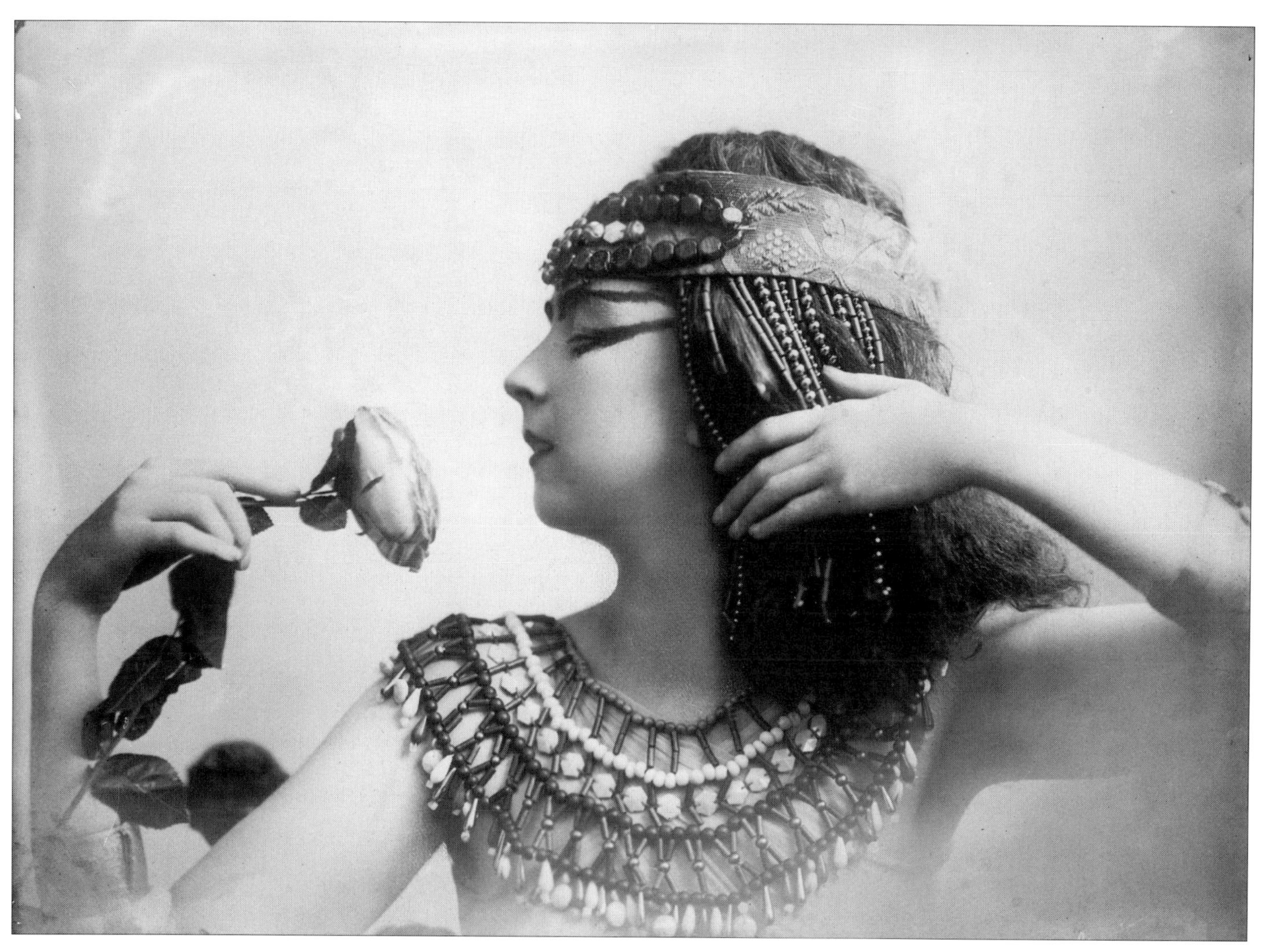

RUTH ST. DENIS (1879–1968)

Ruth St. Denis was a pioneer of modern dance. She started out in vaudeville and was soon discovered by Broadway producer David Belasco. In 1914 St. Denis married Ted Shawn, one of her dance partners, and they established the Denishawn dance school and company in the Los Angeles area. Dancer Martha Graham was one of St. Denis' many students who later became famous. As a dancer with Belasco, St. Denis toured the world and became interested in Eastern cultures, mysticism, and spirituality. Here she portrays the Egyptian goddess Isis.

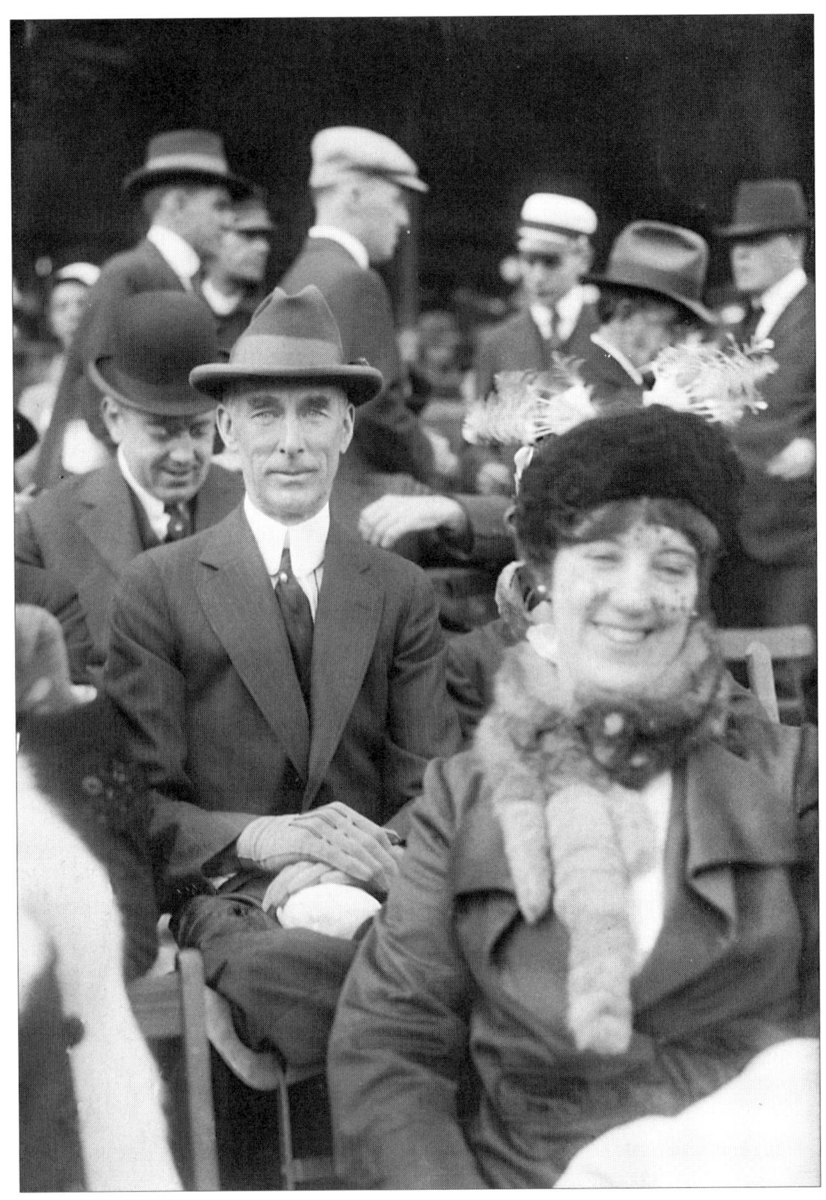

CORNELIUS ALEXANDER McGILLICUDDY "CONNIE" MACK (1862–1956)

Connie Mack was one of the greatest managers in major league baseball history. He holds records for wins (3,731), losses (3,948), and games managed (7,755), with his victory total being almost 1,000 more than any other manager. Mack managed the Philadelphia Athletics for the club's first fifty seasons before retiring at age eighty-seven following the 1950 season. He was the first manager to win the World Series three times, and won five World Series titles in all, third most by a manager, in 1910, 1911, 1913, 1929, and 1930. Connie Mack was elected to the Baseball Hall of Fame in 1937.

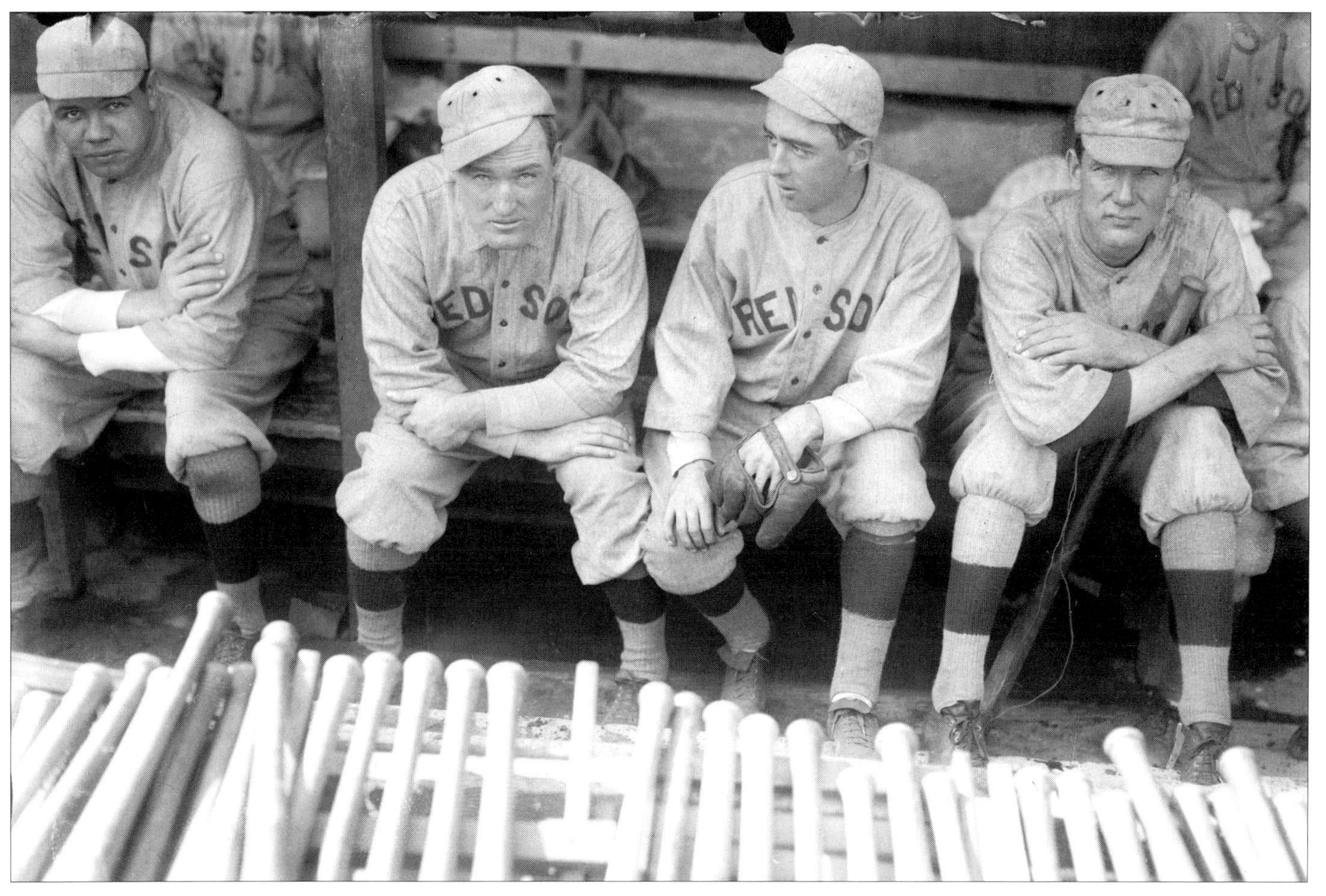

BABE RUTH (1895–1948), BILL CARRIGAN (1883–1969), JACK BARRY (1887–1961), DEL GAINOR (1886–1947)

Babe Ruth, Bill Carrigan, Jack Barry, and Del Gainor *(left to right)* of the Boston Red Sox are seen here in 1916. That was one of the Babe's best years as a pitcher, going 23–12 with a 1.75 ERA in 323 innings. In 1916, the Red Sox won the World Series 4–1 over the Brooklyn Robins. Gainor's pinch-hit single in game two came in the fourteenth inning and ended one of the longest World Series games in history. Ruth was the winning pitcher.

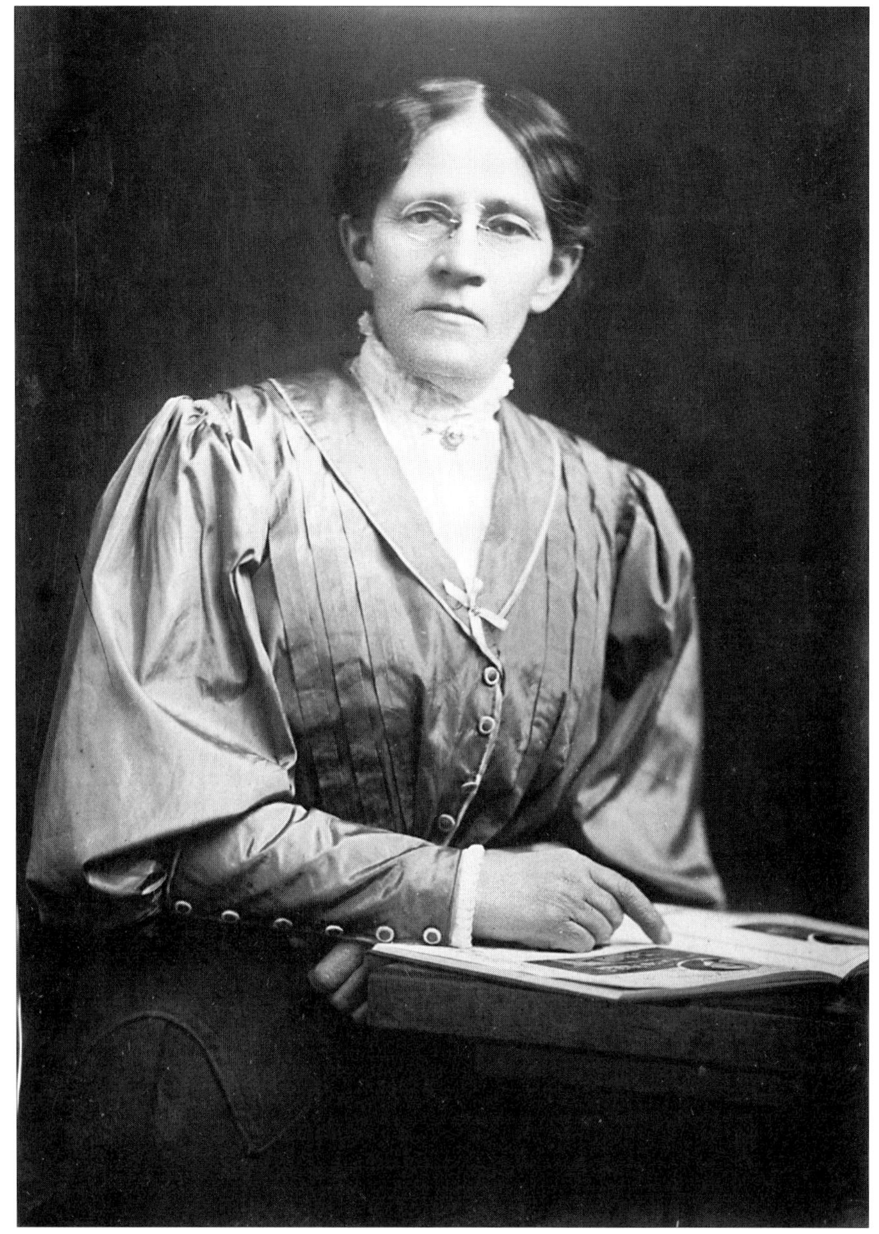

LILLIAN M. N. STEVENS (1844–1914)

Lillian M. N. Stevens was the second president of the National Women's Christian Temperance Union. Under her leadership, the WCTU expanded its membership. During her term, the sale of alcoholic beverages was banned on military bases and prohibition laws were passed in six states: Georgia, Oklahoma, Mississippi, North Carolina, Tennessee, and West Virginia. The WCTU was founded in Evanston, Illinois, and was an increasingly vocal and powerful political force in the United States leading up to the ratification of the Eighteenth Amendment, which established Prohibition in 1919.

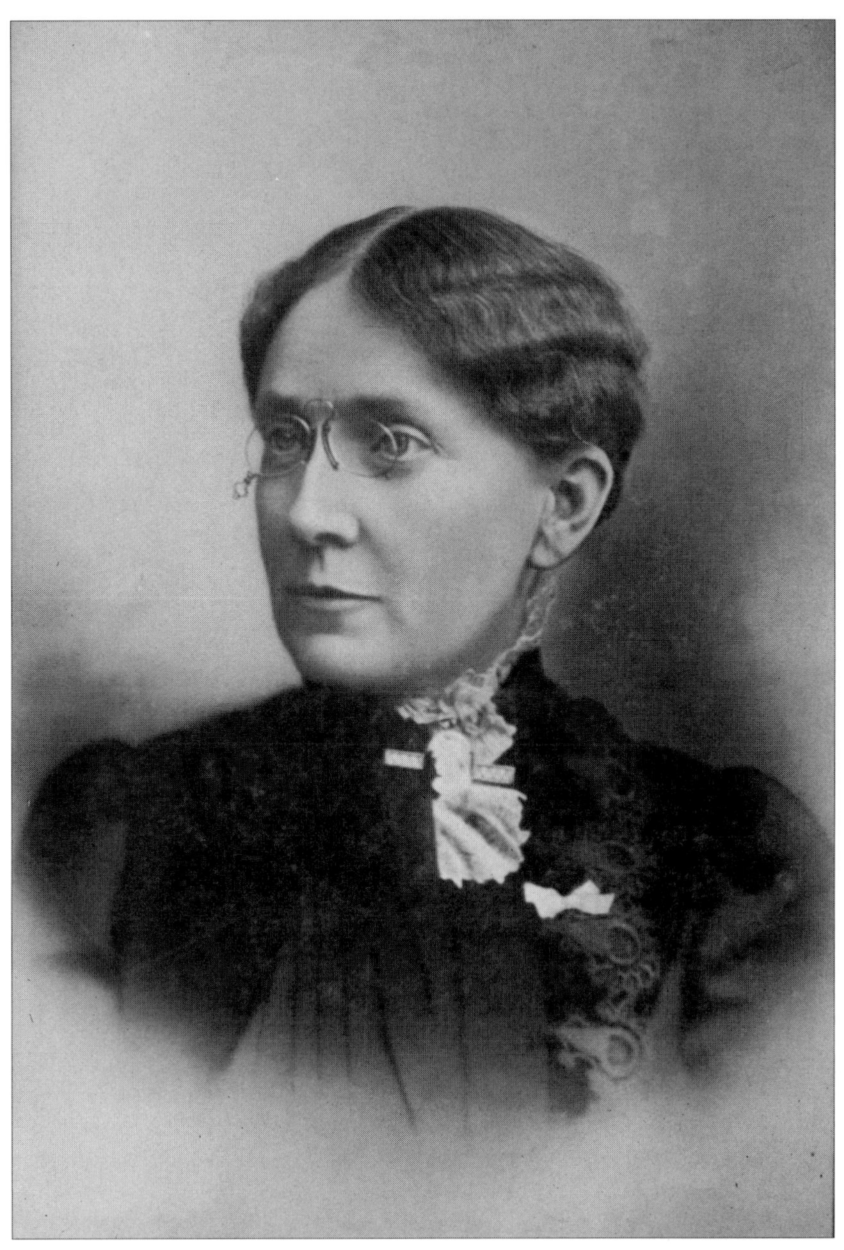

FRANCES WILLARD (1839–1898)

Frances Willard, educator, temperance reformer, and women's suffragist, was elected president of the National Woman's Christian Temperance Union in 1879, a position which she held for life. To promote her causes, she traveled widely and gave hundreds of lectures a year. Her influence was critical to passage of the 1919 Eighteenth (Prohibition) and 1920 Nineteenth (Women's Suffrage) amendments to the U.S. Constitution.

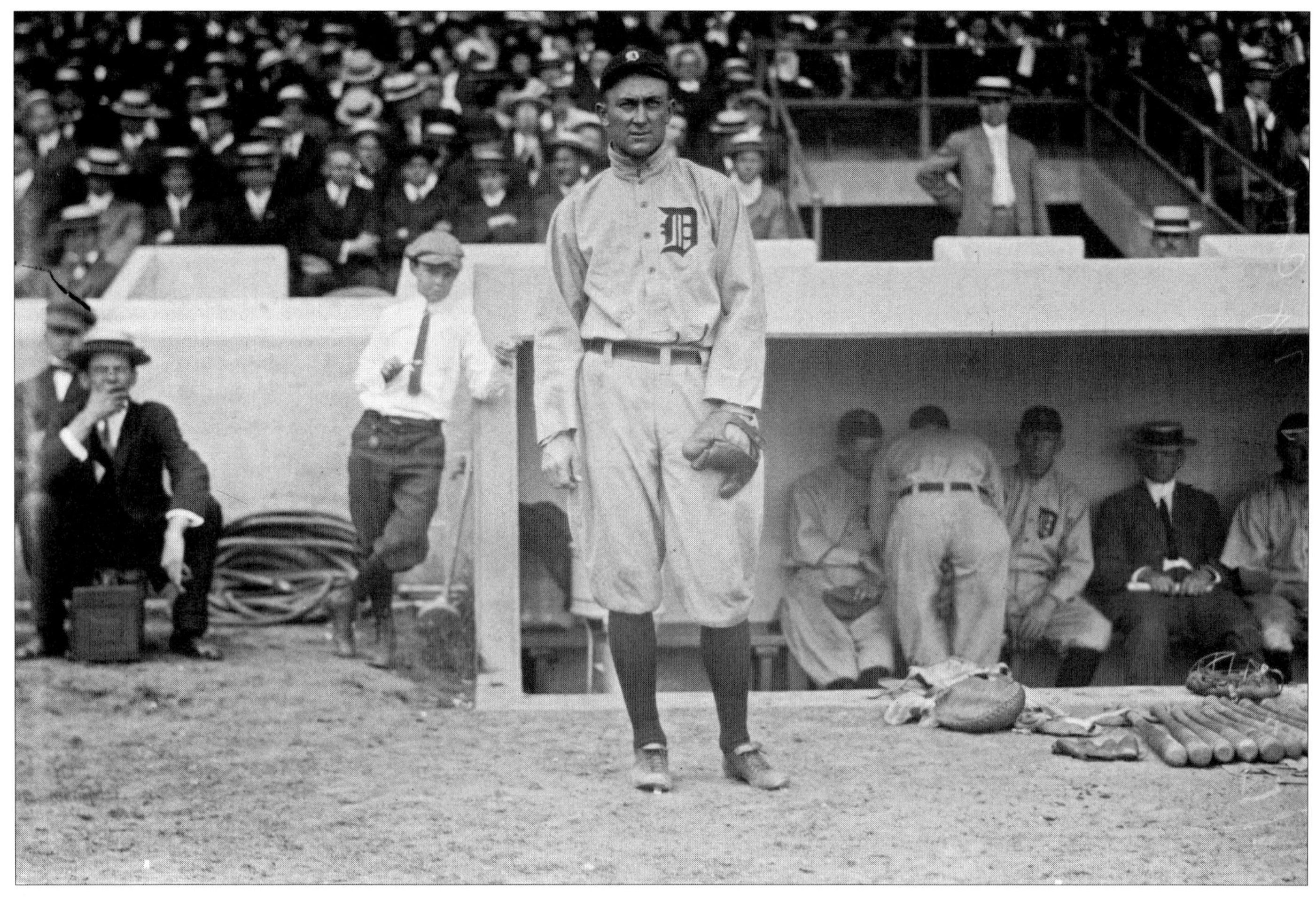

TYRUS RAYMOND "TY" COBB (1886–1961)

Ty Cobb was a Hall of Famer and one of the greatest baseball players of all time. Cobb is credited with setting ninety major league baseball records during his career. He still holds the record for highest career batting average (.367) and most career batting titles (11). Cobb had a mad temper and was often criticized for his overly aggressive—sometimes hostile—behavior on the field. He was elected to the Baseball Hall of Fame in its inaugural year of 1936 along with Babe Ruth, Honus Wagner, Christy Mathewson, and Walter Johnson. Among that stellar group, Cobb received the most votes, 222 out of a possible 226.

JIM THORPE (1888–1953)

Jim Thorpe was one of the most versatile athletes in modern sports. He won gold medals in the pentathlon and decathlon at the 1912 Stockholm Olympics, but was stripped of his Olympic titles and medals when the International Olympic Committee learned that he had professionally played minor league baseball in North Carolina in 1909 and 1910. Decades later his amateur status in terms of the Olympics was reinstated, and his children received commemorative medals in place of the originals, which had been lost. Thorpe also played major league baseball for several teams and football in the new National Football League in the 1920s. Though remembered as one of the greatest athletes in American history, he never had a stable career after his playing days. In 1950, an Associated Press poll of nearly 400 sportswriters and broadcasters voted Thorpe the greatest athlete of the first half of the twentieth century. Of mixed Native American and white ancestry, Thorpe struggled with racism throughout much of his life.

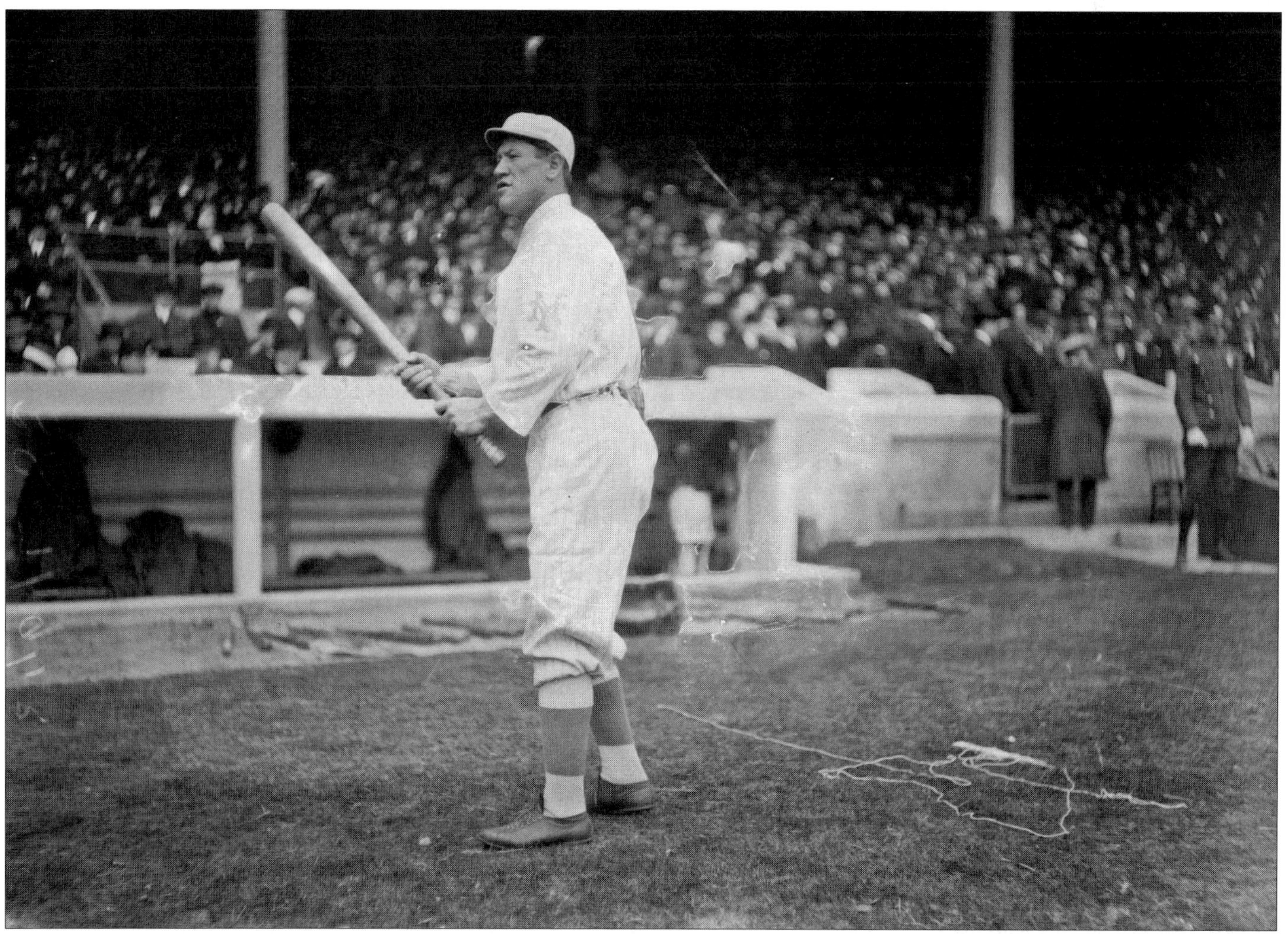

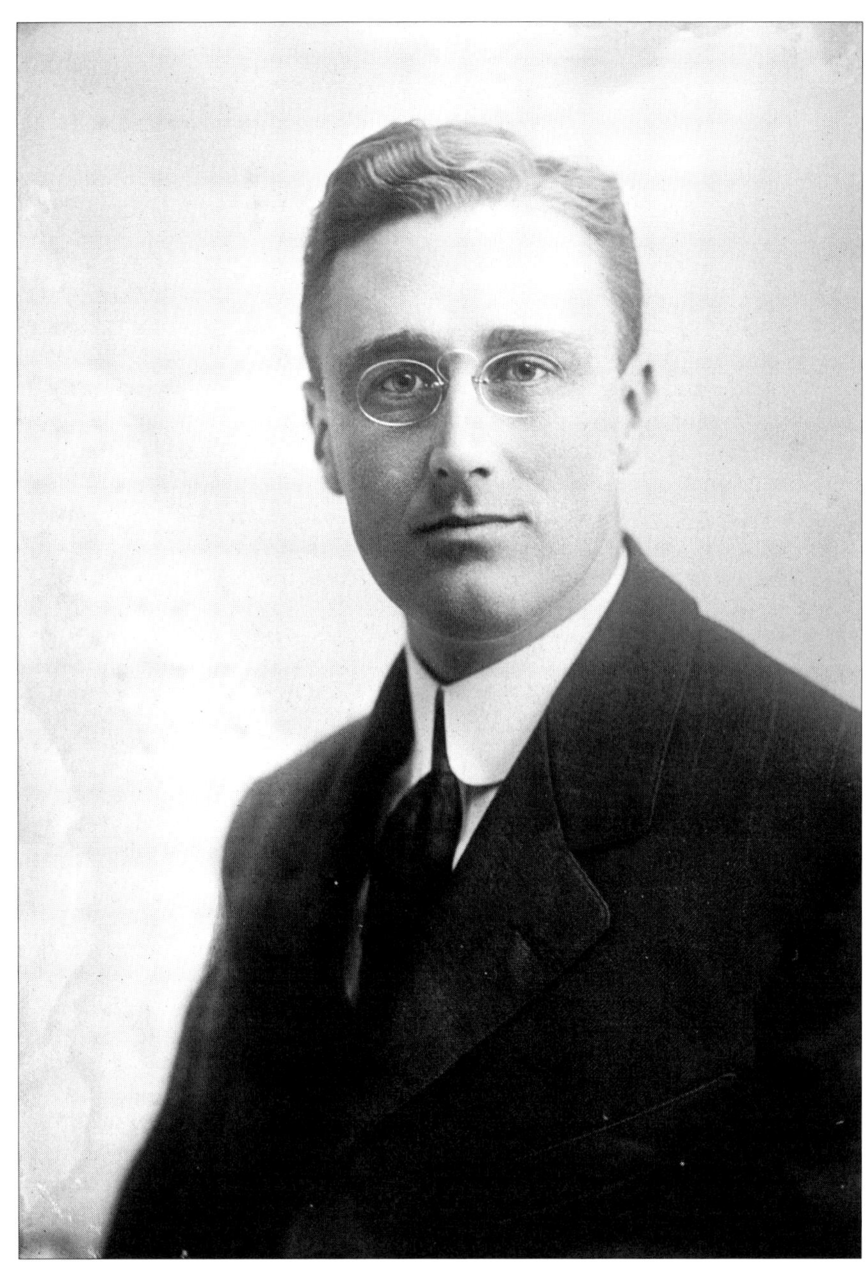

FRANKLIN D. ROOSEVELT (1882–1945)

The thirty-second president of the United States, Franklin D. Roosevelt brought hope to Americans suffering through the Great Depression by implementing New Deal programs. Roosevelt had lost the use of his legs after contracting polio in 1921, but his disability did not prevent him from ably guiding the nation through World War II after the Japanese attacked Pearl Harbor in 1941. He had just started an unprecedented fourth term when he died at the age of sixty-three on April 12, 1945.

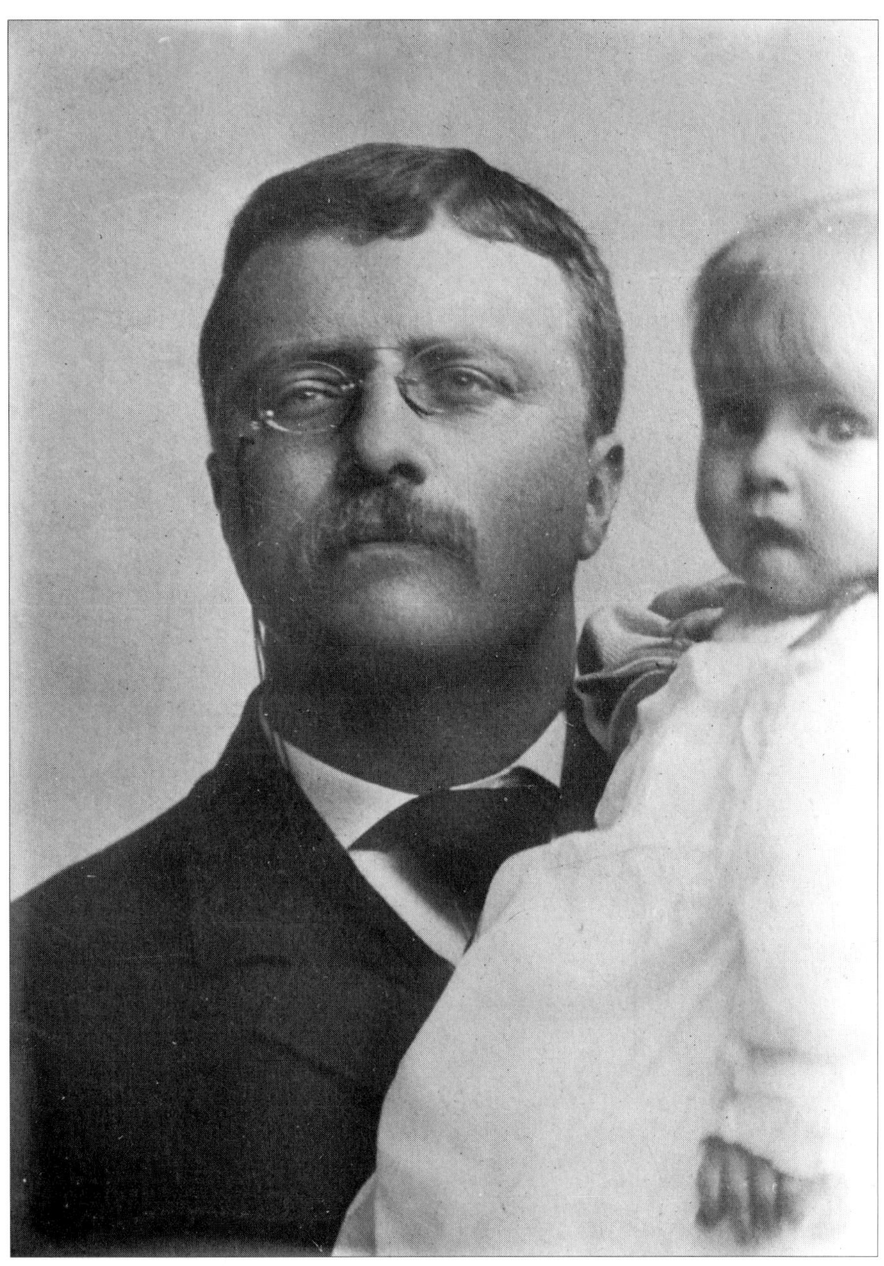

THEODORE ROOSEVELT (1858–1919)

Theodore Roosevelt was the twenty-sixth president of the United States, a hunter, soldier, naturalist, and an entertaining father. During his term in office, he was often seen encouraging his children Alice, Theodore Jr., Kermit, Ethel, Archie, and Quentin in raucous play. Here, in an 1895 photograph, he is holding Archie.

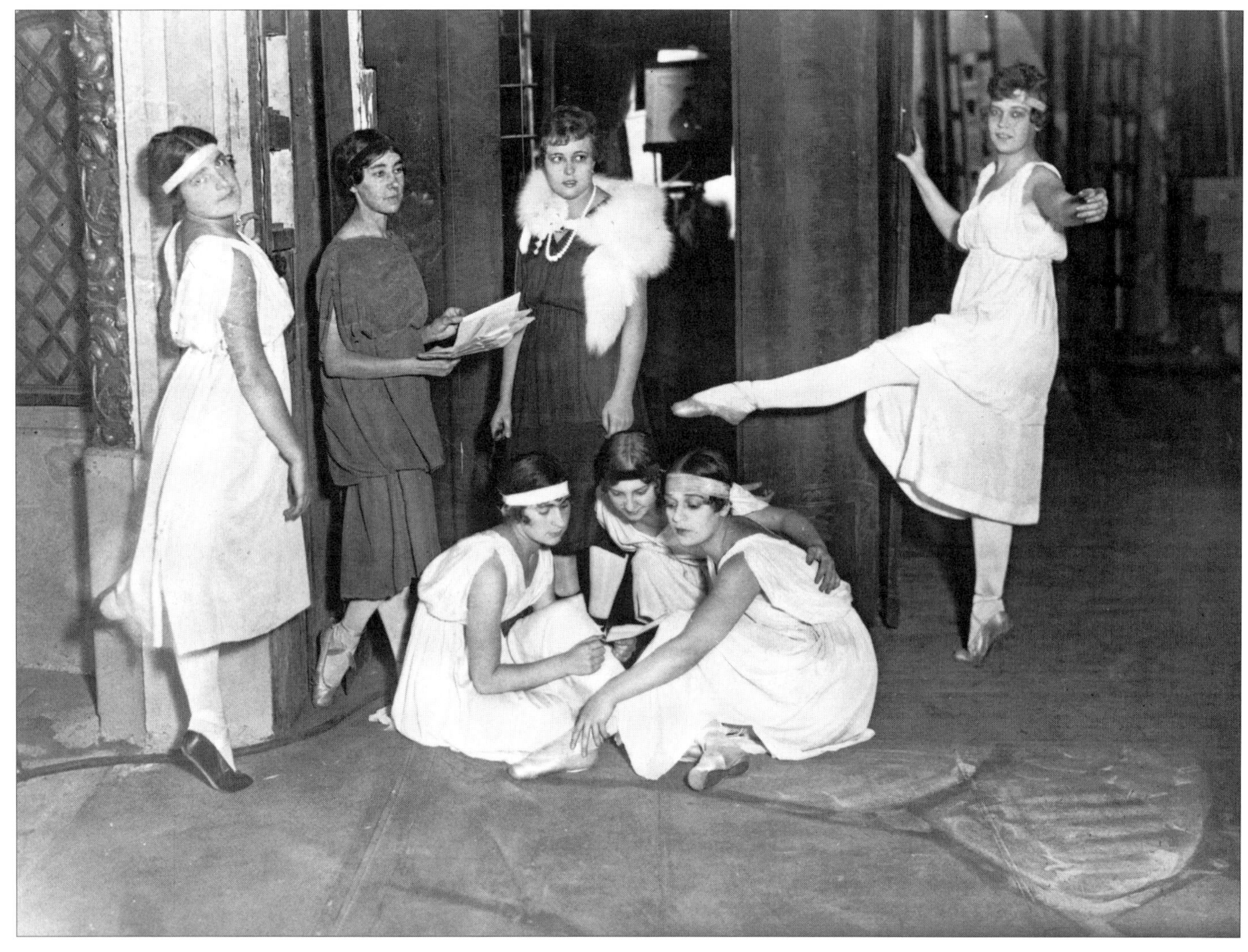

BALLETS RUSSES (1909–1929)

The Ballets Russes was established in 1909 by the Russian impresario Sergei Diaghilev and performed until his death in 1929. Its members were primarily Russians who were trained in St. Petersburg and immigrated to Paris both before and after the Russian Revolution. Featuring works by great choreographers Marius Petipa, Michel Fokine, Bronislava Nijinska, Leonide Massine, Vaslav Nijinsky, and a young George Balanchine, it became one of the most influential ballet companies of the twentieth century. The Ballets Russes was noted for the collaboration among memorable dancers, composers, choreographers, and artists. Composer Igor Stravinsky's career was launched by the ballets he composed for Diaghilev including *Firebird* (1910). Sets and costumes were designed by a who's who of twentieth century art including Braque, Picasso, Matisse and Dalí. Prominent dancers included Anna Pavlova, Tamara Karsavina, Lydia Lopokova, Vaslav Nijinsky, Michel Fokine, and Serge Lifar.

SOCIETY WOMEN IN GREEK PAGEANT, (N.D.)

Society women in Greek pageant *(left to right)*: Grace Walters, Mrs. Arthur Scott Burden, Mr. A. Herter, Mrs. J. B. Eustis, Martha White, and Miss M. R. White.

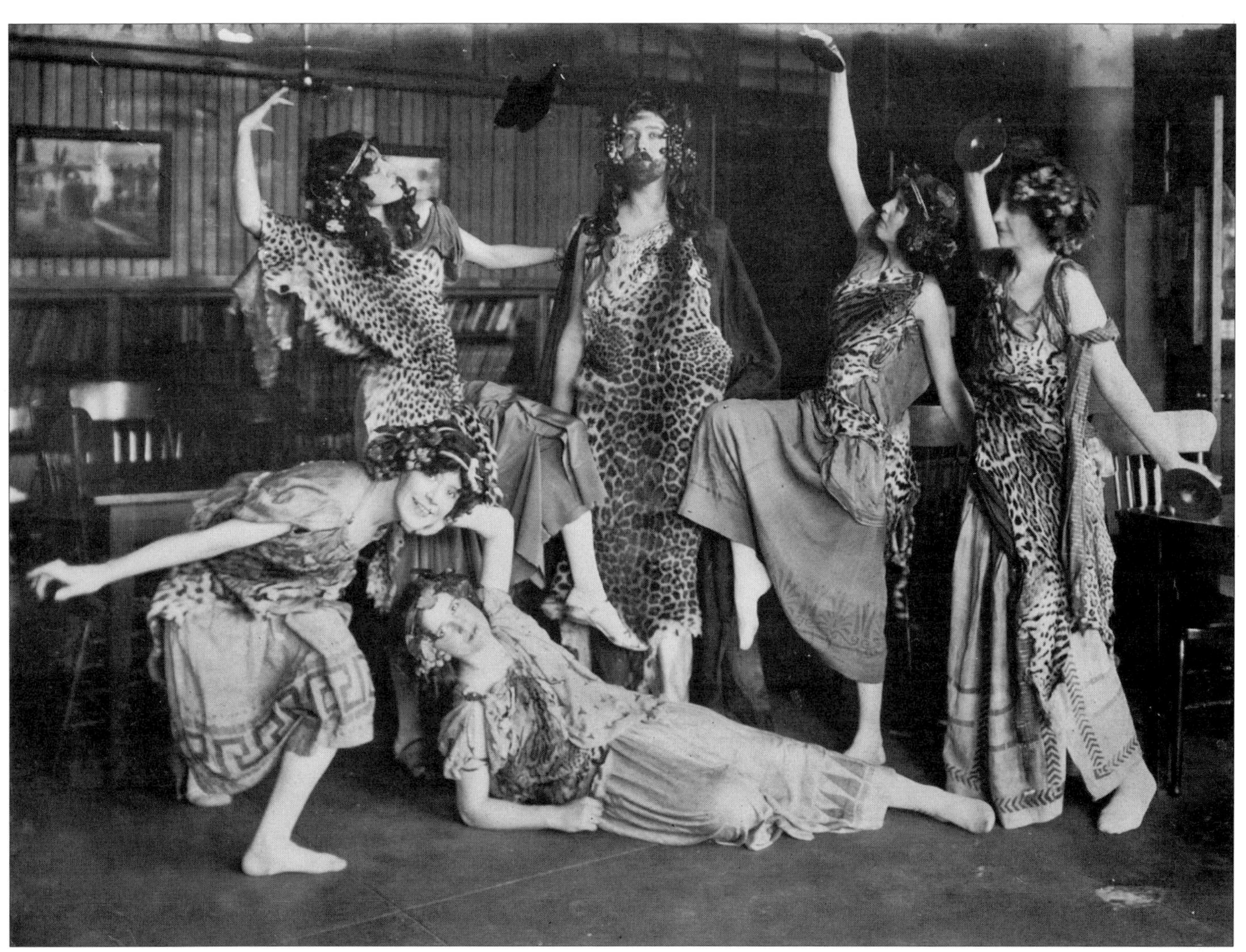

Alphabetical List of the Photos